Dan Storty

D1798851

JOB GENERATION AND LABOUR MARKET CHANGE

Also by D. J. Storey

ENTREPRENEURSHIP AND THE NEW FIRM
THE SMALL FIRM: An International Survey (*edtior*)
THE PERFORMANCE OF SMALL FIRMS
(*with K. Keasey, R. Watson and P. Wynarczyk*)
SMALL FIRMS AND REGIONAL ECONOMIC DEVELOPMENT (*editor*)

Job Generation and Labour Market Change

D. J. Storey
Principal Research Associate
Centre for Urban and Regional Development Studies
University of Newcastle upon Tyne

and

S. Johnson
Research Associate
Centre for Urban and Regional Development Studies
University of Newcastle upon Tyne

MACMILLAN
PRESS

First published 1987

Published by
THE MACMILLAN PRESS LTD
Houndmills, Basingstoke, Hampshire RG21 2XS
and London
Companies and representatives
throughout the world

Filmsetting by Vantage Photosetting Co. Ltd
Eastleigh and London

Printed in Great Britain by
Anchor Brendon Ltd
Tiptree, Essex

British Library Cataloguing in Publication Data

Storey, D.J. (David John), *1947–*
Job generation and labour market change
1. Labour supply   2. Small business
3. Job vacancies
I. Title   II. Johnson, S. *1959–*
331.13'77   HD5710.5
ISBN 0–333–43607–5 (hardcover)
ISBN 0–333–43608–3 (paperback)

Contents

List of Tables

List of Figures

Preface

This book derives from an invitation from the UK Economic and Social Research Council to provide a review of research currently being undertaken throughout the world on job generation.

During this study we have been assisted by a large number of individuals who have contributed substantially to our knowledge. We would particularly like to thank (in no particular order of importance) Konrad Stahl and Wolfgang Eckhard from Dortmund University and Chris Hull and Eberhard von Einem from the IIM in Berlin. In the United States we had particularly helpful discussions with David Birch, formerly of MIT, with Marjorie Odle formerly of the Brookings Institute, Joe Duncan of Dun and Bradstreet, Bruce Phillips of the Small Business Administration, Mike Teitz of University of California at Berkeley, Barry Bluestone at Boston College, and John Sower and Michael Schwartz both of the National Development Council, Washington, DC.

Our studies of Italy would not have been possible without the contribution of our colleagues at Newcastle, Ash Amin who drafted much of the Italian Section of Chapter 5. The material for this came from a visit to Italy in October 1985, with Ash Amin, organised by FOR. We wish to extend our thanks to the FOR for their help in this project particularly Gilberto Gabrielli and Enrico Ricotta. Whilst in Italy we had many fruitful discussions with, amongst others, Professors Alfredo del Monte, Sebastiano Brusco, and Bruno Contini. Our interest in Italian developments, however, was initially stimulated by Sergio Arzeni of OECD. We are most grateful for his helpful insights. Finally at OECD we were greatly assisted by Naoki Mitani.

Nearer home we have benefited from discussions with many UK academics and policy-makers in this area, notably Colin Gallagher, Patrick O'Farrell, and Henry Stewart. Seminars on this material have been presented at the London School of Economics, Newcastle City Action Team, South Bank Polytechnic, the House of Lords Employment Committee, ESRC, Acton Society Trust, and Nene College, Northampton. The contributions made by those attending the Seminars have helped us considerably. We also wish to formally express our thanks to the Economic and Social Research Council for initiating and funding the project and to Dr John Malin for his help and encouragement. The hardest task, however, fell to Ian Molho of the Economics Department at Newcastle University who devoted his

Christmas break to reading the 'final' manuscript. We sincerely thank him for his helpful and constructive comments.

Finally we wish to express grateful thanks to our typist Mrs Betty Robson and the secretarial and administrative staff in CURDS for all the excellent work which they undertake for us.

Of course, we alone are responsible for the text.

D.J. STOREY
S. JOHNSON

1 Introduction and Summary

The oil crisis of the early and mid-1970s triggered or coincided with a number of major developments in the world economy. The slowdown in economic growth in most developed countries which followed the increase in energy prices led firms either to search for substitute forms of energy or to use less energy intensive methods of production.

The period coincided with the growth in economic stature of several countries in South East Asia such as Taiwan and South Korea, which proved to be as effective in competing for European and North American markets as did Japan. The 1970s saw also the start of a major technological revolution with the growth of computers and microprocessors with their application to every form of industrial and domestic life.

Finally the 1970s saw a change in fashion, perhaps best exemplified in the phrase 'small is beautiful'. It became a popular view, at least amongst the young, that large firms provided both a boring and repetitive working environment for the workforce and a bureaucratic environment for management. It was felt by significant numbers of young talented individuals that large firms inhibited creative expression and that working for themselves, or with other like-minded individuals in small organisations, would provide a more creative environment.

In particular the technological changes and the changes in fashion meant that young creative individuals with computing skills were able start firms in high-technology sectors and were able to be highly successful over a short period of time. This was particularly true for those providing software services rather than manufacturing.

The late 1970s and the early 1980s also saw major political changes in both Europe and North America. Ronald Reagan, Margaret Thatcher and Helmut Kohl all came to power at a similar time and replaced administrations which, to a greater or lesser extent, had emphasised the role of the state in the creation of employment opportunities. By the end of the 1970s it had become clear, however, that unemployment was rising in most OECD countries and that inflation was also increasing. A loss of faith in the old fashioned Keynesian demand management policies occurred and the new Western leaders set about trying to change the somewhat comfortable economic consensus which existed in the 1960s and early 1970s.

Both Ronald Reagan and Margaret Thatcher were elected on a manifesto of 'rolling back the frontiers of the state', the implication of which was to provide greater opportunities for individuals to become responsible for themselves. The reduction in the power of the state meant that functions previously conducted by the state and paid for either out of taxation revenues or by 'printing' money were either not provided at all or purchased privately. In this view of society the individual was given more control over the goods and services which he or she chose to purchase but by implication, given less protection if he or she was unable to compete in the market place.

The late 1970s were then a period of rapidly rising unemployment and newly elected governments with a 'new right' philosophy searching with missionary zeal to justify their individualistic policies. It is this context in which the work of David Birch and his *Job Generation* results have to be placed. Having access to a major database covering employment change in 5.6 million establishments Birch was able to show that in the United States between 1969 and 1976, two-thirds of the increase in employment was in firms with less than 20 workers.

For the newly elected governments these results demonstrated that a policy of creating a climate in which small businesses could grow and prosper could make a major contribution to new job creation. Birch's results became the prime justification for policies to promote small businesses, even though, as the UK Secretary of State of Industry recognised, they also possessed a number of other qualities which are attractive to a Conservative administration.

Owner managed small businesses are bastions of freedom, the seed-bed of growth companies, the source of much innovation – and generally have excellent industrial relations. (*Hansard*, 21 May 1979)

It is the purpose of this book to explore the implications for the labour market of changes in the world economy since the early 1970s. In particular we investigate the causes and implications of the relative shift in employment from large to small firms. It is not a change which has necessarily occurred in all countries or at the same rates. It appears, for example, to have taken place most rapidly in the United States, United Kingdom and Germany, whereas in several smaller developed countries such trends are less clear. Nevertheless even amongst the former group of countries the changes have not been particularly striking over a decade and in all OECD countries more than half of all employment continues to be found in large rather than small businesses.

In writing the book we have two main purposes. The first is to provide a statement on the nature and scale of the change in the size structure of employment units. Second to provide a more complete *explanation* of why these changes have occurred. What is the relative importance of technological change, 'fashion', recession, the shift to services, and the growth of competition from the newly industrialised countries in explaining such developments?

To answer these questions we begin in Chapter 2 with a review of the relative importance of small employment units (firms) in the major OECD countries. We assess the extent and nature of the changes in the relative importance of small firms which have occurred over the last decade. This serves to provide a benchmark on the importance of small firms in OECD countries. It also tests the implicit thrust of much current economic policy which suggests that, because small firms are more flexible, responsive to change, and well represented amongst the high technology sectors, then *ceteris paribus* those countries with a higher proportion of employment in small firms would be expected to 'perform' better than those of whose employment is concentrated in large firms.

Whilst it is difficult, because of the data problems, to be satisfied that the international comparisons are fully adequate, there appears to be no evidence to support the view that, once the extreme values of the UK and Japan are excluded, countries which have a high proportion of employment in small firms perform better than those with a low proportion in such firms. There also appears to be no evidence to support the view that those countries in which small firms increased their share of employment most rapidly performed better than other countries. In both cases 'performance' is indicated by net employment change and by change in unemployment.

The results tentatively suggest that policies designed to increase the number of small businesses in an economy are unlikely to have a major impact upon employment creation/unemployment reduction. However, examining changes over time in the share of employment of different sized firms can present a misleading picture of the importance of small firms in job creation. The work of Birch in the United States showed that when employment in individual establishments or enterprises was traced it indicated that small firms were the major source of employment growth in the United States between 1969 and 1976. In Chapter 3 we provide a comprehensive critique of the Birch results. We note that, after their publication, whilst these results had a major impact upon public policy makers, they were also the subject of strong criticism from Armington, Odle and Harris at the Brookings Institute. After reviewing the complex evidence we conclude that whilst Birch almost certainly overestimated the contribution made by small firms, and that Brookings were probably more accurate in their analysis, it is still true that in the United States since the end of the 1960s, small firms have been significant creators of new jobs. The results also show that large firms are net losers of jobs with medium-sized industry broadly maintaining its share.

The unique feature of the analysis conducted by both Birch and by Brookings was that they had access to data on employment on individual enterprises and establishments. They did not have to rely on aggregate data but were able to track employment changes over a period of time within individual corporations, and it is this *dynamic* element which led to the coining of the term 'job generation'. The fact that the term was first introduced by Birch and that his most quoted result relates to the small business share of employment growth does not mean that job generation and small businesses are necessarily linked. Rather the term 'job generation' is more accurately an accounting convention for identifying the contribution to employment change of different types of firms whether these are distinguished by size, sector, ownership, region or any other relevant characteristics.

The interest in the contribution of different sized enterprises to employment change led to a number of attempts to replicate the Birch studies using establishment databases inside and outside the United States. In Chapter 4 we provide a review of these studies and highlight their limitations. In most cases the studies are limited to the manufacturing sector and the vast majority cover only part of a country. For other studies the time period covered is very short and so it is difficult to determine whether any changes which are observed in the size structure of employment units are attributable to cyclical changes or to longer term developments. Finally some studies do not include establishments or enterprises which have ceased trading and hence bias the results. For all these reasons it is unwise to place undue emphasis upon the results of any single study but again the general thrust of the results indicate that large firms are shedding labour and that the very small firm sector is a net creator of jobs.

Nevertheless two major provisos need to be mentioned. The first is that the scale of net job creation by small enterprises is not as significant as that indicated by the original Birch study. Secondly it is unclear whether these results indicate a new trend in developed economies or whether they are simply a reflection of the life cycle or 'trees of the forest' view of the birth, growth and death of firms.

Chapters 3 and 4 are primarily concerned with measuring the contribution to job generation made by different sized firms in a number of different economies. Chapter 5 represents a preliminary attempt to *explain* these developments. We argue that although a number of simple explanations are offered for the relative increase in the importance of small firms – growth of the service sector, technical change, competition, recession, energy prices, fashion, etc., there is no single explanation which is satisfactory. To illustrate the point we examine three areas: Birmingham (UK), Boston (USA) and Bologna (Italy) and demonstrate that small firms have become relatively more important in all these areas but for very different reasons. In Birmingham small firms become relatively more important bcause of the decline of large firms. In Boston small firms become more important because the wealth created by high technology firms lead to a massive increase in consumer-based service sector demand which tends to be satisfied by small firms. In Bologna the growth of small firms stems from the system of small enterprises in industrial districts which specialise in the production of a single high quality product. The small firms are co-ordinated by merchants in the major towns and cities such as Bologna.

One reason for setting out these 'models' is to demonstrate that increases in the relative importance of the small firm sector can occur for very different reasons, and that it is vital to understand the mechanisms of change before appropriate policies can be introduced. It should not be taken to infer that the United States is only characterised by the Boston model, or that the UK is characterised by Birmingham. In most advanced countries there will be elements of all three models; the purpose of the characterisation is to recognise that the policy implications in each of the three areas is very different. Furthermore it is not suggested that the models are necessarily exhaustive and it is also possible that small firms have exhibited relative growth for reasons other than those identified in the Birmingham, Boston or Bologna models.

The models demonstrate that there is no single explanation for the relative growth of small firms. Indeed the explanations for the growth of small firms in the 'successful' models, i.e. Boston and Bologna indicate that there are a set of factors which appear to be associated with successful small business development but which are either ignored or understated by many commentators. For example in Boston the role of defence expenditure and of the concentration of higher education institutions is crucial in facilitating the growth of new high technology businesses. In the Bologna area the international linkages of the merchants in the major towns and the growth of interdependent links between firms growing from agricultural traditions with a system of production are key elements. The 'unsuccessful' Birmingham model on the other hand is characterised by the declining international competitive position of large firms which results in restructuring amongst large firms and of labour shedding leading to 'forced' entrepreneurship.

Having recognised that the relative growth of small firms can stem from a variety of causes, Chapter 6 is devoted to a study of the implications of these developments for the labour market as a whole and for particular groups within the labour market. It assesses the types of jobs which are provided in small firms in terms of the wages paid and conditions of employment. It also analyses the labour which small firms seek in terms of hours worked, skill level and age profile, and considers the implications for changes in labour market policy and for training. Broadly it concludes that small firms are interested in recruiting either skilled labour or highly flexible and cheap labour. The international evidence available suggests that small firms pay lower wages than larger firms and that they generally offer poorer terms and conditions. Their unskilled labour tends to be recruited from the very young and the very old and from part-time (primarily female) workers. Thus if an increased proportion of new jobs are in small firms this could present major problems for the recruitment of middle-aged unskilled male workers. This group is not required by the firms which are creating jobs and there is a considerable risk that they will constitute a long term unemployment problem. Furthermore it is extremely difficult to devise a suitable training package for such individuals since most small firms, by their nature, do not have highly developed forward plans, their aim being to have sufficient flexibility to respond quickly to changing market conditions. The relative growth of the small firm sector constitutes a serious difficulty for governments attempting to introduce appropriate employment policies and to provide a skills training package for the unemployed.

In Chapter 7 the implications for public policy in the United Kingdom of the foregoing analyses are examined. In this chapter the lessons from the Birmingham, Boston and Bologna models are considered together with the wider international evidence on the growth of small firms and self-employment reviewed in Chapter 2. It concludes that much, but by no means all, of the United Kingdom has strong similarities to the Birmingham model, and that present policies being pursued by both local and national government are largely inappropriate since these are designed to promote an enterprise culture through encouraging large numbers of individuals to start their own businesses. The chapter calls for radical rethinking of such policies since the fundamental factor which distinguishes Birmingham from Boston or Bologna is the relatively poor international competitiveness of firms in the former location. In the latter the high technology firms in Boston are highly internationally competitive. Similarly the textile and clothing firms in the Bologna area are highly competitive whereas Birmingham firms have been losing world market share for some years. Unfortunately public policy is directed towards encouraging individuals to start new businesses rather than directing explicit attention towards overcoming this lack of competitiveness. The emphasis is upon increasing the *quantity* rather than the quality of small businesses.

The lesson to be learned by areas approximating to the Birmingham model is that the focus of public policy towards small firms should be of *selective* assistance to those firms which are, in principle, capable of becoming internationally competitive. An examination of the small firm sector shows that over a period of time, growth in employment takes place in relatively few firms. Indeed our data show that approximately half of the growth in employment in new firms over a decade takes place in about 4 per cent of all new firms. The chapter also argues that these fast growth firms are those which are most likely to be selling nationally and internationally and are therefore most likely to overcome the lack of competitiveness which has characterised much of UK industry. The familiar arguments against a strategy of 'selectivity' are discussed, but it is argued that because the performance of small firms is particularly diverse and because there are relatively few which are able to exhibit substantial growth, a non-selective policy is likely to lead to major inefficiencies. We conclude with an indication of how, in practice, a policy of selective assistance might work.

2 Small Firms and Self-Employment in the OECD Countries

2.1 INTRODUCTION

Throughout the 1960s the major concern of industrial economists was with large firms which were seen as the prime movers in an economy. It seemed wholly appropriate to consider whether there were any clear limits to the size of firms. The main emphasis of literature on this matter was to test for the existence of scale economies at the plant level and to consider whether or not increasing levels of industrial concentration were harmful. If small firms were considered at all then they were either relegated to the status of a footnote or the subject of some speculation on the circumstances under which they might be expected to survive.

It would be an overstatement to suggest that matters have reversed, but it is now clear that the rhetoric has changed. Clearly major multinational companies remain the dominant force in the world economy and indeed their power may even have increased. Furthermore, the majority of the employed workforce in the non-government sector continues in all OECD countries to be employed in large firms, and there appears to be no abating in the scale at which mergers between companies are taking place.

Despite all these developments there has been a change in the attitudes both of governments and of economists to the small firm sector. It is no longer asked whether the small firm sector will survive, but rather what role it has in an advanced economy. No longer is self-employment regarded as an inferior status imposed by employers in the agricultural and construction industries. Instead some of the most wealthy *new* groups in society have opted for the status of being self-employed. There is hardly a government in the western world which does not have industrial policies designed to promote the growth and development of the small firm sector – many of these policies having been introduced during the last five to ten years.

This book traces the reasons for, and implications of this change, but in this chapter some basic data are presented on the relative importance of small firms in the developed countries. It is recognised that the information which is available is not always of the highest quality but in this chapter only information presented by OECD is used in an attempt to provide a standardised format. Other international comparisons are available (Ganguly 1985, Storey 1982, 1983, Bannock 1981) but since the OECD data were collected from member states with the explicit purpose of making direct comparisons we have chosen to work with this source of data alone.

2.2 THE IMPORTANCE OF SMALL FIRMS IN DEVELOPED ECONOMIES

Any discussion of the role of small firms in an economy immediately encounters problems of definition. As Beesley and Wilson (1984) point out, within the United Kingdom alone there are more than 30 different definitions. A small firm in the chemical industry is likely to be substantially larger than a small firm in retailing, and so definitions vary between sectors. Some definitions are based upon the number of employees, some are based upon the value of the turnover of the business, whilst others are based upon the number of productive units. In the UK a small firm in road transport is defined according to the number of lorries in its fleet, whilst small firms in catering are defined according to whether or not they are part of a group, i.e. in terms of ownership.

All these measures are unsatisfactory since, even within the context of the UK economy, it is not possible to compare small firms in the road transport sector, where measurement is in terms of numbers of lorries, with small firms in the manufacturing sector where measurement is in terms of employees. Secondly, even where the measurement index is the same – such as number of employees – actual definitions vary. For example in the UK a small firm is defined in the construction sector as having less than 20 employees, but in the manufacturing sector as less than 200. Finally, for many sectors within services small firms are defined according to the value of the turnover of the business. Here, not only does the definition vary according to the sector so that, for example, in 1983 a small firm in retailing had a turnover of less than £185 000 whereas in wholesaling the figure was £730 000, but major problems occur in making comparisons over a period of time because of the effect of inflation. Particular problems occur where some sectors experience a relatively fast or a relatively slow rate of inflation. In any event analysis of time series data where firm size is defined in monetary terms presents substantial problems.

Although it is difficult to obtain a consistently satisfactory operational definition of a small firm, the Bolton Committee (1971) did provide an important conceptual framework. Bolton said that a small firm had three major characteristics:

– it was owned and managed by the same individuals, rather than by professionals on behalf of shareholders.
– it normally had a small share of the market – or, exceptionally, a larger share of a very small market.
– it was legally independent, in the sense of not being owned by another business.

Whilst the Bolton definition highlights the distinctive conceptual dimensions of small businesses, problems of obtaining an operationally satisfactory definition remain. Such difficulties multiply when international comparisons are undertaken. Leah Hertz (1982) in fact devoted a whole book to attempting to provide a consistent definition of small business in the USA, Japan, Israel and the UK. The definition problems which occur in a single country quickly multiply when international comparisons are made. Particular problems occur with the service sector where we noted above that small business definitions tend to be in monetary terms. This means that definitions have to be 'normalised' to account for exchange rate fluctuations. Finally, whilst the collection of data on small firms varies substantially between countries, small businessmen throughout the world are noted for their unwillingness to complete government statistical forms. Coverage tends to be poor in most countries but perhaps particularly so in countries such as Italy where many small firms are thought to operate in the 'black economy' (Mattera 1985).

The effect of these problems means that those international comparisons which are undertaken tend to concentrate upon the role of small firms in the manufacturing sector, where size of firm is defined in terms of employment, rather than according to any other criteria. Whilst this has the advantage of enabling direct comparisons to be undertaken, it has considerable disadvantages. Firstly small firms in manufacturing generally constitute less than 10 per cent of all small firms in a developed economy. Secondly manufacturing is in some countries declining in absolute terms and in most countries is declining in relative terms. Hence, whilst the available international manufacturing data facilitate reasonable comparisons, they understate the changes which are occurring in the small firms sector which is more widely defined.

The terms 'enterprise' and 'establishment' also must be defined since data on small firms can lead to confusion on these matters. An *establishment* is defined as a site at which economic activity takes place, normally a factory, whereas an *enterprise* is the legal business entity – normally called a firm. In many cases where an enterprise has only a single factory then the terms enterprise and establishment are synonymous. However, large enterprises often own numerous small establishments. Clearly these small establishments do not have the characteristics of a small firm since, according to the Bolton definition, they are *not* owned and managed by the same individuals.

Subsequent comparisons of the importance of the small firm sector in the major OECD countries draw heavily upon the authoritative *OECD Employment Outlook* (1985). Table 2.1 presents data on the distribution of employment by enterprise size for the whole private economy, for the most recent years that such information is available. Unfortunately, only seven countries were able to provide this information; for the United States the most recent year's data is for 1977, whereas for the other countries the data are for 1981 onwards. Whilst the reader's

Table 2.1   Distribution of employment by enterprise size: whole private economy[a] (percentages)

| | | Enterprise size (number of persons employed) | | | | |
		Very small 1–19	Small 20–99	Medium 100–499	Large 500 +	Total
Austria	1981	26.2	20.9	19.4	33.4	100.0
Belgium	1983	25.0	20.9	21.5	32.6	100.0
France[b,c]	1981	19.7	22.3	18.7	39.2	100.0
Japan[b]	1983	38.8[d]	17.5[e]	16.5	27.1	100.0
Netherlands[b]	1982	25.9	22.7	[− 51.4 −]		100.0
Sweden[a,b]	1983	15.6	12.4	13.3	58.6	100.0
United States[b,c]	1977	21.6	18.5	12.4	47.5	100.0

[a] Data for Sweden also include the public sector.
[b] Wage earners and salaried employees only.
[c] Service sector coverage is only partial.
[d] 1–29.
[e] 30–99.
Source: OECD (1985).

attention is drawn to the footnotes indicating the difficulties of making comparisons, the table is thought to be the best international guide currently available on the relative importance of small firms throughout the whole economy. It shows that very small firms (enterprises) with less than 20 workers in 1983 provide 15.6 per cent of *all* jobs in Sweden, whereas in Japan firms with less than 30 workers provide 38.8 per cent. In Belgium, Austria and the Netherlands approximately one-quarter of *all* jobs are in firms with less than 20 workers, whereas in the United States 21.6 per cent are in this group. Conversely, Japan has the lowest proportion of employment in large firms – less than half of that in Sweden.

Whilst it is helpful to have data on the whole of the private sector economy (except Sweden where public sector employment is included) it

Table 2.2   Distribution of employment by enterprise size: manufacturing sector (percentages)

		Enterprise size (number of persons employed)				
		Very small 1–19	Small 20–99	Medium 100–499	Large 500 +	Total
Australia	1982	12.6	17.4	21.3	48.6	100.0
Austria[a]	1981	17.4	19.6	24.9	38.2	100.0
Belgium	1983	12.1	20.7	25.8	41.3	100.0
Denmark[a]	1983	9.2[b]	25.9	29.6	35.3	100.0
Finland	1980	9.1	14.8	18.5	57.6	100.0
France[a]	1981	8.7	19.0	22.8	49.4	100.0
Germany	1982		15.1	24.7	60.2	100.0[d]
Ireland	1979		25.9	36.3	37.9	100.0[d]
Italy	1981		24.6	19.1	46.4	100.0[d]
Japan[a]	1983	27.8[e]	19.3[f]	19.6	33.3	100.0
Luxembourg	1980	7.7	11.5	25.8	55.0	100.0
Netherlands[a]	1982	13.0	21.6	[– 65.4 –]		100.0
Sweden[a,g]	1983	10.2	15.8	19.8	54.1	100.0
United Kingdom	1981	[– 20.3 –]		23.4	66.3	100.0
United States[a]	1977	4.9	11.3	12.8	71.0	100.0

[a] Wage earners and salaried employees only.
[b] 6–19.
[c] 6 +.
[d] 20 +.
[e] 1–29.
[f] 30–99.
[g] Data include public sector manufacturing.
Source: OECD (1985).

is difficult to observe any pattern amongst only seven countries. Table 2.2 therefore presents data, restricted to the manufacturing sector, on employment in different sized enterprises. Data for this classification are available for 15 OECD countries but again, notably for the United States, the information is somewhat out of date. A further problem is that for several countries, data are not available for very small firms with less than 20 workers.

Table 2.2 again shows that within OECD countries there is considerable variation in the size distribution of manufacturing firms. The three countries where large firms, with 500 workers or more, provide more than 60 per cent of all manufacturing employment are USA (71 per cent), UK (66.3 per cent) and Germany (60.2 per cent). Conversely, the countries where manufacturing firms with between 20 and 99 workers are important are Denmark (25.9 per cent), Ireland (25.9 per cent), Italy (24.6 per cent). For countries providing data for manufacturing firms with less than 20 workers Japan is clearly exceptional, with more than 27 per cent of all manufacturing jobs being found in such firms.

Within OECD countries there is considerable variation in the relative importance of small firms. It is broadly true that small firms are of the least importance in those countries which were the first to industrialise – notably UK, Germany and the USA. A less clear pattern is apparent from the other countries with, for example, the Japanese manufacturing sector characterised by a few internationally famous giant companies, the strength of which depends crucially upon a myriad of tiny subcontractors (Anthony 1983). It is these businesses which provide almost 28 per cent of employment within Japanese manufacturing.

2.3 CHANGES IN THE IMPORTANCE OF SMALL FIRMS

Our interest within this book, however, is not only the current proportion of output or employment in small firms but in the changes in the shares of small firms over a period of time and most particularly over the period of the 1970s. Information on these changing shares over time is difficult to obtain but OECD (1985) does present some data in the form of graphs.

We have taken these data and expressed them in tabular form. The basic data are in four tables. The first two tables (Tables 2.3 and 2.4) cover the manufacturing sector and the second two cover the whole economy (Tables 2.5 and 2.6). A second distinction is made between data by Enterprise Size (Table 2.3 and Table 2.5) and data by Establishment Size (Tables 2.4 and 2.6).

Table 2.3 Percentage of employment in different sized enterprises:manufacturing in OECD countries

Country		1970	1971	1972	1973	1974	1975	1976	1977	1978	1979	1980	1981	1982	1983	Comment
Australia	1–19						11.6			11.3	11.2	11.8	11.8	12.6		Generally increase in small
	500+						49.6			50.2	50.8	49.5	49.7	48.6		
Austria	1–19				15.8								17.4			
	500+				40.7								38.2			
Belgium	1–19									11.8	11.9	11.8	12.1	12.5	12.1	Very small and very large have grown
	500+									40.7	41.8	41.7	41.6	41.6	41.3	
Denmark	1–19				6.8	7.5	8.4	7.9	8.7	8.6	8.5	8.7	9.3	9.1	9.2	Increase in small
	500+				37.0	38.1	37.0	35.6	35.4	36.8	37.0	37.2	36.6	36.1	35.3	Decrease in large
Finland	1–19	8.8		8.4		7.7		7.8		8.6		9.1				Generally increasing small after 1974
	500+	59.0		59.1		59.5		59.9		58.9		57.6				
France	1–19	6.5		6.8		7.0	7.6	7.7	6.6	7.5	7.6	8.0	8.7			General increase in small. 1977 is a 'blip'
	500+	52.5		53.1		53.1	52.2	52.0	52.1	51.8	51.3	50.7	49.4			
Luxembourg	1–19				8.2				7.5	7.5	7.6	7.7				Little change in small since 1977
	500+				62.4				60.9	58.8	56.4	55.0				Decline in large
Netherlands	1–19									12.5	12.7	12.6	12.8	13.0		Increasing small
	500+									N.A.	N.A.	N.A.	N.A.	N.A.		
Japan	1–29	26.5	26.1	26.5	26.9	26.4	27.1	27.9	29.0	29.4	29.3	28.8	28.3	28.2	27.8	Small peaks in 1978 and after for small
	500+	36.2	36.5	36.8	35.8	36.9	35.4	33.9	32.9	32.4	31.7	32.3	32.7	32.9	33.3	Declining for large
Sweden	1–19				9.8	9.9	9.8	10.0	9.7	9.9	9.8	9.5	9.8	9.8	10.2	No change in small or large
	500+				56.3	55.9	56.4	56.2	56.3	55.7	55.7	56.7	55.8	55.2	54.1	
United Kingdom	1–19	N.A.			N.A.		N.A.	N.A.	N.A.	N.A.	N.A.	N.A.	N.A.			Continuous decline of large since 1973
	500+	70.3			71.5		70.5	69.9	70.1	69.9	69.6	68.2	66.3			
United States	1–19		4.8						4.9							Little change
	500+		71.1						71.0							

Source: OECD (1985)

Table 2.3 presents data on the proportion of total manufacturing employment in small enterprises (generally with less than 20 workers), over the period 1970–83. These data are presented in the upper row for each country. Some data are available for each of twelve countries over that time but only for Japan are data available for each year. At the other extreme, data for both Austria and the United States are available for only two of these years. Furthermore, data for small enterprises are not available for the United Kingdom and data for large enterprises shown in the lower row of the table are not available for the Netherlands. Finally whilst every effort is made to provide a broadly comparable time series across countries it has to be recognised that the original data sources vary considerably and so the figures presented should only be seen to be indicative of developments.

Given these reservations several important points emerge from the table. First that in ten out of the eleven countries small enterprises with (generally) less than 20 workers provided a higher proportion of manufacturing jobs in the final year for which data are available than in the first year. Only in Luxembourg does the share of small enterprises in manufacturing employment actually decline.

The lack of data for all years makes it difficult to assess whether this is a continuous development throughout the period, or whether it is of relatively short duration. In fact it possibly varies between countries; the data for Japan for example clearly show that small enterprises provide an increasing share of total employment in the period until 1978, but after that year the small firm share of employment declines. Very large enterprises in Japan with more than 500 workers are the mirror-image, providing a decreasing share of total employment in the period until 1978 and an increasing share after that time. The results for other countries are less clear but the data suggest that small enterprises have taken an increasing, and large enterprises a decreasing, share of total employment in most years in France, Australia, Denmark and the Netherlands. In the UK it is clear that large firms with more than 500 workers have been continuously reducing their share of employment.

Nevertheless, whilst it is broadly true that the share of total employment in small enterprises has been increasing and that of large enterprises declining during the 1970s and 1980s, the changes in shares are relatively modest in all countries. The largest changes over the period are recorded in Denmark where small enterprises increased their share of total employment from 6.8 per cent to 9.2 per cent over a decade. This suggests that the size structure of enterprises over time cannot be changed quickly.

Table 2.4 Percentage of employment in different sized establishments: manufacturing in OECD countries

Country		1970	1971	1972	1973	1974	1975	1976	1977	1978	1979	1980	1981	1982	1983	Comment
Australia	1–19						13.3	13.5	13.5	13.2	13.3	13.8	13.9	14.6	N.A.	Increase in very small
	500+						N.A.	N.A.	N.A.	N.A.	N.A.	N.A.	N.A.	N.A.	N.A.	
Austria	1–19				19.0								20.8			Decline in large
	500+				27.8								26.3			Increase in small
Belgium	1–19			12.7		12.3	12.9	13.2	13.6	13.9	14.0	13.8	14.1	14.4	14.4	Decline in large
	500+			30.6		31.8	31.2	31.3	32.3	31.8	32.7	33.0	32.4	32.1	32.3	Increase in small
Denmark	1–19	8.6			8.0		9.7				9.6			10.1		Decline in large
	500+	27.0			27.4		27.8				25.7			25.6		Increase in small
Finland	1–19	7.9	6.7	6.3	5.7	5.2	5.0	5.3	5.6	6.4	6.4	6.3	6.3	7.2		Declining small share 1970–75
	500+	30.8	32.6	33.0	33.8	33.8	33.8	32.8	31.5	30.7	29.9	30.4	29.8	27.9		Increasing small share 1976–82
France	1–19						11.3			11.9	12.2			13.5	14.1	Increasing small
	500+						35.5			35.0	34.0			31.9	31.3	Decreasing large
Japan	1–29			26.3			28.5			30.1			30.4			Increasing small
	500+			24.4			23.5			20.5			19.8			Decreasing large
Sweden	1–19	11.8	11.7	11.7	11.0	10.6	7.6	7.3	7.2	6.8	6.4	6.4	6.3	6.5		Break in 1974/5
	500+	30.8	31.2	31.1	31.9	32.9	42.2	41.5	40.7	40.7	40.9	40.2	40.2	39.6		Both very large and very small decline
United Kingdom	1–24							9.0	9.0	9.2			12.4			Increasing small
	500+							42.7	43.0	42.3			37.3			Decreasing large
United States	1–19	6.1	6.4	6.3	6.1	6.2	7.0			6.4			6.7			Break 1975/78 but generally increasing small and decreasing large
	500+	44.2	42.7	42.0	42.4	42.8	41.8			41.9			41.2			

Source: OECD (1985)

Table 2.4 provides manufacturing employment data for ten OECD countries over the 1970–83 period. The upper row shows the proportion of manufacturing employment in very small establishments for certain years during that period, whereas the lower row provides data on the proportion of manufacturing employment in the largest size of establishment. Here data are available for partial time series for ten countries but only for Japan and Finland are there continuous data for the 1970–82 period. Eight countries out of the ten show an increased share of manufacturing employment in small establishments, the exceptions being Sweden and Finland.

The data in Table 2.4 show a broadly similar pattern to that in Table 2.3 with generally modest increases in the importance of the very small establishments and a clear decline in importance of large establishments. The only exception appears to be Belgium where large establishments have become increasingly important and where very small establishments have also become increasingly important.

Tables 2.5 and 2.6 provide a time series for the *total* economy with Table 2.5 providing data on enterprise size and Table 2.6 providing data on establishment size. As noted earlier, data for the whole economy are more difficult to obtain, with only seven countries providing time series data, and two of these countries – United States and Austria – providing data for only two years. Of the remaining five, in France and Belgium it is clear that small enterprises accounted for an increasing share of employment throughout the period. In Japan, as noted in Table 2.3, small enterprises became increasingly important until 1978, after which time their relative importance declined. In the Netherlands there does not appear to be any evidence of change in the relative importance of small enterprises for the few years for which data are available, whilst in Sweden small enterprises became relatively *less* important throughout the period.

An examination of changes in the size distribution of establishments is shown in Table 2.6 but with the data being restricted to six countries only. The general pattern appears to be one of an increase in the importance of small establishments throughout the time period, together with a decline in importance of very large establishments. Only Belgium shows a contrary pattern.

To summarise, it appears from all four tables that there has been an increase in the relative importance of small enterprises and establishments and a decline in the relative importance of very large establishments and enterprises. Such trends appear clearest amongst small establishments within the whole economy. These trends, however, do

Table 2.5 Percentage of total employment in different sized enterprises: all sectors in OECD countries

Country		1970	1971	1972	1973	1974	1975	1976	1977	1978	1979	1980	1981	1982	1983	Comment
Australia	1–19				23.1								26.2			Increased small
	500+				36.2								33.4			Decreased large
Belgium	1–19				20.6	20.4	21.1	21.9	22.7	23.4	23.6	23.8	24.3	24.7	25.0	Increased small
	500+				34.9	35.3	35.0	34.1	33.6	33.0	33.3	33.2	32.8	32.7	32.6	Declining large
France	1–19			15.2		16.0	17.3	17.8	15.1	17.7	17.8	18.5	19.7			Increase in small
	500+			43.5		42.6	41.8	41.3	44.3	41.4	41.0	40.4	39.2			Decreased large
Japan	1–29	37.3	36.8	37.3	37.6	37.6	38.3	38.7	39.6	40.3	39.9	39.4	39.5	39.2	38.8	Increase in small to 1978 then decline in small. Decline in large
	500+	29.9	29.9	30.0	29.1	29.4	28.7	27.8	27.1	26.3	26.3	26.4	26.4	26.8	27.1	
Netherlands	1–19									25.8	25.7	25.5	24.6	25.9		No change in small
	500+									N.A.	N.A.	N.A.	N.A.	N.A.		N.A.
Sweden	1–19				17.4	17.5	17.0	17.6	16.8	16.5	16.4	15.5	15.9	15.1	15.6	Decreased small
	500+				53.2	53.4	55.6	54.6	56.1	57.9	57.7	59.6	59.1	60.6	58.6	Increased large
United States	1–19		22.0						21.6							
	500+		46.5						47.5							

Source: OECD (1985)

Table 2.6 Percentage of total employment in different sized establishments: all sectors in OECD countries

Country		1970	1971	1972	1973	1974	1975	1976	1977	1978	1979	1980	1981	1982	1983	Comment
Austria	1–19				31.1								33.6			Increased small
	500+				17.5								15.4			
Belgium	1–19				21.7	21.4	21.9	22.4	21.7	22.0	21.9	21.8	22.0	22.1	22.2	Slight increase in small
	500+				28.2	28.9	28.2	27.8	29.0	28.2	29.1	29.2	29.0	29.0	29.1	
France	1–19						27.4			28.8	29.5			31.4	32.1	Increase in small
	500+						20.7			19.9	18.9			17.1	16.5	
Japan	1–29			44.5			46.9			48.8			49.4			Increase in small
	500+			11.5			10.6			8.9			8.2			
United Kingdom	1–19					22.0	21.9	23.9	24.0	24.0	24.0			26.1		Increase in small
	500+				32.9	32.8	29.5	28.0	27.9	27.5			25.2			
United States	1–19	24.3	24.9	24.7	24.3	25.8	27.1				26.9		26.1			Increase in small
	500+	26.9	26.1	25.6	25.5	24.3	23.4				22.4		21.5			

Source: OECD (1985)

not apply in all countries and are occurring at very different rates. Nevertheless even in those countries where change is most rapid the size structure of employment units changes only slowly.

2.4   SOME EXPLANATIONS FOR THE CHANGE

The fact that these developments are occurring across a spectrum of developed countries over a similar time period requires some explanation. The key question is whether these changes are a single response to a common set of pressures or whether they are individual responses by firms and governments within those countries which coincidentally happen to have resulted in an increased share of small firm employment. It is imperative to reach a judgement on such matters before implementing public policy in this area.

Five possible 'explanations' have been provided for these developments. First it is suggested that the increased relative importance of small enterprises in developed economies as a whole is a reflection of the growing importance of the Service Sector – where average enterprise size tends to be smaller – at the expense of manufacturing – where average enterprise size tends to be larger. OECD (1985) conducted a shift-share analysis of changes and confirmed that this 'compositional' effect explains only about one-quarter of the shift in Austria, about half in Belgium and France, three-quarters in Japan and 100 per cent in the Netherlands. This suggests that changes in the relative importance of small firms are significantly affected in many countries by the move towards the service economy, but it does not explain why, *within* manufacturing, there is also an increasingly important contribution to employment and output being made by small firms.

A second possible explanation for these developments lies in recent technical developments. For example, it is argued that increased use of microprocessors, CNC machine tools, etc., which can be installed cheaply by small firms, has eliminated many of the scale economies previously available only to large firms. Whilst scale economies at the plant level have been reducing, organisational economies have apparently been moving in the same direction. As we shall show in Chapter 5 much of industry is becoming increasingly fragmented with activities which were formally undertaken *within* a large company now being sub-contracted out to smaller firms. Examples include data input services, advertising and public relations, transport and catering. It is argued that a large company cannot provide the incentives and motivation which are available to workers and owners of a small firm, where the performance of the firm (and hence their own jobs) is much more clearly related to their own performance. The small firm may therefore generate a stronger sense of team spirit amongst the workforce and a greater element of commitment by management. Technological changes therefore enabled many of the traditional organisational advantages of small firms to be realised.

A third possible explanation is that of recession. Here it is argued that during a recession large firms shed labour rapidly, and because redundant individuals are unable to obtain employment within the formal labour market they may establish their own small businesses – particularly in sectors where entry barriers are low. This argument may be counter-intuitive in the sense that smaller marginal firms might be expected to have higher unit costs and, in the event of a reduction in demand, be eliminated from the market. Indeed the high failure rates amongst small firms could indicate the importance of this factor. Contini *et al.* (1984) however, argue that the overall cost structure of businesses has become increasingly rigid partly, but by no means exclusively, because of labour rigidity. This combined with increasing uncertainty in both the product and factor markets, means there is an increased likelihood of fixed structures being under-utilised, and that it is this risk which promotes the search for alternative organisational structures. It may be that vertical *dis*integration provides the large firm with the additional flexibility in which there are cost advantages under conditions of shrinking and uncertain demand. It is these factors that have led to an increased role for subcontracting small firms, which are providing goods and services formerly provided 'in-house' by large firms.

Fourthly it is argued that although recession may have been initially a major stimulus to the growth of small firms, their merits are increasingly apparent to management such that small units are likely to be retained in the event of an upswing in the economy. This is not simply a reflection of a 'small is beautiful' fashion but stems instead from a recognition by management that labour tends to be more flexible in smaller units. It is not possible to have strict demarcation of responsibilities; instead labour has to switch between tasks. It also means that part-time labour can be more easily employed both because the smaller plant is less likely to be unionised, and because the variations in output – and hence demand for labour – can best be met by flexible part-time staff. Since the small firm is itself responding to, and absorbing the variations in demand in the economy as a whole, it has to be flexible in the sense of being able to increase substantially or reduce to zero its own output. The small firm therefore demands flexibility of its own inputs; so fixed assets are low and labour is required to be available for employment – even though the firm cannot necessarily offer a commitment to employment. Bradley Schiller (1985) for example shows that in the United States small firms are major employers of school leavers seeking their first job and of part-time female workers. The low levels of unionisation, the employment of part-time workers, the absence of fringe benefits and the ability in many cases to circumvent health and safety and other worker protection legislation mean that such small firms can have low unit labour costs which enable them to produce additional output at very low cost.

Finally, it is argued that overall motivation in small firms may be better than in large. This argument has several dimensions. It is suggested that the employee in a small firm is more likely to be satisfied with his or her work than is his/her equivalent in a large firm, partly because the tasks in a small firm are less routine and provide more direct job satisfaction, and partly because management is closer and more approachable. Key decisions can then be reached on a more informal basis, leading to lower absenteeism, fewer strikes etc. The evidence on this, however, is far from convincing, Curran and Stanworth (1986) and Storey (1982) suggesting instead that there are few real differences in attitude which reflect the size of the firm, although variations are found between sectors, between locations and between points in time.

More recently, however, it has been suggested that the prime benefit of the growing number of smaller units in an economy lies in the additional motivation given to the management rather than the workforce. In many developed economies middle and often senior management in large firms have very restricted areas of responsibility. Frequently, if they had developed a career in, for example, personnel, this can lead them to lose touch with developments in production and vice versa. This, in turn, makes it more difficult for individual managers when promoted to positions of responsibility to take strategic decisions about the company. It can also lead either to disaffection by less senior groups of managers or to empire-building which may not necessarily be in the overall interest of the company. The growth of forms of vertical disintegration such as management buy-outs and the additional use by large companies of out-workers, consultants and the 'hiving-off' of functions such as catering, transport and cleaning has meant that managers become aware of all aspects of running a business. Since it is their livelihood and often their own money which has been invested, the small firm provides a major stimulus to improved management and efficiency.

2.5 SMALL FIRMS AND ECONOMIC PERFORMANCE: SOME INTERNATIONAL EVIDENCE

The key result of the work by David Birch, in the USA, which excited interest among many politicians was that small firms were a major source of new job creation. If this result was widely applicable it would be expected that those advanced countries having a high proportion of employment in small firms would be expected to have, for example, faster rates of economic growth, lower levels of unemployment and lower rates of job shedding than economies dominated by large firms.

Three points need to be made immediately. First, although we will examine the relationship between the importance of small firms in the *manufacturing* sector with *economy-wide* performance in terms of unemployment rates, this approach is less questionable than might initially appear. For those countries which did provide data for the manufacturing and non-manufacturing sectors there was a strong positive correlation between the importance of small firms in both sectors. Countries with a high proportion of employment in small firms in the service sector tended to have a high proportion of employment in small firms in the manufacturing sector and so it is possible to use small firm employment in manufacturing as a proxy for the whole economy. Secondly, we have already noted that the year for which the data available applies in each country varies considerably. Clearly it would be desirable to have all data being for a single year but this is not possible. Again, however, this should not concern us unduly since, as Table 2.3 shows, the proportions of total manufacturing employment in different firm sizes normally only change a maximum of two or three percentage points over a decade. Thirdly, in all countries a small firm is defined as an enterprise having less than 100 workers. However for three of the countries, Germany, Ireland and Italy, data are not collected for firms employing less than 20 workers, whilst in the Swedish case the data include some public sector establishments. To overcome the shortage of data for the 0–19 worker group we have firstly used the unadjusted figures. In a second set of calculations we have added to the unadjusted figures a proportion which represents the average contribution made by firms with less than 20 workers in all the remaining 11 countries. This we call the adjusted data.

The proportion of employment in manufacturing firms with less than 100 employees is plotted against job shedding in manufacturing 1980–82 in Figure 2.1 (a) and against rates of unemployment in 1983 in Figure 2.1 (b). The positions of Japan and the United Kingdom stand out immediately and it is easy to see why it is inferred that, if only these

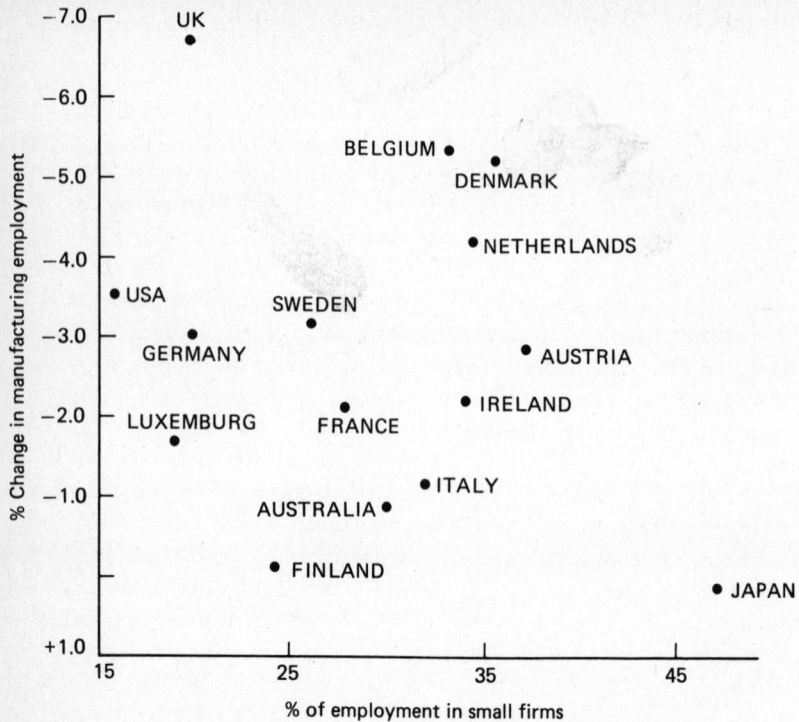

Figure 2.1 (a)   Manufacturing employment change (%) 1980–82 and percentage employment in small firms in the OECD countries

countries are considered, both unemployment and job shedding are positively related to the proportion of employment in large firms. However it is the UK and Japan which are the exceptional cases when all OECD countries are included. To demonstrate the effect of their inclusion/exclusion, Table 2.7 shows the simple correlation coefficients.

First none of the correlation coefficients are significant at the 5 per cent level either including or excluding UK and Japan or with or without the adjustments made for Ireland, Italy and Germany. Secondly it can be seen that these correlation coefficients are sensitive to the exclusion/inclusion of UK and Japan but relatively insensitive to the adjustments made for Italy, Ireland and Germany. The inclusion of Japan and the UK indicate that job shedding and unemployment are highest in those countries where small firms are less important, but it is interesting to

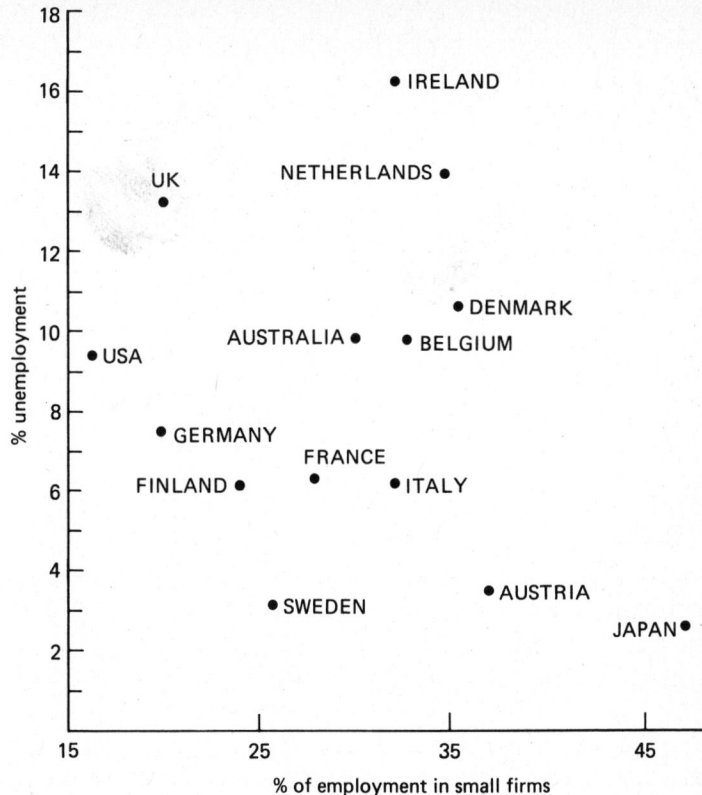

Figure 2.1 (b)   Unemployment rates and share of small firm manufacturing
employment in the OECD countries, 1983

note that this observation depends exclusively on the presence of the UK
and Japan. Once these countries are excluded, as in columns 3 and 4 of
the table the signs on the coefficients are reversed and those countries
which are more dependent on small firms in fact 'perform' *worse* than
those more dependent on large firms.

In conclusion it appears that there is no evidence whatsoever for the
assertion that the economies of those countries where small firms are
dominant perform better than those where small firms are less
important. Hence increasing the number, or relative importance, of
small firms in an economy will not necessarily lead either to increasing
employment or reduced unemployment.

Table 2.7 Correlation coefficients: percentage of manufacturing employment in small firms, (EMP) with unemployment in 1983 (UN 83) and manufacturing job loss 1980–82 (MF LOSS)

	1 EMP	*2* EMP	*3* EMP	*4* EMP
UN 83	− 0.2638	− 0.1953	+ 0.1017	+ 0.2398
MF LOSS	+ 0.2042	+ 0.2990	− 0.3229	− 0.2104
	N = 14	N = 14	N = 12	N = 12
	Unadjusted	Adjusted	Unadjusted	Adjusted

Note: Adjusted means that data for Ireland, Italy and Germany are adjusted to take into account that no data for employment in firms with less than 20 workers are provided.
N = 14   includes UK and Japan.
N = 12   excludes UK and Japan.
Source: OECD (1985)

2.6 THE EFFECTS OF CHANGES IN THE IMPORTANCE OF SMALL FIRMS

The absence of any clear unambiguous relationship at the level of the national economy between firm size and employment creation/reduction in unemployment is due either to the absence of any real relationship or to specification errors. Any relationship between the size structure of employment units and job creation/unemployment reduction is considerably more complex than the unvariate function outlined above and hence specification errors are likely to be present. For example, in explaining changes in employment, factors such as productivity changes, manufacturing/service employment, public/private sector employment are all potentially relevant variables. In examining changes in unemployment, additional forces such as activity rates, demographic changes and migration patterns also have to be included. To include these factors when only fourteen observations are available, whilst it would increase explanatory power, would make it impossible to adequately interpret the equations.

A second possible specification error is that any relationship between firm size and employment creation should examine *changes* in rather than the absolute value of these variables. It has already been noted above that many of the explanations for the relative increase in importance of small firms are related to developments in the 1970s – technical change, recession, third world competition, etc. On the other hand Tables 2.3–2.6 showed that whilst there was a general increase in importance of small firms in most economies the change rarely exceeded 2–3 per cent over a decade, whereas there were, during the 1970s, absolute differences between countries of more than 20 per cent.

In this situation it may be more relevant to test whether, during the 1970s, those countries which experienced the greatest increase in the relative importance of small firms were those which experienced the greatest/smallest reduction in employment within the manufacturing sector.

To test this hypothesis, data was used on employment change in the 1970s in the twelve OECD countries, providing data on enterprise size in manufacturing, as identified in Table 2.8. For all countries with the exception of Austria it is possible to distinguish between changes in the share of very small firms (generally with less than 20 workers) in the early 1970s and changes in their share over the late 1970s and early 1980s. The actual years which are used in the analysis are shown in Table 2.8. For Austria it is not possible to distinguish changes over two periods and so only changes over the whole of the period 1973–81 are included.

Table 2.8   Comparison of employment change in small manufacturing enterprises: years selected

	Early 1970s	Key	Late 1970s Early 1980s	Key
Australia			1975–82	A1
Austria	1973–81	A2		
Belgium			1978–83	B
Denmark	1973–78	D1	1978–83	D2
Finland	1970–76	F1	1976–80	F2
France	1971–76	FR1	1976–81	FR2
Luxembourg	1973–77	L1	1977–80	L2
Netherlands			1978–82	N
Japan	1971–78	J1	1978–83	J2
Sweden	1973–77	S1	1977–82	S2
United Kingdom	1973–76	UK1	1976–81	UK2
United States	1972–77	USA		

Small Firms defined as those manufacturing enterprises having less than 20 workers, except in Sweden where small is defined as less than 21 workers, in Japan where it is less than 30 workers and in the United Kingdom where it is less than 100 workers.

Sources: *OECD Employment Review* 1985 and unpublished data for Finland, France, Luxembourg and Netherlands data on manufacturing employment taken from *OECD Labour Force Statistics*.

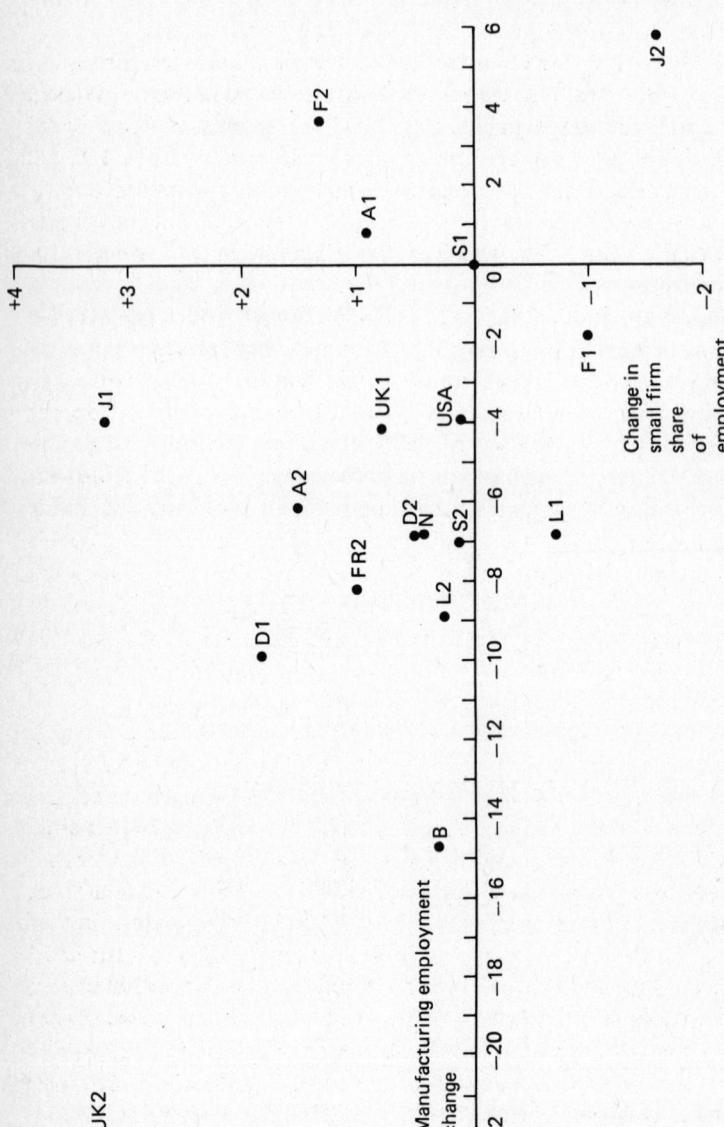

Figure 2.2 Manufacturing employment change and change in share of employment in small enterprises
Source: OECD (1985)

Furthermore, early period data for Australia, Belgium and Netherlands are missing, whilst later period data for the United States are not available.

In Figure 2.2, changes in the share of manufacturing enterprises with (generally) less than 20 employees over the relevant time period are compared with changes in manufacturing employment in that economy over the same time period. It might therefore be expected that if small firms were major new job creators then those countries where small firms were experiencing the largest increase in their share of employment would be those with the largest increase/smallest decrease in employment.

An examination of Figure 2.2 shows that there is considerable variation in the performance of the various countries and that Japan and the UK in the latter 1970s (J2 and UK2) are both significantly out of line with other OECD countries, but for very different reasons. In the case of the UK this may be because the small firm sector is defined as less than 100 workers rather than 20 workers. The UK however experienced a massive *reduction* in manufacturing employment and a massive *increase* in the share of small firms. From our knowledge of the UK economy we do not believe that if the data were available for the 1–20 employment range that the UK would be less out of line. Indeed it is probable that during this period it was the smallest size grouping which experienced an even faster growth than the 1–99 size group, and so the UK would have been even more 'exceptional' than Figure 2.2 suggests.

The other exception is Japan in the the later period (J2). During this time Japan experienced a major *increase* in manufacturing employment and a *reduction* in the share of employment in very small enterprises. With the exception of these two 'extremes' the data for the remaining countries are not incompatible with the hypothesis that increases in manufacturing employment are associated with an increase in the share of manufacturing employment in very small enterprises, but the association is weak. The role of these extreme values is illustrated in Equations 1 (a) and 1 (b) of Table 2.9. Equation 1 (a) shows that when all eighteen data points are included in the analysis an *increased* share of employment in small firms is significantly associated with a *reduction* in employment. In the framework of the current analysis a reduction in manufacturing employment leads to small firms becoming relatively more important i.e. having a large share of employment. Even so the overall explanatory power of the equations is relatively low with $R^2 = 0.202$.

Once the extreme values of UK2 and J2 are excluded, however, any relationship disappears completely, as is shown in Equation 1 (b) of Table 2.9. Amongst the remaining countries there is no relationship between manufacturing employment change and changes in the average size structure of manufacturing employment units. Whilst the above tests broadly take the early 1970s as one period, and the late 1970s and early 1980s as the second period, the actual number of years over which the tests are conducted vary. Furthermore, in countries such as Japan, the share of small enterprises increases in the early period and declines in the later period so that these short periods may merely reflect trade cycle conditions rather than longer term developments.

An alternative test is to compare employment change and the change in the relative importance of small enterprises over as long a period as possible. Unfortunately as was shown in Table 2.3 the period covered by data for each country varies considerably. In some countries such as the Netherlands, data are not available until 1978 and then available annually until 1982, whereas data are not available for the United States beyond 1977. Clearly if the relative growth of small firms is a reflection of the particular economic conditions of the mid to late 1970s it is unfortunate that data on these matters are not available for all countries for comparable years.

It is possible to partly overcome these problems by taking. for each country, base year data for 1973 or the year closest to 1973 and comparing *annualised* percentage changes in both total manufacturing employment and the share of small enterprises with (generally) less than 20 employees over the period 1973–1983, or year closest to 1983. The results of this comparison are shown in Figure 2.3. Again the results

Table 2.9 Regression results: changes in employment in small firms and changes in manufacturing employment/unemployment

Equation 1(a)
$$\Delta\ \mathrm{EMP}\ = 0.231 - 0.09\ \Delta\ \mathrm{SF} \qquad R^2 = 0.202$$
$$\qquad\qquad\ \ (0.614)\ (2.01) \qquad\qquad\ N\ = 18$$

Equation 1 (b)
$$\Delta\ \mathrm{EMP}\ = 0.791 + 0.125\ \Delta\ \mathrm{SF} \qquad R^2 = 0.003$$
$$\qquad\qquad\ \ (1.838)\ (0.199) \qquad\qquad N\ = 16$$

Equation 2
$$\Delta\ \mathrm{EMP}\ = 0.122 - 0.006\ \Delta\ \mathrm{SF} \qquad R^2 = 0.026$$
$$\qquad\qquad\ \ (3.707)\ (0.490) \qquad\qquad N\ = 11$$

Equation 3
$$\Delta\ \mathrm{UN}\ \ = 0.079 + 0.11\ \Delta\ \mathrm{SF} \qquad R^2 = 0.323$$
$$\qquad\qquad\ \ (2.29)\ (1.96) \qquad\qquad\ \ N\ = 10$$

Source: OECD (1985)

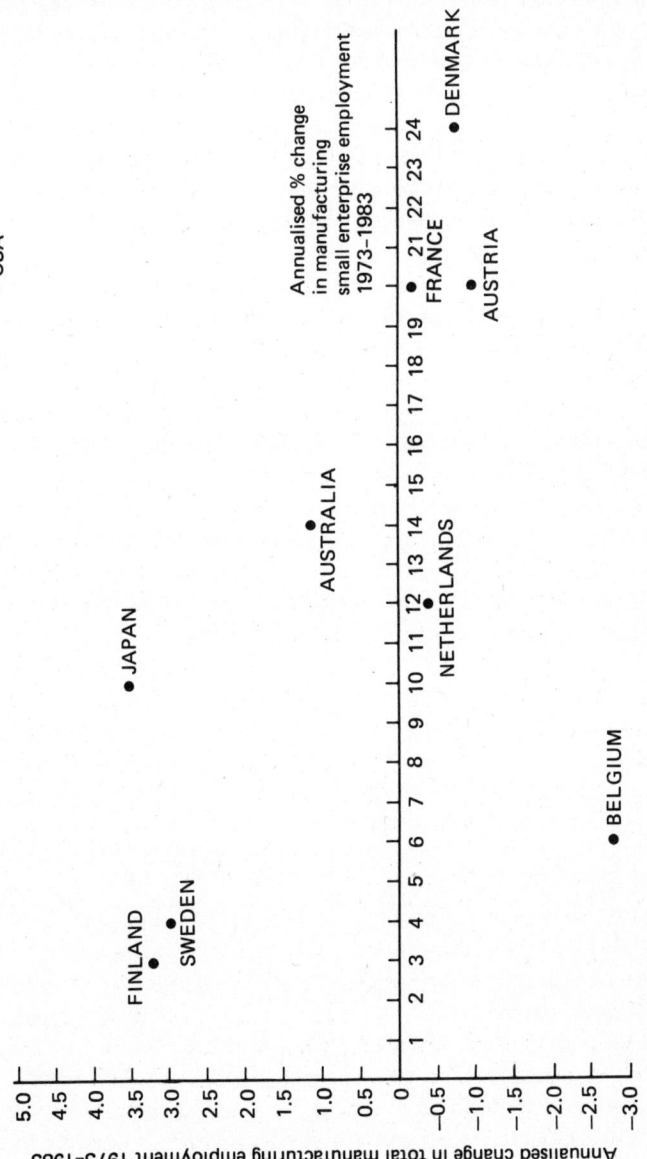

Figure 2.3 Manufacturing employment change and changes in the share of employment in small firms 1973–83
Source: OECD (1985)

indicate a considerable spread in performance. The countries which fit the 'expected' pattern best are the United States where total manufacturing employment increased rapidly and where the share of small firms also rose, and Belgium where manufacturing employment declined and where the increase in the share of manufacturing employment in small enterprises was smallest. The remaining countries, however, fail to support the 'expected' hypothesis. Indeed it would appear that, if anything, the relationship is again the opposite of that predicted. For example, Finland, Sweden and Japan all experienced a substantial increase in manufacturing employment yet the increase in the share of employment in small firms was modest. On the other hand France, Denmark and Austria each experienced either the low rates of manufacturing employment growth or absolute decline yet had the fastest rate of increase in the proportion of employment in small firms.

This diversity of performance is reflected in Equation 2 of Table 2.9 which shows that over the 1973–83 period changes in manufacturing employment are unrelated to changes in the average size structure of manufacturing enterprises across the eleven countries providing broadly comparable data. Finally we examine changes in unemployment in the 1973–83 period in ten OECD countries with changing shares of manufacturing employment in small firms. Here it would be expected that those countries where the small firm sector is expanding fastest – as reflected in its increasing share of employment – would be those where unemployment rose most slowly over the decade. Again it has to be recognised that small enterprise data apply only to the manufacturing sector and in addition that unemployment rates are affected by a variety of factors other than employment opportunities. Nevertheless the policy thrust within many developed countries has been to see an increasingly active and growing small firm sector as a panacea for increasing unemployment.

The results of Figure 2.4 provide no support for the view that an increasingly important small manufacturing sector is associated with smaller increases in male unemployment rates. If anything, the evidence again points to the opposite inference with Finland and Sweden experiencing both small increases in unemployment and a small increase in the share of manufacturing employment in small firms. Conversely Denmark experiences a major rise in both unemployment and of the share of manufacturing employment in small firms. With the exception of these Scandinavian countries there appears to be little pattern to the relationship.

Equation 3 of Table 2.9 provides the regression coefficients for this

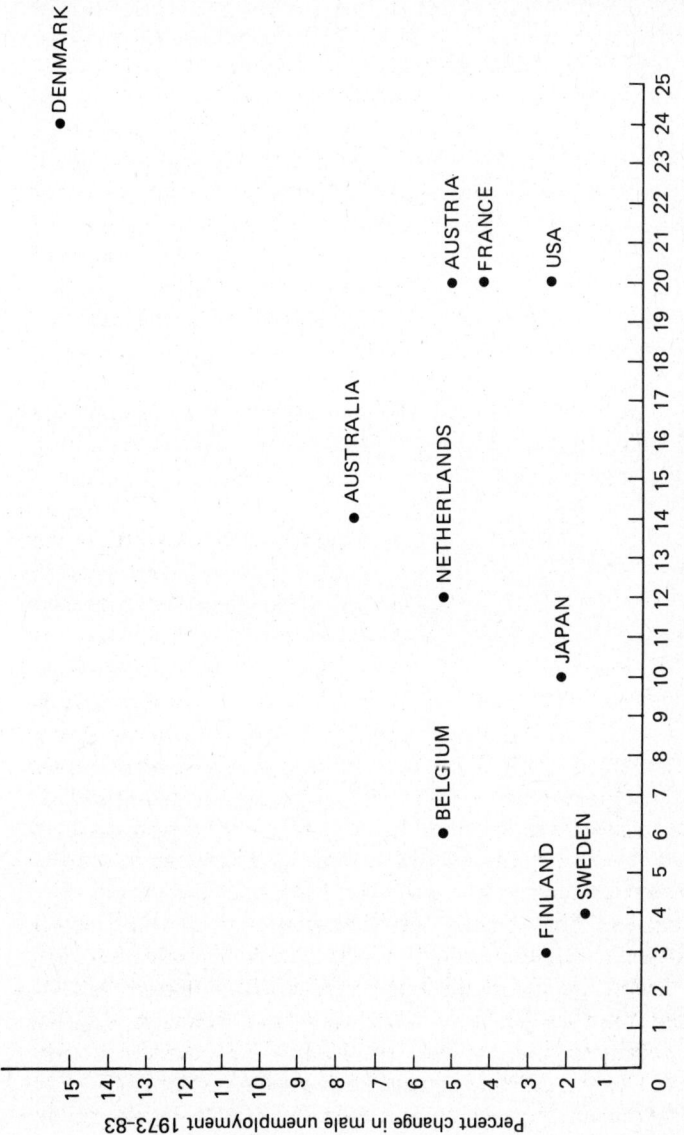

Figure 2.4 Changes in male unemployment and changes in the share of employment in small firms, 1973–83
Source: OECD (1985)

analysis and shows that *increases* in unemployment are significantly positively associated with *increasing* shares of manufacturing employment in small firms i.e. the opposite to that which is currently predicted. As we showed in Figure 2.4 these results depend upon the role of the Scandinavian countries. We therefore conclude that for most countries the changing size structure of manufacturing enterprises is not clearly related to the performance of the national economy either in terms of job creation or in terms of reductions in unemployment.

The limitations imposed by the data mean that our conclusions from this section are somewhat negative. All that can justifiably be inferred is that there is no clear relationship between the performance of an economy in terms of job creation/unemployment reduction and the size structure of its employment units. If anything our analysis suggests that Britain and Japan are closer to being 'special' cases, rather than being at opposite ends of a continuous relationship.

2.7 SELF-EMPLOYMENT

In several major developed countries interest in self-employment has paralleled interest in the role of small businesses as a major source of job creation. Self-employment is generally defined as employers, own account workers, members of producer co-operatives and in some cases unpaid family workers. Clearly the growth of new businesses is likely to parallel growth in the numbers of employers but interest amongst employment policy-makers is also expressed in changes in the number of 'own account' workers. The latter group, although they currently do not employ other individuals, in some instances may be thought of as 'apprentice' employers. In some cases they may start a business as an 'own account' worker but, in the event of an increase in demand for their product/service become an employer. Indeed if the objective of policy is to raise either the rate of new firm formation or the total stock of businesses in the economy then an increase in self-employment may be a good 'leading indicator'. Nevertheless it should be stressed that self-employment is not identical to new firm formation (Johnson 1981) and that the characteristics of self-employed individuals becoming employers is likely to differ significantly from self-employed individuals who are own account workers (Pickles and O'Farrell 1987). It also seems likely that they will differ from self-employed individuals participating in co-operative enterprises.

From the earlier results in this chapter it might be expected that increases in self-employment would be taking place in many countries

Table 2.10   Proportion of self-employment to civilian employment in the non-agricultural sector (percentages)

	1969	1973	1979	1981	1984	Comment
Australia	9.3	9.5	12.4	12.1	12.4	r
Austria[a]	13.1	11.7	8.9	8.6	7.9	f
Belgium	11.9[b]	11.0	11.2	11.5	12.3	r
Canada	—	5.8[c]	6.7	6.4	7.4	r
Denmark	—	9.7[c]	9.2	8.3	8.4[d]	f
Finland	—	—	—	—	6.9	nc
France	—	9.7	8.7	8.7	9.1[d]	f/r
Germany	8.3	7.6	7.7	7.6	8.2	f/r
Greece	—	—	—	27.8	27.3	nc
Iceland [a]	10.2	8.3	7.0	7.0	7.3[d]	f/r
Ireland	9.6[e]	10.1	10.4	9.6	11.4	nc
Italy	—	17.8	18.7	19.6	20.6[d]	r
Japan	14.6	14.1	14.0	13.6	13.0	f
Netherlands	—	3.7[c]	4.1	5.6	4.9[d]	r
New Zealand	7.5[e]	9.1[f]	—	8.4	—	r/f
Norway	7.9[g]	7.8	6.5	6.8	6.4	f
Portugal	—	11.5[h]	12.1	11.6	—	nc
Spain	16.1[b]	16.3	15.9	16.3	17.9	nc
Sweden	5.6[b]	4.8	4.5	4.6	4.7	nc
Switzerland	7.6[b]	—	7.5[i]	—	—	nc
Turkey	25.0[b]	25.0[c]	20.8[i]	—	—	nc
United Kingdom[a]	6.5	7.3	6.6	7.9	8.7[d]	r
United States	7.0	6.7	7.1	7.3	7.6	r
Unweighted average [j]	—	9.5	9.4	9.5	9.9	—
Coefficient of variation (%)[j]	—	40	42	42	44	—

[a] The data include unpaid family workers.
[b] 1970.
[c] 1975.
[d] 1983.
[e] 1971.
[f] 1976.
[g] 1972.
[h] 1974.
[i] 1980.
[j] Summary statistics are calculated excluding Finland, Greece, New Zealand, Portugal, Switzerland and Turkey.
Note: f = falling: r = rising: n.c. = no clear change.
Source: OECD (1986)

during the 1970s. Table 2.10, however, shows that during the years 1969–84, self employment in the non-agricultural sector rose in about one third of OECD countries, remained broadly constant in another third and fell in the remaining third.

The countries which experienced a significant rise were the United States, United Kingdom, Canada, Italy, Australia and the Netherlands. The presence of such 'influential' countries within this group is the probable reason why it is now a popular view that the growth of self-employment is a major and widespread trend amongst developed countries. Table 2.10, however, makes it clear that these developments are far from uniform, with Germany experiencing a decline in self employment between 1969 and 1973, followed by an increase.

Amongst the countries experiencing a general decline in self-employment are Japan where the proportion fell in each year from 1969 onwards. Others experiencing a fall include Austria, Denmark and Norway, whilst almost all the remaining countries experience no clear rise or fall over the period.

Finally it should be noted that the change in the proportion of the non-agricultural labour force which is self-employed is very small over the decade of the 1970s. The largest change has been in the United Kingdom where self-employment grew from 6.6 per cent in 1979 to 8.7 per cent in 1983. The strong impression from the data presented in Table 2.10 is of some movement, perhaps in a slightly upward direction since 1979, but no consistent changes over the longer period 1969–1984. OECD (1986) attribute the changes which have taken place since 1979 to three main factors. The first is the now familiar one of increasing unemployment, the second is the growth of business and professional services which can be more flexibly supplied by the self-employed and thirdly the growth of politically inspired measures by governments to promote self-employment.

The evidence on the importance of unemployment as a factor explaining the growth of self-employment is documented by OECD. They find that the proportion of self-employment to civilian employment fluctuates counter cyclically in almost all OECD countries except for Japan and Australia. Their regression coefficients suggest that a 1 per cent rise in unemployment has tended to increase the proportion of self employment by less than 0.3 per cent.

Structural changes in the characteristics of the self-employed work-force are apparent. Over the last ten years the major growth in self-employment has been amongst technical, professional and related workers particularly in the service sector. These groups have increased substantially whereas others which formerly dominated the ranks of the self-employed, such as production and transport workers, as well as general labourers, have experienced little growth in numbers.

It is not clear to what extent the growth in self-employment is a response to government policies i.e. genuinely additional activity which would not have been generated in the absence of a policy initiative, as opposed to government policy merely financing a development which would have taken place anyway (deadweight). Policies to promote self-employment, particularly amongst the unemployed, have been introduced in France, Ireland, UK and the Netherlands whereby unemployed workers do not lose entitlement to state financial assistance if they start a business. In France, for example, the unemployed worker may be provided with a capital sum equivalent to six months of benefits if he or she wishes to start a business.

It therefore appears that whilst the relative importance of self-employment in developed countries has not risen as consistently as has the share of small firms in total employment there has certainly been an increase amongst the major industrialised nations with the exception of Japan. Since 1979 the relative importance of self-employment appears to have increased in several countries.

2.8 CONCLUSION

This chapter has shown that the relative importance of small firms varies markedly from one OECD country to another. In Japan, for instance nearly 40 per cent of all workers are employed in firms with less than 30 workers, compared with only 15 per cent in Sweden.

During the 1970s and early 1980s there appears to be strong evidence of a changing size structure of employment units, with large firms reducing their share of total employment and small firms increasing their share. Whilst these developments are occurring in most OECD countries the magnitude of the change should not be overestimated. Even where the change has been most rapid the shares of large and small firms have only altered by a few percentage points over the period.

It is hypothesised that during this period small firms are the major source of new jobs in developed countries since they have the ability both to respond flexibly during recessions and to take advantage of the new technologies developed during the period. It might therefore be expected that those countries which had a high proportion of employment in small firms would have a better record of job creation than countries where the economy tended to be dominated by large firms.

If the hypotheses were correct then it would suggest that countries with a poor economic performance should pursue policies to raise the rate of small firm formation (and survival). Unfortunately the data available for testing this hypothesis are relatively weak but the preliminary results suggest that only the 'extreme' cases of UK and Japan support such a hypothesis. The remaining OECD countries offer no support for such a view. It appears that there is no clear relationship between the size structure of employment units in a country and its economic performance in terms of employment creation/reductions in unemployment throughout the 1970s and early 1980s. It would therefore be very unwise for countries experiencing economic difficulties to believe that increasing the number of small businesses in an economy is *necessarily* likely to lead to improved performance.

The examination of self-employment trends suggests that this has risen in about one third of OECD countries since the early 1970s, but has remained static in another third and declined in the remainder. Since 1979 it appears, however, that self-employment has risen in rather more countries than it has fallen.

Several theories have been advanced to explain these developments – technical change, recession, fashion, government initiatives, increased energy prices, Third World competition etc. At this stage it is not possible to favour any single or combination of explanations although it has been noted that the role of recessionary conditions is consistently important in explaining both the relative growth of small firms and the growth in self employment.

One major difficulty with testing these theories is that, from an examination of data on the share of total employment by different sized units, it is not possible to determine the underlying dynamics of employment change. For example it is quite possible for small firms to be a major source of employment growth and yet their *share* of employment to be falling between two points in time. Similarly, an increase in the small firm share of employment does not necessarily imply that small firms are major generators of jobs. This may simply reflect the fact that large firms are contracting and becoming small firms. Only by examining employment growth at the level of the individual enterprise is it possible, in principle, to determine the relative contribution of different sized enterprises. It is the tracking of births, deaths, expansions and contractions of employment within individual enterprises that is called 'Job Generation' and it is to a review of that material which we now turn.

3 Job Generation in North America

3.1 INTRODUCTION

In 1979 David Birch, of MIT, produced the seminal report 'The Job Generation Process', which purported to show that two thirds of the increase in employment in the United States between 1969 and 1976 was in firms employing less than 20 workers.

The implications of this report were clearly that if new employment opportunities were to be created then it was the task of the government to provide conditions most suited to inducing growth amongst small firms. The report coincided with the election to office of Ronald Reagan in the USA and Margaret Thatcher in Britain, both of whom were politically highly sympathetic to such arguments. Indeed the cynics in the UK suggested that if David Birch had not existed then Margaret Thatcher would probably have invented him!

Any work as massively influential as that of Birch will inevitably be the target of criticism, and on both sides of the Atlantic his work was attacked, sometimes on grounds of ideology and sometimes on grounds of methodology. In this chapter we shall examine the latter challenges within the United States, notably those from Catherine Armington and Marjorie Odle, then at the Brookings Institution. To place that challenge in context we begin with a brief description of the purpose of job generation studies.

The major objective of this chapter is to demonstrate that although current computing technology enables analysis to be conducted on massive data bases including annual data on five million establishments and four million enterprises (US Government 1985, p. 21), considerable judgement on the part of the researchers has to be exercised in producing 'simple' summary statistics. This judgement is needed because those entrepreneurs and establishments included in the data base may have significantly different characteristics from those not included. Unfortunately, these judgements can lead to major differences in results obtained on key issues such as the contribution of small firms to job creation. It is our task to set out, as clearly as possible, the nature of these judgements and offer an outsider's view on the debate between MIT and Brookings. The minimum which we expect the reader to gain from this chapter is a recognition that statistics on jobs created by small or large firms are to be treated with even more than normal caution.

3.2 JOB GENERATION – COMPONENTS OF CHANGE ANALYSIS

'Job Generation' studies attempt to examine within the private market sector, the magnitude of job losses and job gains at the micro level (i.e. at the level of the individual firm and/or establishment). Emphasis is placed upon which 'types' of firm or establishment (size, age, sector, etc) are responsible for the generation of new jobs, and for the loss of jobs.

It is argued that the availability of micro level data facilitates a better understanding of the factors underlying employment change. For example, an increase in the share of total employment accounted for by small firms does not necessarily imply that small firms are generating large numbers of new jobs. It may simply be the (arithmetic) result of large firms contracting. Similarly, a decrease in the small business share of employment could indicate that small firms are growing rapidly and moving into higher size bands. Only micro level data can quantify the relative importance of these effects.

In order to investigate the micro-level changes which give rise to changes in the aggregate distribution, it is necessary to trace the employment changes which take place within each individual firm/establishment over a period of years. The 'components of change' approach identifies six possible ways in which employment may change in each individual unit. These 'gross components' are:

(i) employment generated from the opening of new establishments
(ii) employment loss from closure of existing establishments
(iii) employment generated by expansion at 'in situ' establishments
(iv) employment lost by contraction at 'in situ' establishments
(v) employment generated by in-migrants to the area
(vi) employment lost by out-migrants from the area

The way in which these gross components combine to give the overall net employment change can be summarised in Figure 3.1.

Data requirements

In order to carry out a components of change analysis of a particular country, region, area or sector, it is clearly necessary to obtain longitudinal data on individual establishments over the time period,

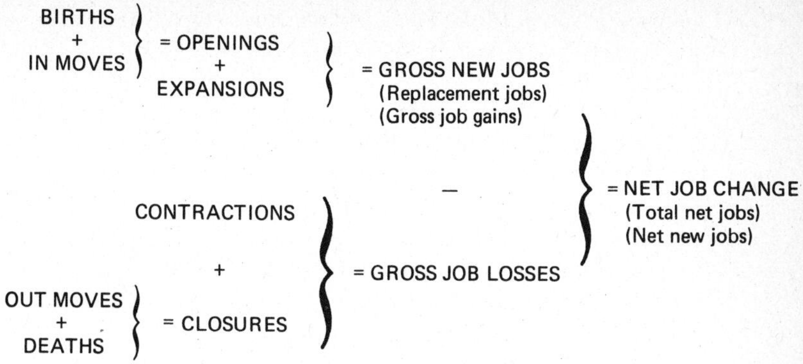

Figure 3.1   The job generation process

Source: Storey (1980)

covered by the analysis. Accurate information on 'deaths' of existing units and 'births' of new firms or establishments is also a pre-requisite. The importance of obtaining as accurate and representative a data base as possible cannot be over-emphasised. Any errors, omissions and biases within the original data base are likely to be translated into highly misleading results. This is, or course, true for any form of empirical research, but when emphasis is placed upon particular components, notably births, coverage of which is frequently patchy, the conclusions from the study become highly dependent upon the quality of the input data.

The data base which has been used extensively by 'job generation' researchers in the United States and Canada is derived from data collected by the Dun and Bradstreet credit company. The following section summarises the principal findings of these studies. The remainder of the Chapter will discuss the nature of the Dun and Bradstreet data base, its limitations, and the ways in which different researchers have attempted to overcome these problems. Most importantly, the extent to which different approaches to the analysis of the raw data give rise to significantly different results, will be illustrated and discussed.

3.3   RESULTS DERIVED FROM THE DUN AND BRADSTREET DATA BASE IN THE UNITED STATES AND CANADA

The Dun and Bradstreet data base has been utilised by three main groups of researchers in the United States – the Program on Neighborhood and Regional Change at the Massachusetts Institute of Technology (MIT), the Business Microdata Project at the Brookings Institution and the US Small Business Administration (SBA). In Canada, the Department of Regional Industrial Expansion has also undertaken a job generation study using the Canadian Dun and Bradstreet data base, with the assistance of David Birch. A major problem with any comparative analysis of job generation studies is that the results can be presented in various ways, using different definitions, industrial and regional groupings, and covering different time periods. Here we present the results in such a way that comparisons can be made across different studies, and wherever possible major discrepancies are pointed out in footnotes to the tables.

3.3.1   Job generation by size of firm

The prime focus of attention in the job generation literature has been upon the comparative job creating potential of small and large firms. This derives from the Birch study which suggested that the vast majority of new jobs created in the United States during the period 1969–1976 were in small firms. Following the Birch study, the research team at Brookings (Armington and Odle, 1982) undertook an analysis of the Dun and Bradstreet data for the period 1978–1980, and found that small firms (with less than 100 employees) created around 40 per cent of net new jobs over this period, only slightly more than their share of employment in the base year, thus questioning the view expressed by Birch that small firms were the overwhelming source of new jobs. The results of these two studies, along with analyses of various time periods by both Brookings and the SBA[1] and the Canadian study of the 1974–82 time period, are summarised in Table 3.1. Several points emerge from these figures:

(i)   There appears to be a substantial variation over time in the figure for the percentage of net new jobs created by small firms (defined as firms with less than 100 employees). This varies from 36 per cent in 1978–80 to 223 per cent in 1980–82.

(ii)   The results for the 1980–82 period illustrates the problems involved in using a 'percentage of jobs generated' figure, where employment change within some size bands is negative. This problem is discussed in Storey (1982) pp. 19–21.

(iii)   The 'percentage of jobs generated' figure tells us nothing about the absolute number of jobs created by firms in each size band. It only illustrates the relative performance of the different size groups

Table 3.1 Percentage of net new jobs generated by size of firm – results from various studies of the 1969–82 time period

Time period	Source	Size of firm (no. of employees)					Net Employment Change (000)
		0–19	20–99	<100	100–499	500+	
USA							
1969–76	A	66.0	15.5	81.5	5.2	13.3	6759
1969–72	A			82.0			
1972–74	A			53.0			
1974–76	A			65.0			
1976–82	B	38.5	14.1	52.6	9.8	37.6	11871
1976–80 (1)	B	29.1	13.4	42.5	10.6	46.9	10892
1976–80(2)	C	36.0	15.0	51.0			11533
1976–78	B	36.3	15.8	52.1	10.4	37.5	6427
1978–80 (1)	B	29.9	5.9	35.8	7.3	56.9	4465
1978–80 (2)	D			39.1			7104
1978–80 (3)	E			70.0			4849
1980–82	B	232.6	–9.8	222.8	–31.4	–91.4	979
Canada							
1974–84	F	54.7	9.1	63.8	–3.2	39.4	1122

Sources:
  A Birch (1979)
  B US Small Business Administration (1985)
  C Armington (1983)
  D Armington and Odle (1982)
  E Birch and McCracken (1983)
  F Government of Canada (1984)

over a given time period. For instance, the figure of 232.6 per cent for the 0–19 size group in 1980–82 represents 2.3 million jobs, whereas the apparently much smaller figure of 36.3 per cent for the 1976–78 period for the same size grouping represents the same absolute number of jobs created by very small firms, because in this latter period the US economy was highly successful in creating new jobs in all sizes of firms.

(iv) For the two time periods for which different studies overlap (1976–80 and 1978–80), substantially different results are achieved by the research groups concerned. This is particularly noticeable for the 1978–80 period, where Brookings, both in their own work and that for the SBA, calculate a small firm share of net job change of less than 40 per cent, but the results of the MIT team suggest a substantially higher figure (70 per cent). This discrepancy occurs despite the fact that all three studies use the same data base. Such significant differences in results suggest that it is necessary to examine the methodologies employed by the research teams in dealing with the Dun and Bradstreet data base. This issue will be discussed in detail later in the Chapter.

3.3.2   Job generation by age of firm

It has been suggested that it is not only the size of a firm, but also its age which influences the rate of job generation. Specifically, the hypothesis is that young firms create jobs at a faster rate than older firms within the same size group. This issue has not been studied in as much detail as the influence of size on job generation, but the Birch (1979) study of the 1974–76 period suggests that around 80 per cent of net new jobs are created by firms which are less than four years old.[2]

There are no comparable figures in the other US studies, but the results presented by Armington (1983) for the 1976–1980 period tend to support the hypothesis that young firms grow more rapidly than older-established firms. Armington found that young (under four years old) independent firms existing in 1976 lost jobs at a slower rate than firms which were five years old or more, despite a higher rate of job loss due to closure among the younger firms. A similar result is found for small independent firms, with the youngest age group being the only group to exhibit positive employment growth. Again the youngest firms exhibited the highest rate of job loss through closure (25 per cent of 1976 employment), which suggests that the surviving small, young firms must have grown at a rapid rate in order to achieve an overall employment gain of 2.4 per cent.

3.3.3   Job generation by industry

Another issue which has been addressed by researchers using the Dun and Bradstreet data base has been to indentify those industry groups which have been growing most rapidly. Studies of the 1976–82 period, and of the various sub-periods, by Brookings and the SBA have shown that employment in manufacturing has grown at a relatively slow rate, with services and finance and related sectors exhibiting the fastest growth rates, along with the mining industry, which grew by 38 per cent over the 1976–82 period (see Table 3.2).[3]

Table 3.2   Employment growth by industry division for selected time periods (per cent)

Industry Division	1976–1982	1976–1978	1978–1980	1980–1982
All Industries	**15.6**	**8.5**	**5.4**	**–1.1**
Agriculture, Forestry & Fishing	4.9	4.3	–2.7	3.4
Mining	37.6	13.1	9.8	10.8
Construction	7.9	7.9	1.0	–1.1
Manufacturing	5.3	6.5	5.0	–5.8
Transportation, Communications & Utilities	13.0	5.4	6.6	0.6
Wholesale Trade	15.2	8.9	5.2	0.5
Retail Trade	15.6	8.1	5.3	1.6
Finance, Insurance & Real Estate	19.3	7.0	3.8	7.5
Services	29.3	12.4	7.4	7.0

Source: US Government (1985) table A1.15 p. 29

Table 3.3   Per cent change in job generation by industry division and employment size of firm, 1976–1982

Industry Division	Employment size of firm				
	< 20	20–99	100–499	500+	Total
All Industries	**29.3**	**13.1**	**10.7**	**12.2**	**15.6**
Agriculture, Forestry & Fishing	21.8	–7.7	–10.9	–13.8	4.9
Mining	72.1	52.3	59.2	24.1	37.6
Construction	24.8	–2.1	–14.1	–1.4	7.9
Manufacturing	42.7	10.7	2.1	1.1	5.3
Transportation, Communications & Utilities	33.9	11.4	8.0	10.3	13.0
Wholesale Trade	28.9	8.2	12.7	4.7	15.2
Retail Trade	9.5	10.7	20.4	24.6	15.6
Finance, Insurance & Real Estate	46.6	14.3	7.6	13.9	19.3
Services	52.6	26.2	19.6	26.2	29.3

Source: US Government (1985) Table A1.16 p.30

Table 3.3 illustrates employment growth rates by firm size and industry, 1976–1982. In all industries (except Retail) employment growth was most rapid for the smallest size groups. Indeed, in the agriculture, manufacturing and construction sectors, small firms appear to be the only significant source of new jobs. It is also interesting to note that in some industries (notably Services, Finance and Transport/ Communication) the largest size group (500 +) grew rapidly, with the medium-sized firms (100–499) exhibiting the lowest rates of employment growth.

The Canadian study also reveals that manufacturing employment is the slowest-growing sector (7.3 per cent over the 1974–82 period compared with around 50 per cent for Services, Finance and Mining– see Table 3.4). The Canadian results suggest that very large enterprises performed well, as compared with medium-sized firms, within most sectors. For instance, in the manufacturing sector, the only size groups to exhibit any employment growth are the very large (500 +) and very small (less than 50) firms. This is also true of Construction, a result which is in direct contrast to the US employment figures which suggest that very large firms performed particularly badly in manufacturing and construction. It is also interesting to note that, although manufacturing was the slowest growing sector in terms of employment in the Canadian economy, it still provided 10 per cent of the net jobs created over the 1974–82 period. The bulk of new jobs (nearly 70 per cent) were provided by three sectors – Services, Finance and Trade (Table 3.5).

Table 3.4   Net employment change (1974–82) by industry and enterprise size expressed as a percentage of 1974 base employment (Canada)

Industry	\	\	\	\	\	\	\
	Enterprise employment size group						
	0–19	*20–49*	*50–99*	*100–199*	*200–499*	*500 +*	*Total*
Agriculture	62.1	4.6	−13.6	−3.9	50.8	450.6	44.5
Forestry	40.0	−1.9	−26.4	−23.0	133.0	57.6	19.2
Fishing	167.1	32.9	87.2	−81.2	12.5	−56.1	37.2
Mines	90.4	62.2	41.9	1.0	12.4	66.3	52.6
Manufacturing	57.4	12.6	−8.9	−14.5	−14.4	12.8	7.3
Construction	44.9	−7.5	−21.3	−29.3	−3.6	24.6	14.8
Transport	56.7	13.3	2.6	8.4	12.8	51.0	36.6
Trade	29.0	7.6	−4.9	−10.3	−8.4	48.6	21.7
Finance	95.6	43.2	20.1	7.6	12.9	49.6	49.6
Services	75.6	48.9	42.3	35.3	21.1	42.3	51.0
Total	48.9	17.3	1.6	−5.0	−3.1	31.1	24.7

Source: Government of Canada (1984) Table III.3 p. 15.

Table 3.5 Percentage distribution of net employment change (1974–82) by industry and enterprise size (Canada)

Industry	0–19	20–49	50–99	100–199	200–499	500+	Total
			Enterprise employment size group				
Agriculture	1.1	0.0	0.0	0.0	0.1	0.2	1.3
Forestry	0.3	0.0	−0.1	−0.1	0.1	0.2	0.4
Fishing	0.1	0.0	0.0	0.0	0.0	0.0	0.1
Mines	0.8	0.3	0.1	0.0	0.2	3.0	4.5
Manufacturing	7.4	1.7	−1.2	−2.3	−3.1	7.7	10.0
Construction	6.7	−0.5	−0.8	−0.9	−0.1	0.6	5.0
Transport	3.0	0.4	0.1	0.2	0.3	5.9	9.9
Trade	14.0	1.0	−0.4	−0.7	−0.5	7.9	21.4
Finance	4.1	0.6	0.3	0.1	0.3	4.6	10.0
Services	17.1	4.0	2.7	1.9	1.4	9.4	37.4
Total	54.7	8.5	0.6	−1.8	−1.4	39.4	100.0

(Total net change in employment is 1 121 592)

Source: Government of Canada (1985) Table III.2C p. 13

3.3.4 Job generation by corporate status

Birch (1979) found that 58 per cent of net jobs created between 1969 and 1976 were in independent firms most of which were small. He also found that the opening of new branches by multi-plant firms accounted for a large proportion of jobs in births, but that expansion took place mainly in independent establishments. Figures derived from Armington (1983) suggest that between 1976 and 1980, about 37 per cent of net new jobs arose from (mostly small) single-plant firms, with the remaining 63 per cent being accounted for by the headquarters and branches of multi-plant firms, most of which are large.

3.3.5 Regional variations in job generation

Results from the US Dun and Bradstreet studies suggest that the rate of job loss through closure and contractions is fairly constant across regions (approximately 8 per cent per year between 1969 and 1976). Similarly, the Canadian study (Government of Canada, 1984) showed little regional variation in gross job loss (around 40 per cent of jobs over an eight year period). The difference between fast and slow growing regions appears to lie in the rate of job creation in expansions and births of new firms. In Canada, variations in job creation through births account for most of the observed regional differences in net job generation. The Birch study of the US also suggests that inter-regional migration accounts for an insignificant percentage of regional employment change. These findings are confirmed by the Brookings studies (Armington and Odle, 1982; Armington, 1983)

An interesting result arising from studies of job generation by region is that small firms create the largest percentage of new jobs in the slowest growing regions. For instance, Birch (1979) found that firms with less than 50 employees accounted for all net job growth in the North East region of the USA, and almost 80 per cent of net new jobs in the North Central region. Results presented by the SBA (Small Business Administration, 1985) also suggest that small firms were the overwhelming source of new jobs in the slowest-growing regions, whereas in the faster-growing regions, all sizes of firm grew rapidly (Table 3.6).

This, however, may simply reflect the observation made in Table 3.1 that, during times of prosperity, large firms appear to expand their labour force proportionately more rapidly than small firms. When large numbers of jobs are being created the large firm is likely to be a very

Table 3.6   Job generation by census region and employment size of firm, 1976–82 (per cent)

Region	Total	*Employment size of firm*					
		0–19	*20–99*	*<100*	*100–499*	*<500*	*500 +*
US Total	15.6	29.3	13.1	22.0	10.7	18.9	12.2
New England	12.7	25.5	7.6	17.0	6.2	13.8	11.5
Middle Atlantic	4.3	19.9	2.5	11.9	−0.8	8.1	0.0
East North Central	6.5	17.4	4.6	11.4	4.3	9.4	3.9
West North Central	15.6	18.8	10.4	15.3	11.5	14.3	17.2
South Atlantic	17.6	33.8	16.1	25.7	12.8	22.0	12.8
East South Central	11.3	17.3	9.7	14.0	9.7	12.8	9.8
West South Central	34.6	44.8	32.9	39.5	25.3	35.7	33.4
Mountain	38.9	47.5	30.1	40.4	35.8	39.3	38.4
Pacific	26.4	48.4	22.5	36.6	21.0	32.6	19.4

Source: US Government (1985) Table A1.18, p. 32.

important source of new jobs whereas in recessions large firms seem to decrease their labour force proportionately more than small firms. Hence in depressed regions, where proportionately fewer jobs are being created than in prosperous regions, it is to be expected that small firms will be *proportionately* more important, even though they may create fewer jobs in absolute terms than do small firms in prosperous regions. In short it is the contribution to job generation of large firms that determines prosperity at a regional level.

3.3.6 Synthesis

The Dun and Bradstreet data base has been used to produce a large number of tabulations of job generation with respect to a number of key variables, notably firm size. Given that the job-generating capacity of different-sized firms has been the major focus of attention in the job generation literature, it is unfortunate that such a wide variation in results is achieved by different researchers using the same data base. The outstanding example of this problem is the 1978–80 period, where researchers from Brookings and MIT achieved markedly different results for the percentage of new jobs generated by small firms (39 per cent and 70 per cent respectively for firms with less than 100 employees). Such discrepancies suggest that a detailed analysis of the methodologies employed by the two research groups is necessary.

3.4 THE DUN AND BRADSTREET DATA BASE AND THE BIRCH/BROOKINGS DEBATE

Dun and Bradstreet is a commercial organisation whose principal purpose is to provide credit rating information on businesses. To this end, a large amount of information is collected regarding establishment age, location, employment, sales and any branch or subsidiary relationship, for a large number of business establishments in the United States (5.6 million establishments in 1976, representing 82 per cent of all private sector employment)[4] This data is contained in the Duns Market Identifier (DMI) file. The Dun and Bradstreet DMI file, along with other credit rating and marketing information collected by private companies, has several advantages over other sources of company information, such as those collected by public authorities. Firstly, the data is for the most part publicly available, and confidentiality is not an issue. Secondly, Dun and Bradstreet have a commercial incentive for ensuring that the information collected is current and accurate. The same is true for the responding establishments. A business is more likely to provide accurate information to a credit-rating company (which may have a significant impact upon the performance or even survival of the company) than to a government body as there is no direct commerical interest in supplying accurate information to the latter. If, however, the commercial information is potentially damaging the business may be reluctant to provide it quickly.

The Dun and Bradstreet DMI file also suffers from problems and potential biases from the point of view of the academic researcher. Some of these problems arise from the fact that the data is not collected specifically for the purpose of academic research (inaccurate employment information, incomplete coverage, inconsistencies, etc). Others are due to the inevitable problems associated with such a huge data base (clerical errors, missing records, etc). Each specific problem is discussed below, along with an explanation of how these problems were approached by the two main groups of job generation researchers in the United States – the Massachusetts Institute of Technology (MIT) team under the direction of David Birch, and the Business Micro-data Project, based at the Brookings Institution.

3.4.1　Dun and Bradstreet – the major problems

The problems associated with the analysis of the Dun and Bradstreet data base will be considered under two broad headlines – those concerning the representativeness of the sample, and those related to the analysis of change over time.

Sample coverage

It is important to recognise that the DMI file is not a census of the business population, but is in fact only a sample (albeit a very large one). As such, there may be biases in the sample (i.e. under- or over-representation of certain sectors), which relate to the purpose for which the information is collected, and the methods used to collect it. The most important biases which appear to exist in the Dun and Bradstreet sample are the under-reporting of branches of multi-establishment businesses, and the under-reporting of small firms, particularly in the retail and service sectors.

Missing branch records　As discussed above, the Dun and Bradstreet files are used primarily for the purpose of credit rating. Branches of multi-establishment firms are unlikely to require credit independently from the owning company, therefore a lower priority is given to the collection of data from these branches, as opposed to data at the enterprise level. Both the MIT and Brookings research teams noted the under-reporting of branches by multi-establishment firms. About 50 per cent of multi-establishment firms do not report disaggregated data for their branch establishments. However the MIT and Brookings research teams treated this under-reporting of branches in markedly different ways.

The DMI files provide two employment figures for multi-establishment businesses – the establishment's employment, and the aggregate employment of all affiliated establishments in the business. In many cases there appeared to be a large discrepancy between the aggregates of the two figures reported; in other words, the sum of the establishment employment figures was often less than the reported employment for the enterprise as a whole. This discrepancy was seen as a major problem by the Brookings group, who suggested that almost 50 per cent of employment in branch establishments is missing from the DMI files, whereas MIT estimated the figure to be around 8 per cent.

The MIT team, in its earlier work, chose to believe the establishment figures, and total enterprise employment was calculated as the sum of the employment figures for each reported establishment within a given enterprise. The Brookings researchers, on the other hand, accepted the enterprise figures as the 'true' level of employment, and created proxy (or 'imputed') records to represent missing branches on the basis of the distribution of employment size of reported branches in the same industry. Brookings created approximately 430 000 establishments in this way in 1977, and added nearly 20 million employees to the employment reported by establishments.[5]

This process was criticised by the MIT team, who pointed out that the total number of jobs recorded in the Brookings cross-sectional (USEEM)[6] file exceeded the estimates of the US Bureau of Labor Statistics by over 20 million in 1978. MIT suggested that, in most cases, the total enterprise employment recorded in the DMI files included overseas as well as domestic employment. This was confirmed by a spot-check, and it was estimated that nearly 10 million jobs in foreign affiliates may have found their way into the DMI files in 1980 (Birch and McCracken, 1983, p. 11).

It is clear, then, that the MIT research team under-estimate the extent of employment in multi-establishment companies, whereas Brookings probably over-estimates this employment by wrongly including foreign as well as domestic employment.[7]

From the point of view of our analysis, it is necessary to estimate the extent to which these different approaches may affect the results of the two research teams' analyses of job generation by firm size. Two points can be illustrated here.

Firstly, if foreign employment is growing at a faster rate than domestic employment, as appeared to be the case for some sectors of the US economy in the late 1970s (Birch and McCracken, 1983, p. 11), the Brookings approach will inflate the employment growth performance of multi-establishment firms, most of which are in the larger size bracket.

Secondly, it is possible that the MIT approach (summing reported establishment employment to estimate total enterprise employment) may lead to some firms being classified into the smaller size bracket whereas their actual total enterprise employment warrants their categorisation as large firms. The extent of this potential problem depends largely upon whether Armington and Odle (1981) are correct in asserting that 'Dun and Bradstreet frequently reported relatively small central administrative offices, while not covering the large productive branch establishments' (p. 73). If this is correct, the MIT 'bottom up' approach may place some large manufacturing firms in the small size bracket because of the non-reporting of employment in the larger branches. For instance, a manufacturing firm employing 1000 people in two or three plants, but only 90 in its administrative offices may be classified as a small firm according to the MIT approach, and any employment growth in this firm will be attributed to the small firm sector. This would be a particular problem if Dun and Bradstreet added employment in the manufacturing plants to the file, and they were wrongly classified by the MIT team as 'branch births', as opposed to new coverage of already existing branches.

In summary, the Brookings approach to the problem of missing branch records may lead to an over-estimate of employment growth in large firms whereas the MIT methodology has the potential of bias towards small firm employment growth. This may go some way towards explaining the large difference between the Brookings and MIT estimates of the contribution of small firms to employment growth between 1978 and 1980, although we shall see later than the treatment of births and deaths appears to be the crucial factor accounting for the different results.

Sectoral variations in coverage   Harris points out that 'one of the more serious shortcomings of the DMI files is the under-reporting of small retail and service establishments' (1984, p. 12). Comparisons with

County Business Patterns and tax return data show Dun and Bradstreet to be missing many restaurants and bars, medical and legal offices, real estate and insurance brokers, dry cleaners and hairdressers (Harris, 1981). Neither the MIT nor the Brookings research teams appear to have made adjustments to the raw data, such as a weighting system to statistically correct for this sample bias.

The effect of this possible sample bias on the results of the employment change analysis is difficult to discern, but is probably not great. However, it is likely that those small firms which do enter the DMI files are amongst the more dynamic in the small firm sector, and those which do not enter the file may be stagnant or declining (i.e. not in need of a great deal of credit). Hence the extent of employment growth in small firms may be overstated.

Branches wrongly classified as independent firms It is suggested by Eckhart, von Einem and Stahl (1985) that, in some cases, branches are classified by Dun and Bradstreet as legally independent firms. This occurs where branches carry out their own profit-and-loss calculations,[8] which quite often appears to be the case in the USA. If this problem is not corrected, it will lead to employment growth in these branches being attributed to the small firm sector, instead of the larger firms to which they belong. The scale of this problem is unknown, and is not referred to by either MIT or Brookings, but it is clear that there exists the potential for bias towards employment growth in small firms.

The Dun and Bradstreet DMI file therefore is not a complete census of the business population, and suffers from serious shortcomings in the reporting of branch plants and of smaller firms, particularly in the retail and service sectors. This needs to be borne in mind when considering the results of job generation studies.

Job generation 1978–80: MIT versus Brooking

Far more serious problems emerge in studies of changes over time, particularly in relation to 'births' and 'deaths' of business establishments, especially branch plants. The way in which these problems are dealt with can significantly affect the results of job generation studies. This is most clearly illustrated by a comparison of job generation results obtained by MIT and by Brookings, using exactly the same data base for the period 1978 to 1980.[9]

From Table 3.1 it will be recalled that firms with less than 100 workers created 70 per cent of new jobs according to Birch compared with 39.1

per cent according to Armington and Odle even though both were using *identical* data. We now attempt both to explain the basis of these differences and tentatively suggest some alternative calculations.

The differences between MIT and Brookings' approach to the analysis of changes over time will be discussed under five broad headings:

- Treatment of non-updated records.
- Treatment of 'hyperactive growth' records.
- Treatment of non-branch births.
- Treatment of branch births.
- Treatment of closures.

Non-updated records   A large percentage of small firm records had not been updated from one period to the next (42 per cent of all records between 1978 and 1980). The Brookings team excluded the non-updated records from their longitudinal analysis, although continuing to use them as part of the 'target employment' upon which their weighting scheme was based. MIT included the non-updated records in their growth calculations. Harris argues that the MIT approach may bias downwards employment growth rates, particularly in the small firm sector, but it should not affect the relative shares of employment growth of small and large firms [1984, p. 15]. However, it is probable that a proportion of the non-updated firms will actually have died and some may have reduced their employment. This may be particularly true for smaller firms, which are more difficult to trace than larger ones. Some of the non-updated firms may have expanded, but it seems likely that these would be the firms whose records are most regularly updated (expansion generally requires credit). It could be argued therefore, that we might expect the 'non-updated' firms, which appear in the MIT study as firms with an average growth rate of employment equal to zero to exhibit, on average, a decline in employment. Inclusion of these records may therefore bias upwards the employment growth in small firms.

The Brookings approach to the problem of non-updated records is to devise a complex weighting system to ensure that the longitudinal (USELM) file, which contains only records which are deemed suitable for analysis of employment change over time, is representative of the entire USEEM (cross-section) file, which also includes non-updated and imputed branch records. The USEEM file is divided into sampling cells according to the size and structure of the firm, the industry division and the type of record (birth, death or 'match'). This represents the target population from which weights are calculated to inflate the longitudinal file in order to ensure that it is representative of the USEEM file, which in turn is assumed to be representative of the US business population as a whole.[10]

This weighting process is based on the assumption that 'the distributions of employment change in the non-updated records is identical to that in the updated records' (Armington, Odle and Harris, 1983, p. 12). In fact it would seem likely that the records which are most likely to be regularly updated are those of large firms, whose employment figures are fairly easily obtainable, and those of the faster growing firms in the smaller size bracket. Hence, it can be argued that the Brookings weighting system will tend to over-estimate employment growth in the small firm sector by assuming that the non-updated firms behave in the same way as the firms whose records have been updated.

Insufficient information is available regarding the Brookings weighting system to accurately quantify this effect. However, the figures presented by Birch and McCracken (1983) suggest that the net effect of the Brookings weighting system is to increase the overall employment change between 1978 and 1980 by over 1.8 million jobs. It is not known what proportion of this increase is allocated to small firms, but intuition suggests that, as small firms tend to be less regularly updated than large ones, smaller firms will receive a relatively heavy weight (the maximum weight allowed is 10). Hence a disproportionate amount of the 1.8m job growth estimated by the weighting procedure is probably allocated to small firms.

It is also possible, as suggested above, that the 'neutral' MIT approach is biased towards over estimating small firm growth. This will be the case, however, only on the stronger assumption that real employment change in the 'non-updated' firms is negative. As the actual employment change associated with non-updated records is, by definition, unknown, we can do little more than point to possible biases introduced by the procedures used to deal with these records. The conclusion of this section is that both the Brookings and the MIT approach lead to a potential bias in favour of small firm employment growth, with this bias being more severe in the case of the Brookings weighting system.

'Hyperactive growth'   Clerical errors in the recording of employment occasionally yield employment growth (and decline) rates which are highly improbable. Both MIT and Brookings have complex editing techniques to 'screen out' these errors. Both define allowable changes in employment. Brookings use a single liberal cut-off (plus or minus 200

times base year employment), whereas MIT has several cut-offs for groups of businesses in two size classes and two broad industry classes.[11] Harris argues that 'MIT's restrictions on allowable changes in employment in larger businesses are particularly stringent and may exclude some large businesses with high but feasible rates of employment change' (1984, p. 16). In particular, it is argued that growth through acquisition (which tends to take place mainly within the large firm sector) could be excluded, whereas the employment loss from the apparent death of the acquired firm may still be included, exerting a downward bias to employment change in large firms.

Indeed, it is unclear from the available publications of the MIT and Brookings research groups, how changes of legal status are dealt with in the Dun and Bradstreet files. One possibility is that firms which have been taken over retain their identification numbers and the 'organisational status' code is simply altered. This procedure should not distort the picture of employment change by firm size. However, it has been suggested by Eckhart, von Einem and Stahl (1985) that firms which change legal status are allocated new identification numbers. This would appear to the job generation researcher as the death of one firm and the birth of another. In the case of the takeover of a small independent firm by a larger enterprise, this would appear in any tabulation as a job loss through death in the small firm sector, and an increase in large firm employment through the birth of a new branch or subsidiary. This imparts a bias in favour of large firm employment growth. In the absence of any detail regarding the treatment of changes in legal status by Dun and Bradstreet, and regarding the extent of such changes and their size distribution, one can only speculate about the effect of changes in legal status on the results of job generation studies.

MIT's application of their editing technique to the 1978–80 Brookings data removed about 2.7 per cent of the 1978 employment in non-imputed establishment records, as opposed to only 0.4 per cent removed by Brookings. The MIT adjustments have neglible effect on net employment change (140 000 jobs out of a total change of about 6 million). This overall change is comprised of the dropping of a net expansion of 310 000 in small firms and a net contraction of 168 000 in large firms (Birch and McCracken, 1983, table 4, p. 15). In addition to checking changes in *establishment* employment, the Brookings longitudinal editing techniques must consider radical changes in reported *enterprise* employment upon which their branch imputations are based. Birch and McCracken discovered two such errors which went undetected by the Brookings analysis of 1978–80,[12] amounting to a spurious employment growth of 852 000. This amounted to almost half of all the gain in imputed employment in the 400 000 + records for which imputations were made (Birch and McCracken, 1983, p. 12).

It is extremely difficult to discern whether the procedures adopted by the two research teams to deal with 'hyperactive growth' records impart any bias to the final results. It is possibe that some erroneously high-growing small firms have slipped through the editing procedure, but it may be equally true that some large firms which exhibit erroneously high rates of decline are included, thus balancing out any potential bias towards large or small firms.

Non-branch births One of the most serious problems facing job generation researchers using the Dun and Bradstreet files is that 'births' of new firms are not always promptly recorded in the files. It may take up to seven years before all (or almost all) of a particular year's births are finally tracked down and recorded. Fortunately Dun and Bradstreet record the year in which non-branch establishments started business, which is extremely helpful in tracking them. The problem faced by researchers, particularly when a short period of time (e.g. 1978 to 1980) is being examined, is that only a small proportion of that period's births will be reported, and thus techniques need to be developed which will estimate the amount of employment generated in unrecorded births. The potential extent of this problem is illustrated in Figure 3.2, which is taken from Birth and McCracken (1983). After two years, they appear to suggest that perhaps 25 per cent of births which occurred at time zero will be recorded in the DMI flle.[13] Although some of the original firms will have died, the DMI file still seriously under-reports those firms which were born during the period under analysis, and still existed at the end of the period, but which had not yet found their way into the DMI files.

The Brookings team chose to simulate non-branch births during the two-year period by accepting any newly listed business which was established up to five years prior to inclusion in the file, as a 'birth'. This approach was criticised by MIT researchers on two grounds. Firstly, the Brookings approach accepts as 'births', firms which may have actually been born up to five years prior to the period under investigation. 'Since birth rates vary from year to year, there is no clear relationship between birth rates during the one and a half years under study and births that occurred over the previous five years' (Birch and McCracken, 1983, p. 22). Secondly, a 'growth bias' may be introduced, in that firms which are up to five years old may have actually crossed over into a higher

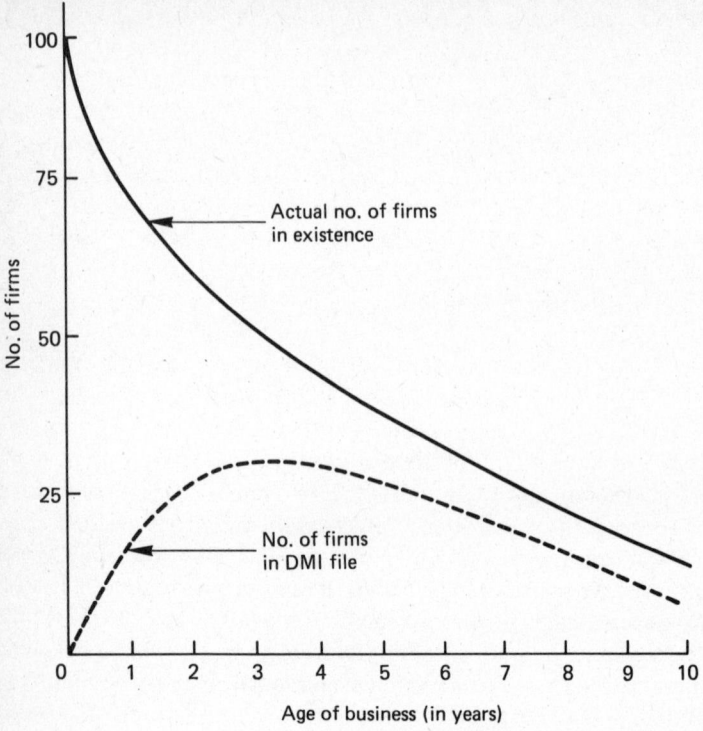

Figure 3.2   Actual firm population vs. Dun & Bradstreet's measurement of that population

employment size band since their birth and thus employment growth may be wrongly attributed to the larger rather than the smaller size group. Evidence suggests that only a very small number of firms actually grew out of the small business class (under 100 employees) during their first four years of operation (see Teitz 1981, p. 35). Furthermore, these rapidly expanding firms are likely to be those which Dun and Bradstreet pick up quickly. Firms which only enter Dun and Bradstreet files after five years are likely to be slower-growing businesses which have not required a great deal of credit and have therefore not come to the attention of Dun and Bradstreet. It seems, therefore, that the 'growth bias' suggested by Birch and McCracken is unlikely to have a great deal of effect, if any, on the Brookings' results. MIT, in their analysis of the 1978–80 Brookings data, chose to divide the newly listed non-branch establishments into 'regular births' – those which started up in 1979 or

Table 3.7 Adjustment required to Dun & Bradstreet's birth data to estimate actual births

Factors by which to multiply D & B Births to estimate actual births when the interval (in years) over which births are measured is:

Industry	1	2	3	4	5
Agriculture	6.4	4.4	3.4	2.8	2.4
Manufacturing	2.1	1.9	1.8	1.7	1.6
Other Industry	2.6	2.3	2.0	1.8	1.7
Trade	1.8	1.7	1.6	1.5	1.5
Service	7.0	4.9	3.9	3.2	2.8

Source: Birch and McCracken (1983) Table 7, p. 23.

1980 – and 'known new listings' – those which started up some time during the five year period up to 1979. MIT estimates that the Brookings file only contains about 19 per cent of the business births which actually occurred during 1979 and 1980. Drawing upon an analysis of the rate at which births which actually occurred in 1969 were absorbed into the Dun and Bradstreet files over the 1969–1980 period, the MIT team calculated a number of 'absorption factors' by which recorded births must be multiplied in order to estimate actual births in the 'real world'. Different absorption factors were calculated for five industry groups, and for different time intervals. These factors are shown in Table 3.7. It shows, for instance, that if a two-year period is being studied, recorded births in the service sector must be multiplied by 4.9 in order to estimate the actual employment in firms which were born during the period, and which still existed at the end of the period.[14]

The effect of the MIT approach can be seen by comparing Tables 3.8 and 3.9. Table 3.8 shows the components of employment change derived by MIT from the Brookings file after removal of imputed branches and records deemed to be in error. Table 3.9 shows the revised components of change after the MIT adjustments to the birth and death figures.[15] Brookings estimated employment in non-branch births to be 2 613 000 (2 082 000 in the small firm sector and 531 000 in large firms).[16] The MIT adjustments yielded a total figure of 4 275 000. Most of the 1.7 million increase (1.25m) was allocated to the small firm sector. Hence, the MIT method of estimating actual non-branch births increases the proportion of employment growth attributable to small firms. If no other adjustments had been made by MIT apart from this, the small firm share of employment growth would have increased from 35 per cent to 48 per cent.

Table 3.8   Components of employment change by enterprise size and type in reduced Brookings file (All figures in '000s)

Enterprise Type	Regular births	New list. births	Death	Expan.	Contr.	Net change
Small						
Head Office	1 152	930	2 032	2 517	1 234	1 333
Branch	—	329	202	87	23	191
Sm. Total	1 152	1 259	2 234	2 604	1 257	1 524
Large						
Head Office	306	225	938	1 547	1 096	44
Branch	—	3 645	1 399	1 185	641	2 790
Lg. Total	306	3 870	2 337	2 732	1 737	2 834
Grand Total	1 458	5 129	4 571	5 336	2 994	4 358
Small Business Share	79%	25%	49%	49%	42%	35%

Source: Birch and McCracken (1983) Table 6, p. 18.

Table 3.9   Revised components of employment change by enterprise size and type after MIT adjustments to Brookings data

Enterprise Type	Regular births	New list. births	Death	Expan.	Contr.	Net change
Small						
Head Office	3 327	0	1 258	2 517	1 234	3 352
Branch	0	157	166	87	23	55
Sm. Total	3 327	157	1 424	2 604	1 257	3 407
Large						
Head Office	948	0	911	1 547	1 096	488
Branch	0	1 746	1 336	1 185	641	954
Lg. Total	948	1 746	2 247	2 732	1 737	1 442
Grand Total	4 275	1 903	3 671	5 336	2 994	4 849
Small Business Share	78%	8%	39%	49%	42%	70%

Source: Birch and McCracken (1983) Table 8, p. 33.

Two criticisms can be levelled at the MIT approach to non-branch births. Firstly, the 'absorption factors' are based on an analysis of the absorption of 1969 births into the DMI file. As Birch and McCracken themselves point out 'Dun and Bradstreet is constantly improving the coverage and the currentness and accuracy of its file' (1983, p. 25). It might be expected therefore that Dun and Bradstreet would absorb 1979 and 1980 births more quickly than was the case for firms which were born in 1969. If this is the case, the MIT absorption factors are too high, leading to an overestimate of births.

A more important aspect of this approach which can be criticised is the (implicit) assumption that the average level of employment of the unrecorded births is the same as that of the births which are promptly recorded in the file. It seem likely, as argued above, that the firms which are picked up fairly quickly by Dun and Bradstreet will be at the larger end of the small business scale and will be expanding rapidly. The unrecorded firms, on the other hand, might be expected to be less dynamic and have lower average employment levels than those which are recorded promptly. Of course, the level of employment in unrecorded births is, by definition, unknown, but the assumption that average employment in unrecorded births is equivalent to recorded births is likely to lead to an over-estimate of the birth employment component.

It can be concluded that, although neither approach to the estimation of actual births is entirely satisfactory, the MIT weighting technique is likely to lead to an over-estimate of the birth component (most of which occurs in the small firm sector), and that MIT criticisms of the Brookings approach are unlikely to lead to the large discrepancy in the birth figure which is noted above.

Branch births   The under-reporting of branches of multi-establishment firms by Dun and Bradstreet has already been noted. This problem becomes more acute when change is being analysed over time, because Dun and Bradstreet are continually attempting to improve coverage and therefore some of the branches which are added to the file will not, in fact, be branch births, but simply new coverage of already existing branches. This problem is exacerbated by the fact that Dun and Bradstreet do not report a start date for branch establishments, apart from the date at which the owning company started in business. It becomes a very difficult task to differentiate between genuine branch births and new branch coverage.

The Brookings team developed a technique for estimating the proportion of newly listed branches which represented actual branch births as opposed to new coverage (which would involve replacing some proxy branch records with 'real' records). This procedure is based on the assumption that proxy branches behave in the same way as reported branches with respect to deaths and employment change. (Armington, Odle and Harris, 1983, p. 13). This approach yielded 3 974 000 new jobs in branch births over the 1978–80 period, most of which occurred in the large firm sector, as might be expected.

The Brookings approach was criticised by Birch and McCracken who argued that a significant proportion of Brookings' branch births were, in fact, new listings which were due to the Dun and Bradstreet policy of extending branch coverage, which was vigorously implemented in the late 1970s. For instance, Birch and McCracken point out that the Brookings approach estimated an additional 1.1 million jobs in new manufacturing branches, at a time when manufacturing employment nationally had declined by 200 000 jobs. (Birch and McCracken, 1983, p. 28) MIT used official statistics on employment in multi-plant enterprises for 1967 to 1977 in order to estimate the likely level of employment change due to actual branch births in the 1978–80 period. Birch and McCracken applied the average annual growth rate for 1967– 77 (2.8 per cent) to the Brookings data for 1978–80, and estimated that real branch births added 1 903 000 to total employment (less than half the level estimated by Brookings).[17] Most of the 'spurious births' occurred in the large firm sector, and the final adjustments can be seen by comparing the 'New Listing Births' columns of Tables 3.8 and 3.9. This adjustment alone would have increased the small business share of net employment growth from 35 per cent to 44 per cent. Combined with the non-branch birth adjustments, the small firm share would be 69 per cent. The technique used by MIT to estimate real branch births has been strongly criticised by Harris on two grounds:

> First, employment growth is the dependent variable under investiga-tion. So an assumption that sets the growth for a large segment of the population equal to an average for an earlier period pre-determines the results. Secondly, even this average[18] is based on the subset of industries covered by *Enterprise Statistics*, which excludes many of the industries in which large multi-establishment enterprises are expanding most rapidly – transportation communication and public utilities; finance, insurance and real estate, and numerous other service sector industries.   (Harris, 1984, p. 20).

It seems that, although the Brookings approach clearly over-estimates branch births, the adjustments made by MIT lead to a gross under-estimate of actual branch births.

As with non-branch births, the 'true' level of employment change due to branch births is unknown, and analysts must rely on unsatisfactory estimation techniques and heroic assumptions – not an ideal basis for achieving robust and realistic results.

Deaths   The final major problem facing researchers analysing the Dun and Bradstreet files concerns the reporting of 'deaths' of firms. Records may remain on file for some time after the firm has ceased trading, due to Dun and Bradstreet's reporting lags, particularly in relation to small firms in the service and retail sectors. Conversely records may be removed from the file for firms which have not necessarily 'died'. According to Birch and McCracken, Dun and Bradstreet occasionally undertake purges of their files to remove records which are out of date, or not useful for other reasons. One such purge took place during 1978 to 1980, when Dun and Bradstreet decided to purge all companies which did not respond to first-class mailings (known as 'Nixies').[19] MIT assume that the removed firms (about 180 000 in 1980), which had been recorded in Brookings as deaths, had not in fact died, but possibly had moved a short distance. MIT assumed an average employment in these firms of 5 which gave a 'spurious death' count of approximately 900 000 jobs.[20] These were allocated 90 per cent to small firms and 10 per cent to large firms, giving the adjustment to the 'Death' column which can be seen by comparing Table 3.9 with Table 3.8. The overall effect of this adjustment on the small firm share of employment change was fairly small (43 per cent as opposed to 35 per cent), but this works in the same direction as the other adjustments described above; i.e. the small firm share of employment growth is boosted. The final result of all the MIT adjustments to the Brookings data is shown in Table 3.9, with the small business share of net employment change having increased from 35 per cent to 70 per cent.

Neither MIT nor Brookings appear to take account of the fact that some of the records remaining on the file will actually have died during the period under investigation. MIT can particularly be criticised for assuming that all of the 180 000 records purged in 1980 represented firms which were still in existence. It seems more than likely that a proportion of these firms had, in fact, died. The fact that MIT developed a weighting system to multiply up reported births to represent actual births, but did not carry out a corresponding adjustment to take account of unreported deaths, imparts a bias in favour of net employment growth, particularly in the small firm sector, where the majority of the under-reporting takes place. It could be argued, therefore, that Brookings may have exaggerated the employment loss due to deaths,[21] but that MIT over-compensated for this, and under-estimated deaths.

It can be seen, therefore, that behind the apparently straightforward tabulations of the components of employment change presented by researchers from the Brookings group and from the MIT programme, lies a complex and often confusing amount of data manipulation, estimated figures and 'heroic assumptions'. It would be impossible to adjudicate between the different approaches as to which is 'right' and which is 'wrong', without a great deal more information about the underlying assumptions, weighting systems, etc. Tables 3.8 and 3.9 can be regarded as 'extremes' in the sense that the procedures adopted by the MIT group tend to bias the results in favour of a larger share of net employment growth for small firms, whereas the Brookings methodology on balance works in the opposite direction. The possible exception to this statement occurs with regard to the treatment of non-updated records, where the Brookings methodology would appear to be more biased in favour of small firms than is the MIT approach. The impact of different approaches to some aspects of the data base (such as non-updated records, 'hyperactive growth' records and changes in legal status) are impossible to quantify without further detailed knowledge, but a comparison of Tables 3.8 and 3.9 show the extent to which different methods of estimating births and deaths can significantly alter the results of a study of job generation by firm size.

We now attempt to illustrate the potential sensitivity of the results to differing assumptions and methodology, by applying 'reasonable' assumptions, which in most cases give a result somewhere between those obtained by the two groups under discussion here.

3.4.2   Employment change 1978–1980: a 'realistic' analysis[22]

The outcome of the above discussion appears to be that the Brookings study of the 1978–1980 period suffers from a number of problems, particularly in relation to the treatment of branch and non-branch births, but that MIT over-compensate for these problems to such an extent that the small business share of net employment change is likely to be overstated. This section will present a 'realistic' approach, using some of the arguments expressed in Section 3.4.1, which will lead to estimates of non-branch births, branch births and deaths which avoid the extremes of both Brookings and MIT.

Non-branch births

It was argued above, that the MIT estimate of non-branch births was probably too high due to the implicit assumptions that Dun and Bradstreet's promptness in recording births had not improved between 1969 and 1980, and that employment in unrecorded births is the same as in recorded births. A more 'realistic' assumption may be that Dun and Bradstreet's reporting has improved to the extent that 20 per cent more jobs are discovered in years 1–2 for 1978–80, than was the case in 1969.[23] Furthermore, we assume that average employment in unrecorded births is 75 per cent of that in recorded births. We therefore need to add to the Brookings estimates only 60 per cent (75 per cent × 80 per cent) of the employment which was added by MIT. Assuming that the improved reporting and employment differential is the same for both large and small firms, we obtain the 'Regular Birth' column in Table 3.10.

Branch births

The quote from Harris (1984) above illustrates that MIT probably under-estimates the extent of branch births during 1979 and 1980. Equally, the Brookings figure is undoubtedly an over-estimate. In the absence of any further detailed information, we will simply 'split the difference' between the two figures to give a 'realistic' estimate. This adjustment will result in the 'New Listing Births' column of Table 3.10.

Table 3.10   Revised components of employment change by enterprise size and type using 'realistic' assumptions

Enterprise type	Regular births	New list. birth	Death	Expan.	Contr.	Net change
Small						
Head Office	2829	—	2032	2517	1234	2080
Branch	—	180	202	87	23	42
Small Total	2829	180	2234	2604	1257	2122
Large						
Head Office	781	—	938	1547	1096	294
Branch	—	2696	1399	1185	641	1841
Large Total	781	2696	2337	2732	1737	2135
Grand Total	3610	2876	4571	5336	2994	4257
Small Business Share	78%	6%	49%	49%	42%	50%

Deaths

Finally, we consider that any 'spurious deaths' included in the Brookings figures are likely to be balanced by firms remaining on the files which have, in fact, died. Therefore, we will use the unaltered Brookings figures as estimates of 'actual' deaths.

These revised figures yield a small business share of employment growth of 50 per cent. We do not claim that this is the 'correct' figure, but rather that the assumptions which have led to this figure are equally as 'realistic' as those used by both MIT and Brookings. The main object of this exercise has been to illustrate the sensitivity of the results of job generation studies to the assumptions employed in adjusting the raw data to represent the 'real world', and to caution against the quotation of a simple index (small business share of employment growth) without examining what lies behind the analysis.

3.4.3   The 'Dun and Bradstreet' studies – conclusions

The work by Birch and his colleagues at MIT in examining employment change in the United States has been a major factor leading to new government policies designed to assist small firms in many developed countries. Furthermore the techniques of analysis of Dun and Bradstreet and other 'credit-rating' data bases pioneered by Birch have been replicated, with modifications, in Canada, the United Kingdom and Sweden.

Despite this international success it must remain a matter for concern that the results of such an influential study are so sensitive to key assumptions. To demonstrate this sensitivity this section has analysed in detail the database and methodologies used by two separate teams of researchers using the same raw data for employment change in the period 1978 to 1980. We have seen that the research team of MIT radically altered the figures provided for them by the Brookings Business Microdata Project to take account of some of the problems inherent in the Dun and Bradstreet DMI files. These alterations lead to the estimate of the small firm share of net employment change being increased from 35 per cent to 70 per cent. It has been argued in this paper that the MIT approach probably over-estimated employment growth in small firms and a figure somewhat less than 70 per cent, but probably greater than the Brookings estimate, would be more realistic.

Several conclusions can be drawn from this study. First that the summary tables and figures presented by job generation researchers obscure a great deal of data manipulation based upon (often dubious) assumptions, and should be treated with considerable caution.

Second, it is clear that, despite this sensitivity, during most time – periods in the United States from the end of the 1960s, small firms were creating jobs at a faster rate than large firms. This rate of job creation varied, being relatively high in times of recession and relatively low in periods of prosperity. It also remains true that during this time the MIT team generally overestimated the contribution of smaller firms.

Thirdly, it is also generally agreed that the regional *variations* in job loss rates were small and that the geographical areas which created the most net new jobs were those which *created* most new jobs, rather than those which *lost* fewest jobs.

3.5 OTHER NORTH AMERICAN JOB GENERATION STUDIES

This chapter has concentrated upon the most widely-quoted and influential job generation studies conducted in North America – those using the Dun and Bradstreet data base. However several other studies have been undertaken which have received less publicity. This concluding section briefly describes the results of three such studies, one from California and two from Canada.

3.5.1 Small business and employment growth in California

Tcitz, Glasmeier and Svensson (1981) analysed employment change between 1976 and 1979 amongst a sample of 25 000 firms derived from the records of the California Employment Development Department (EDD). The results of their analysis of employment change by firm size are summarised in Table 3.11. This shows that firms with less than 20 employees created 56 per cent of the 121 832 net new jobs which were generated in the sample of firms over the three-year period under investigation. The detailed annual figures, however, show a great deal of variation, and it is worthy of note that during the year in which employment growth was greatest (1977–78), large firms made a significant positive contribution. It is also important to note that the pattern of job generation by firm size varies by sector, with large firms being the most important generators of jobs in the manufacturing sector (Table 3.12). Another important result from the Californian study is illustrated in Table 3.13. This illustrates the development of the 940 firms which were first started in the first quarter of 1976. Over half of the

Table 3.11   Employment change by firm size in California; all sectors

	Net added jobs in employment size class				
Year	1–19	20–99	100–249	250+	Total
1976–77	19 242	10 543	1 262	− 3 964	27 083
1977–78	29 964	15 529	3 583	29 551	78 357
1978–79	19 617	1 274	1 697	− 6 196	16 392
Total					
1976–79	68 553	27 346	6 542	19 391	121 832

	Percent distribution				
1976–77	71.1	38.9	4.7	− 14.7	100.0
1977–78	37.9	19.8	4.6	37.7	100.0
1978–79	119.7	7.8	10.4	− 37.8	100.0
Total					
1976–79	56.3	22.4	5.4	15.9	100.0

Source: Teitz *et al.* (1981) p. 22

Table 3.12   Employment by change by firm size in California; manufacturing

	Net added jobs in employment size class				
Year	1–19	20–99	100–249	250+	Total
1976–77	1 624	3 604	240	1 489	6 957
1977–78	2 787	3 285	1 867	9 262	17 201
1978–79	2 230	2 005	− 280	7 779	11 734
Total					
1976–79	6 641	8 894	1 827	18 530	35 892

	Percent distribution				
1976–77	23.3	51.8	3.5	21.4	100.0
1977–78	16.2	19.1	10.9	53.8	100.0
1978–79	19.0	17.0	− 2.4	66.3	100.0
Total					
1976–79	18.5	24.8	5.1	51.6	100.0

Source: Teitz *et al.* (1981) p. 23

Table 3.13   Employment development of firms which were new in 1976

Size Class	Percentage after four years in size class:						
At entry	Exit	0–9	10–19	20–99	100–249	250+	Total
0–9	52.0	28.0	11.6	8.0	0.3	0.0	100.0
10–19	41.2	16.0	22.1	20.6	0.0	0.0	100.0
20–99	33.1	5.4	11.5	45.9	2.7	1.3	100.0

Source: Teitz *et al.* (1981) p. 54

firms which started with less than 10 employees had ceased to exist by the end of 1979. Of the remaining firms, sixty per cent remained in the 0–9 size category, and only 0.3 per cent of the entire population of small new firms employed more than 100 by 1979. This represents only two firms out of the original 621 which started with less than 10 employees in 1976. This table clearly illustrates that only a small proportion of the new and small firm population creates the vast majority of new jobs in that size group. We shall return to this point in our discussion of job generation outside North America in Chapter 4, and the policy implications will be outlined in Chapter 7.

3.5.2   Job creation in Canadian manufacturing, 1974–1979

A study of a longitudinal data base derived from the annual Statistics Canada Census of Manufactures has been reported by Layne (1982). Employment in manufacturing units (i.e. establishments) which were in existence in 1974 was traced through to 1979. The study excluded new firms which were created between 1974 and 1979. The results show that total employment in the cohort of manufacturing units declined by 9 per cent over the five year period. However, the smallest units (with less than 20 employees) had the same total employment in 1979 as they had in 1974 (Table 3.14). This is despite the fact that over 40 per cent of the small units which existed in 1974 has ceased trading by 1979. In contrast, aggregate employment in the largest size category (100+ employees) declined by 10 per cent, in line with a similar decline in the number of units in existence. Layne therefore calculates that the level of employment in *surviving* small units increased by around 70 per cent, whereas employment in surviving large units remained stable over the five year period. Given that new units (most of which are likely to be

Table 3.14   Employment change by firm size in Canadian manufacturing 1974–1979

Employment size In 1974	1974	1976	1979
0–19	100	102	100
20–49	100	96	93
50–99	100	94	91
100 & over	100	92	90
Total	100	93	91

Source: Layne (1982)

small) are excluded from the analysis, it seems that small units were creating jobs at a more rapid rate than large units in the Canadian manufacturing sector between 1974 and 1979.

3.5.3   Job creation in Canada 1975–82

Wietfeldt (1984) compared the performance of 7749 members of the Canadian Federation of Independent Business (CFIB) with that of 175 firms listed in the 1975 *Canadian Business* list of the largest 400 corporations, over the period 1975 to 1982. It is important to note that these samples cover only surviving firms, and that births and deaths of firms are excluded from the analysis. This means that the figures for

Table 3.15   Employment change as a percentage of initial employment within each size category – CFIB job creation study

Size of firm SME Sector	Percentage increase in employment	
	1975–80	1975–82
1–4	60.7	75.7
5–9	20.5	28.2
10–19	23.5	19.1
20–49	12.0	9.3
50–99	4.4	1.9
100+	7.3	−2.7
Total SME	14.2	12.5
Big Business	5.4	−2.5

Source: Wietfeldt (1984), p.11

Table 3.16 Percentage of net employment growth 1975–1982 by firm size –
CFIB job creation study

Size of firm by no. employed	Percentage of net employment growth	Percentage of total 1975 employment
1–4	36.8	6.1
5–9	25.9	11.4
10–14	14.2	9.0
15–19	9.5	6.4
20–49	17.4	23.5
50–99	2.3	15.5
100+	−6.1	28.1
ALL SIZES	100.0	100.0

Source: Weitfeldt (1984)

small firm employment change, where most births and deaths occur, are likely to be distorted. The results of this analysis are summarised in Tables. 3.15 and 3.16. Between 1975 and 1980, the 'SME' sample increased its employment by 14.2 per cent, whereas the 'Big Business' sample increased by 5.4 per cent. When the period 1975–82 is examined, big businesses actually reduced their level of employment. Within the small firm sector, the most rapid percentage increases in employment were achieved by the smallest firms. This is perhaps not surprising since this group is starting from a low base. However, Table 3.16 shows that firms with less than 10 employees contributed over half of the net new jobs created by the SME sector between 1975 and 1982, suggesting that, in absolute terms, small firm job generation is significant.

3.6 CONCLUSION

There is general agreement amongst the major North American job generation studies that small firms have been a significant source of new jobs, at least since the early 1970's. Most studies indicate that small firms have been increasing their employment faster than either medium or large sized firms. When sectoral analyses are conducted it is apparent that the faster rates of small firm growth are found in services, rather than in the manufacturing sector. Hence whilst the early work by Birch significantly over-estimated the importance of small firms in employment creation it did highlight, for the first time, the sector's importance in job creation in North America.

4 Job Generation in Other OECD Countries

4.1 INTRODUCTION

The pioneering work of Birch, and the subsequent work of the Brookings researchers, discussed in Chapter 3, led to many attempts to replicate these studies in other countries, notably the United Kingdom. Several studies have also been carried out in other European countries, New Zealand and Japan. The aim of this chapter is to provide a critical review of these studies, with particular attention being focused upon the question of firm size and job generation.

The central problem which has faced researchers outside the United States has been the lack of national data bases comparable to the Dun and Bradstreet data base used by the Birch and Brookings research teams. Hence most studies have been based upon local or regional data bases compiled from various sources such as Factory Inspectorate data, Census of Employment data or local surveys. Two notable exceptions to this have been the analyses of the UK Dun and Bradstreet data base for the 1971–81 and 1982–84 periods, undertaken by the research team led by Colin Gallagher at Newcastle University, and the study of manufacturing employment change 1972–1975 carried out by Macey of the UK Department of Industry (DoI), using an internal DoI data base. The results of these studies are summarised in Section 4.2, together with the local and regional studies which have been undertaken in the UK, covering Scotland, the East and West Midlands, Northern England, Northern Ireland and the North West. Job generation studies which have been carried out in West Germany, France, Italy, the Republic of Ireland and New Zealand are discussed in Section 4.3. This chapter concludes with a critical appraisal of these studies, particularly as regards the role of small firms in the job generation process.

4.2 UK JOB GENERATION STUDIES – THE KEY RESULTS

4.2.1 A review of UK job generation studies

Table 4.1 shows that eleven major job generation studies have been undertaken in the UK, i.e. where data on individual employment units are available for two points in time and where these units are either a complete enumeration of all employment units or may be easily scaled-up to provide full enumeration.

Only three studies covering the whole of the United Kingdom have been undertaken. These are Gallagher and Stewart (1986), Doyle and Gallagher (1986) and Macey (1982), with only the first two covering businesses in both the service and the manufacturing sectors. All other studies shown in the table include establishments in the manufacturing sector, except for that by Hubbard and Nutter (1982) which includes services only. Apart from Gallagher and Stewart, Doyle and Gallagher, and Macey, all other studies include only regions or sub-regions of the United Kingdom. In total they provide a fairly extensive picture so that the only area without major job generation studies is Wales.

Whilst the geographical coverage of the studies is adequate the results of the studies cannot be compared directly for a variety of reasons outlined in the remainder of Table 4.1. Thus, for example the duration of the study periods vary considerably; the Macey study of UK manufacturing covers only a three year period, whereas the Hamilton, Moar and Orton (1981) study of Scotland covers twenty years.

Several of the studies, however, cover a period of approximately one decade (Lloyd and Mason (1984), Cross (1981), Gallagher and Stewart (1986)) but even here comparability is difficult since any study which includes the recessionary years from 1976 onwards is likely to produce very different results from those in the more prosperous 1950s and 1960s.

A further source of difficulty in making comparisons is the various data sources used. Fothergill and Gudgin (1979), Lloyd and Mason (1984), Healey and Clark (1985) derive either their lists of establishments and/or the employment in those establishments, from the Factory Inspectorate (FI). Whilst coverage of manufacturing establishments by the Inspectorate is likely to be close to comprehensive the employment identified covers 'blue-collar' workers only. It does not include managers and 'white-collar' workers. A second problem with such data is that the frequency of update depends upon visits by the Inspector which are likely to be more frequent for large establishments than for small. The records collected for some smaller establishments are therefore likely to be somewhat out of date.

It also has to be recognised that there are, at the margin, considerable opportunities for differences in interpretation of these classifications. An example illustrates this point. Take the case of an establishment A ceasing to trade, changing its name to B and moving to alternative premises within the same town. It is possible to classify this as a closure,

Table 4.1 Major UK job generation studies

	Geographical Coverage	Sectoral Coverage	Time Period	Prime Data Source	Coverage	Cut Offs	All Employees	Base year Employment
UK Studies								
1.								
(a) Gallagher & Stewart	UK	All	1971–81	Dun and Bradstreet	Unclear	None specified	All	Not given
(b) Doyle & Gallagher			1982–84					
2. Macey	UK	Manufacturing	1972–5	ROC	88% of ACE	<10 employees	All	6 488 000
Regional UK Studies								
3. Cross	Scotland	Manufacturing	1968–77	Scottish Council data	90% of ACE	<10 employees	All	587 270
4. Firn & Swales	Birmingham Clydeside	Manufacturing Manufacturing	1963–72	Questionnaire ED 871	Survivors only All	<5 employees <5 employees	All	Not given

5. Fothergill & Gudgin	East Midlands	Manufacturing	1968–75	Factory Inspectorate	Good	None specified	Blue Collar Only	576 000
6. Hamilton, Moar & Orton	Scotland	Manufacturing	1954–74		Only post 1954 estabs.	None specified	All	Zero
7. Healey & Clark	Coventry	Manufacturing	1974–82	Interviews & official data	Comprehensive	None	All	115 317
8. Howick & Key	Inner London (Tower Hamlets)	Manufacturing	1973–76	ACE	Good	None	All	27 324
9. Hubbard & Nutter	Merseyside	Manufacturing & Services	1971–75	ACE	Good	None	All	250 520
10. Lloyd & Dicken	Merseyside/Manchester	Manufacturing	1966–75	Factory Inspectorate	Good	None specified	Blue collar only	76 087 91 523
11. Storey	North East England	Manufacturing	1965–81	ACE	Good	None	All	393 000
12. DED	Northern Ireland	Manufacturing	1971–78	ACE	Good	None	All	172 000

followed by an opening. It is equally possible to regard it simply as a transfer. There is no clear 'correct' definition. Furthermore those undertaking such studies might, from public records, be unaware of the connections between A and B, so that the 'closure' and 'opening' combination is probably the most likely, if not necessarily the best informed, classification. However if no name change occurred establishment A is more likely to be classified as a transfer and thus a continuing business. To this extent classification, even with perfect information, may be arbitrary. Particular problems also occur with establishments which move outside a given geographical area of study. In some cases they are classified as closures, whereas, as far as the national economy is concerned, they are merely transfers.

It should be emphasised that these ownership classification problems are not unique to the use of Factory Inspectorate data. Similar problems occur where the basic data is Census of Employment (ACE) such as used by Storey or Hubbard and Nutter, or other employment data such as that used by Firn and Swales. Since each of these data bases has been constructed from raw employment data provided to individual researchers, the classification accuracy depends upon the care and effort devoted to the examination of ownership change. For example in some cases it is clear that ownership is classified according to presence or absence in Directories such as *Who Owns Whom*, whereas in other cases this is supplemented either by telephone calls, interviews or obtaining records from Companies House. It is broadly true that those data bases which use only Directory sources to classify establishments into ownership types generally underestimate (sometimes quite significantly) the extent of multiple ownership of business establishments. Conversely they *inflate* the importance of independent establishments. For a full review of these problems see Healey (1984a).

These problems do not arise with the Dun and Bradstreet data used by Gallagher & Stewart. It will be recalled from Chapter 3 that Dun and Bradstreet are a credit-rating agency who have constructed a data base of UK businesses. To provide credit ratings, Dun and Bradstreet make regular contact with firms to collect information on their ownership, employment, location, sales etc., and they have made the data base available for research purposes, provided that confidentiality controls are strictly observed. Colin Gallagher and Henry Stewart were therefore provided with two 'complete' data bases for 1971 and 1981 and their research has involved the combining of these data bases and the analysis of employment changes during that decade. Unfortunately this creates a set of rather different problems. First the employment data provided by the UK Dun and Bradstreet was in the form of ranges, rather than actual employment. Second, coverage in 1971 was incomplete and so it was often unclear whether an establishment which appeared in 1981 was a genuinely new establishment or whether it had simply been 'missed' in 1971. Thirdly, coverage of new and small firms was weak, because relatively few required credit ratings. Fourthly, some of the employment data was several years out of date because during that period Dun and Bradstreet had not been required to undertake a new credit rating. Some establishments could even have ceased trading. Fifthly it was unclear from individual records whether the employment at an individual establishment referred to employment at that establishment or total employment in the enterprise of which it was part. Hence whilst the UK Dun and Bradstreet data had the considerable advantage of including both the manufacturing and service sectors throughout the whole of the United Kingdom, considerable extra 'cleaning' of the data was needed before it could provide an adequate picture of employment change in the UK. In particular it is likely that those businesses which were included in the data base in 1971 were not necessarily representative of the population of UK businesses in existence at that time. Furthermore those which subsequently appeared in the data base are more likely to be faster growth businesses (seeking credit ratings) than in the population as a whole. There is some debate on whether Gallagher and Stewart adequately took account of these inherent biases in 'scaling-up' their results. This debate is described in section 4.4.1 below.

Of the other data sources available the most reliable and extensive are the Annual Census of Employment (ACE) and the Annual Census of Production (ACOP). Whilst their coverage is good they also have key disadvantages. First the ACE only began in 1971, so that data bases covering prior years have to use other data sources such as Principal Employers Lists. Second, ACE was conducted annually only for the years 1971–78. A further census was conducted in 1981 but in 1984 it became a sample, although data for this year has yet to be released. Thirdly and most importantly, there are severe restrictions imposed upon those allowed access to both ACOP and ACE data. Only government officials have been allowed to use ACOP, whilst only those working directly with or within Local Authorities have been allowed access to ACE.

Table 4.1 also provides a qualitative assessment of coverage of establishments, i.e. the extent to which the establishments in the data base are coincident with those actually present in the area under study. Clearly no establishment data base can hope to be a complete enumeration although some data bases are much better than others. It is broadly true that coverage is best in the two government data bases of

ACOP and ACE, whilst the Factory Inspectorate Data is also thought to be adequate. The studies by Healey and Clark and by Firn and Swales (1978) for the West Midlands are incomplete because they include only surviving businesses, whilst we have noted above the limitations of the Dun and Bradstreet data in this context. The study by Hamilton, Moar and Orton examines only businesses which started to trade in Scotland after 1954 and so it is also an incomplete enumeration of all plants.

Many of the data bases also exclude the smallest sized establishments, whilst those based on Factory Inspectorate data include only employment amongst blue-collar workers. Finally in Table 4.1 we provide an estimate of the size of these data bases in terms of employment in establishments in the base year. Clearly the largest, according to this criteria, should be the Gallagher and Stewart study but they do not provide this information for 1971. The study by Macey uses the largest known data base of approximately $6\frac{1}{2}$ million manufacturing employees. Amongst the regional data bases the largest are those for Scotland, the East Midlands and North East England, with the remaining study area data bases being considerably smaller.

4.2.2   The UK Dun and Bradstreet studies: 1971–1981 and 1982–1984

There is only one group of job generation studies which cover the whole of the UK private sector economy (i.e. manufacturing and service sectors) and which is, in principle, directly comparable with the Birch and Brookings studies of the USA. These have been conducted by a research team under the direction of Colin Gallagher (Gallagher and Stewart, 1986; Doyle and Gallagher, 1986). The Gallagher team were given access to the United Kingdom files of the Dun and Bradstreet corporation for 1971, 1981, 1982, 1983 and 1984. The results of the analysis of employment change between 1971 and 1981 and between 1982 and 1984 have been produced, and are summarised in Tables 4.2 and 4.3.

These tables show that, as with the USA studies, small firms create jobs at a faster rate than do large firms. Indeed, between 1971 and 1981, small firms with less than 20 employees were the only net creators of jobs, with particularly heavy job losses being sustained by firms in the largest size group (with more than 1000 employees). The pattern for 1982 to 1984 is similar. According to the Doyle and Gallagher study, firms with less than 50 employees created almost 700 000 jobs over this period, whilst very large firms (1000+) lost almost half a million jobs. Comparing Tables 4.2 and 4.3 it appears that the rate of job loss from

Table 4.2   Net employment change by firm size 1971–81

No. of employees in 1971	Total employment in 1971 (millions)	Total employment in 1981 (millions)	Net change (Millions)	Percentage of total base year employment
1–19	2.05	3.15	1.10	6.2
20–49	0.97	0.85	− 0.12	− 0.7
50–99	0.96	0.92	− 0.04	− 0.2
100–499	4.28	3.77	− 0.51	− 2.9
500–999	1.97	1.66	− 0.31	− 1.8
1000+	7.47	5.06	− 2.41	− 13.6
TOTAL	17.70	15.41	− 2.29	− 12.9

Source: Gallagher and Stewart (1986)

Table 4.3   Net employment change by firm size 1982–84

No. of employees in 1982	Total employment in 1982 (millions)	Total employment in 1984 (millions)	Net change (Millions)	Percentage of total base year employment
1–19	3.36	3.96	0.60	4.1
20–49	1.57	1.66	0.09	0.6
50–99	1.20	1.19	− 0.01	− 0.1
100–499	2.84	2.55	− 0.29	− 2.0
500–999	1.25	1.07	− 0.18	− 1.2
1000+	4.55	4.07	− 0.48	− 3.2
TOTAL	14.77	14.49	− 0.28	− 1.9

Source: Doyle and Gallagher (1986)

large firms has remained approximately constant over time (around 1½ per cent of total employment per year) whereas the rate of employment growth by small firms has accelerated in the later period. Firms with less than 20 employers created jobs at a net annual rate of 0.6 per cent of total employment between 1971 and 1981; by the 1982 and 1984 period this rate had increased to 2 per cent per year.

In both 1971–81 and 1982–84, the overall net employment change is negative, so it is not possible to directly compare the results of the UK Dun and Bradstreet studies with the USA results reported in Chapter 3, which express small firm job generation as a percentage of *net* new jobs.

Gallagher and Stewart (1986) produced a 'fertility ratio' which describes the relative contribution of different sized firms to *gross* new jobs (i.e. expansions and births) over the 1971 to 1981 period. The percentage of gross new jobs created by firms in each size band is compared to its proportion of employment in 1971. In Table 4.4, it can be seen that firms with less than 20 employees created 36 per cent of new jobs between 1971 and 1981, although they accounted for only 12 per cent of the workforce in 1971. This results in a 'fertility ratio' of 3.1, suggesting that small firms have a high potential for job creation. Conversely, the largest firms accounted for over 40 per cent of the workforce in 1971, but created only 11 per cent of new jobs. Doyle and Gallagher (1986) do not present fertility ratios on a comparable basis for the 1982–84 period, but it is possible to calculate the appropriate figures from the available data. These too are shown in Table 4.4. Once again, the smallest size groups exhibit the highest fertility ratios. Firms employing over 100 people have fertility ratios below unity, suggesting that these firms create less jobs than might be expected on the basis of their proportion of employment in 1982.

The UK Dun and Bradstreet studies, therefore, appear to broadly corroborate the findings of the Birch and Brookings job generation studies in the USA – that small firms are the most important source of new jobs in the UK economy. The main difference between the UK and US studies lies in the fact that, in most cases, all sizes of firm in the US are net creators of jobs, whereas in the UK, medium-sized and large firms are net losers of jobs.

4.2.3   The Macey study of manufacturing employment change 1972–1975

Macey (1982) produced an analysis of employment change in UK manufacturing industry between 1972 and 1975, using an internal Department of Industry data base known as the Regional Office Information System (ROIS). Two points should be noted regarding the ROIS data base: firstly it is based upon establishments as opposed to enterprises, and secondly the data base excludes establishments with less than 10 employees (20 in Greater London). Hence the data base omits a large number of units in the size group which has received the most attention in the job generation literature – very small firms.

Table 4.5 summarises the results obtained by Macey with regard to net employment change by establishment size. This illustrates that establishments in the smallest size band (11–20 employees) are the only

Table 4.4 Fertility ratios by firm size 1971–1981 and 1982–1984

Number of Employees in 1971	1971–81			1982–84		
	% of total employment in base year	% of gross job creation	Fertility ratio	% of total employment in base year	% of gross job creation	Fertility ratio
1–19	12	36	3.1	23	46	2.0
20–49	5	7	1.4	11	13	1.2
50–99	5	8	1.6	8	10	1.3
100–499	24	27	1.1	19	11	0.6
500–999	11	11	1.0	8	4	0.5
1000+	42	11	0.3	31	17	0.5

Source: Gallagher and Stewart (1986); Doyle and Gallagher (1986)

Table 4.5   Net employment change by establishment size: UK manufacturing 1972–1975

| | | | Employment size | | | |
	11–20	21–50	51–200	201–500	500+	Total
Number ('000)	+ 2.1	– 28.0	– 94.7	– 88.8	– 202.0	– 411.4
As % of total 1972 employment	+ 0.0	– 0.4	– 1.5	– 1.4	– 3.1	– 6.3
As % of 1972 employment in size-band	+ 1.3	– 6.4	– 7.6	– 6.8	– 6.1	– 6.3

Source: Macey (1982) p. 19

ones to exhibit net employment growth between 1972 and 1975. All other size bands experienced a net loss of jobs. Even when openings of new establishments are included according to their size group in 1975, a similar pattern prevails. Macey argues that the employment performance of different sized firms is best described by measuring employment change in each size band as a percentage of base year (1972) employment in the size band, rather than as a percentage of total base year employment. If this criterion is utilised, there is an inverse relationship between establishment size and employment performance up to the 200 employee point, but employment performance improves slightly with increased size in establishments with more than 200 workers. These observations lead Macey to conclude that 'at a broad level the data suggests that across GB and over the time period studied, size was not a major determinant of net employment performance' (1982, p. 54). Macey also notes that there are considerable spatial variations in the employment performance of different sized establishments (Table 4.6). In most cases, small units performed better than larger establishments, but there are some exceptions. For instance, in Scotland all size groups experienced a net decline in employment, but in percentage terms the largest size group (over 500 employees) declined least.

The Macey data therefore partially confirm the results of the Dun and Bradstreet analyses in that small manufacturing establishments experienced a net increase in employment at a time when larger units were losing jobs. However, it should be pointed out that the growth of small *establishments* does not necessarily imply that small *firms* are creating jobs. Some small establishments are branches of larger firms and it is probable that part of the growth of small plant employment is

Table 4.6 Employment change by firm size and region: UK manufacturing 1972–1975

| Region | Employment size | | | | | |
	11–20	*21–50*	*51–200*	*201–500*	*501+*	*Total*
South-East	− 4.1	− 9.4	− 12.2	− 12.3	− 8.1	− 9.8
East Anglia	+ 15.6	− 4.6	− 3.2	− 4.4	− 5.7	− 4.2
South-West	− 1.0	− 6.5	− 5.1	− 1.2	− 8.4	− 6.2
West Midlands	− 6.2	− 6.3	− 4.2	− 1.0	− 9.7	− 6.9
East Midlands	+ 8.9	+ 0.3	− 5.3	− 10.1	− 8.3	− 6.9
Yorkshire & Humber-side	+ 3.8	− 2.1	− 8.0	− 4.7	− 2.6	− 4.1
North-West	+ 9.1	− 4.8	− 7.9	− 10.5	− 4.9	− 6.3
North	+ 18.4	− 1.9	− 0.0	− 2.2	− 3.5	− 2.5
Wales	+ 9.8	− 4.4	− 3.9	− 3.3	− 3.0	− 3.1
Scotland	− 5.1	− 9.3	− 8.4	− 4.3	− 1.3	− 4.1
Regional Average	+ 4.9	− 4.9	− 5.8	− 5.4	− 5.5	− 5.4

Source: Macey (1982) p. 46

due to the expansion of these branches. This is also true for new establishments. Macey points out that, of the 79 000 jobs created in establishments born between 1972 and 1975, 67 000 were accounted for by the establishment of new branch plants and only 25 000 by wholly new manufacturing firms.

4.2.4 The Fothergill and Gudgin study of the East Midlands 1968–1975

Fothergill and Gudgin (1979) used a data base covering 10 000 manufacturing establishments in the East Midlands, constructed mainly from the records of the Factory Inspectorate, to analyse employment change in that region between 1968 and 1975. The main results of this analysis are summarised in Table 4.7. Unlike Macey, Fothergill and Gudgin provide details of employment change by ownership type of firm, which makes it possible to separate the contributions of independent firms and multi-plant firms to net employment change. In the three main ownership classes (single plant independent, multi-plant headquarters and multi-plant branches) net employment change is positive for small units (with less than 25 employees) and negative for larger units. The contribution of new firms and new branches to employment change is categorised separately rather than being incorporated into the appropriate size classes. Over a seven-year period, wholly new firms, the majority of which were single plant independents,

Table 4.7 Employment change by plant size: East Midlands manufacturing 1968–75 as percentage of total 1968 manufacturing employment

| | | New firms | New branches, moves in, etc. | Existing plants by size in 1968 | | | | |
				1–25	26–100	101–500	501 +	All Plants
Single-plant firm	Independent	+ 3.7	+ 0.3	+ 0.4	− 0.5	− 0.9	− 0.2	+ 2.8
Multi-plant firm	Subsidiary	—	+ 0.8	0	− 0.1	− 1.1	− 1.7	− 2.0
	HQ	+ 0.3	+ 1.4	+ 0.1	+ 0.2	− 1.1	− 3.2	− 2.3
	Branch	+ 0.1	+ 3.2	+ 0.3	− 0.1	− 1.8	− 1.8	0
	ALL PLANTS	+ 4.1	+ 5.7	+ 0.8	− 0.5	− 4.8	− 6.9	− 1.5

Source: Fothergill and Gudgin (1978) p. 6.

added 4 per cent to 1968 employment. It should be noted that the establishment of new firms, new branches and relocated plants over the 1968 to 1975 period, together with the expansion of small firms was insufficient to offset the job losses incurred in the larger plants, resulting in a net decline in manufacturing employment.

4.2.5 Manufacturing employment change in North East England 1965–81

Storey has undertaken a series of studies of manufacturing employment change in the counties of Tyne and Wear, Durham and Cleveland between 1965 and 1981, using a data base constructed from several sources including data held by the Employment Exchange Area Offices, the County Councils and (after 1971) data from the Annual Census of Employment (ACE). The results of an analysis of employment change by size of establishment for two periods, 1965–76 and 1976–81, are summarised in Table 4.8. This table shows quite clearly that small establishments were net creators of jobs, and large establishments experienced net losses over the entire period under consideration. However, it should be pointed out that the percentage figures in Table 4.8 disguise the fact that absolute employment growth in small establishments has been insufficient to offset the large job losses which have occurred in larger plants, particularly in the latter period. Only in County Durham during the 1965–76 period was there a net growth in total manufacturing employment. It should also be noted that the data refers to establishments rather than firms, and some of the net

Table 4.8 Percentage manufacturing employment change by establishment size in North East England

| County | Time | Size of establishment | | | | |
		< 25	25–99	100–499	500 +	Total
Tyne and Wear	1965–76	+ 37.5	− 0.8	− 14.3	− 19.4	− 13.7
	1976–81	+ 5.6	− 15.9	− 33.4	− 28.4	− 26.5
Durham	1965–76	+ 44.6	+ 26.0	+ 31.6	− 3.1	+ 13.2
	1976–81	+ 32.7	− 10.5	− 23.3	− 34.7	− 25.4
Cleveland	1965–76	+ 134.9	+ 36.1	+ 9.7	− 20.2	− 10.2
	1976–81	+ 39.2	− 6.6	− 25.4	− 33.7	− 27.8

Sources: Cleveland County Council (1985); Durham County Council (1986); Tyne and Wear County Council (1986).

employment growth in small establishments will be accounted for by the establishment and growth of branch plants. Indeed, Storey (1985a) demonstrates that, when classified by ownership type, only non locally controlled subsidiaries exhibited net employment growth in North East England over the 1965–78 period.

4.2.6   Job generation in Scottish manufacturing industry

Three major studies of job generation in Scottish manufacturing industry have been undertaken. Cross (1981) used data provided by the Scottish Council to analyse the contribution of new manufacturing firms to employment change over the period 1968–77. He found that approximately 10 per cent of 1977 manufacturing employment in Scotland was in plants which had opened since 1968. A further examination of the data reveals that, of the 54 000 jobs created in openings, the vast majority (37 600) were accounted for by 'immigrant plants', and only 12 200 jobs were created by wholly new manufacturing firms. In short, new manufacturing firms which had opened since 1968 accounted for only just over 2 per cent of manufacturing employment in 1977.

The Scottish Office (1980) and Hamilton, Moar and Orton (1981) used the Scottish Office Manufacturing Establishments Record (SCOMER) to analyse employment change in Scottish manufacturing industry between 1954 and 1974. The SCOMER data base is similar to that used by Macey (1982) in that it omits units with 10 or fewer employees. The two Scottish studies differ slightly in that the Scottish Office covers all manufacturing units on the file, whereas Hamilton,

Table 4.9   Net Employment change in Scottish manufacturing industry 1954–1974, as percentage of initial employment within each size class

Size of unit at start of period	Time period			
	1954–59	*1959–64*	*1964–69*	*1969–74*
11–24	11	10	25	3
25–49	− 2	5	17	7
50–99	− 3	8	13	4
100–199	− 9	− 1	2	− 7
200 +	− 4	− 2	1	− 8
TOTAL	− 4	0	4	− 5

Source: Scottish Office (1980) p. 18.

Moar and Orton analyse only those establishments which opened during the 1954–74 period. Both studies conclude that small establishments tend to grow on average at a faster rate than large establishments. The results of the Scottish Office study are summarised in Table 4.9 which shows that, for three out of the four sub-periods analysed, small units grew at a more rapid percentage rate in terms of total employment than did large units. In all cases, net employment change amongst plants with 11–24 employees is positive, whereas plants with over 200 employees are net losers of jobs in all time-periods apart from 1964–69. The potentially misleading use of percentage figures must be noted here, as with the Northern results presented in Table 4.8. For instance the 4 per cent decline in large unit employment between 1954 and 1959 represents 19 000 jobs lost, whereas the 11 per cent growth in small unit employment represents only 2700 extra jobs.

4.2.7 Manufacturing employment change in Northern Ireland 1973– 1981

A study conducted by the Northern Ireland Department of Economic Development (1982) and reported by Hart (1985) used Annual Census of Employment (ACE) data to examine the contribution of small firms to manufacturing employment growth in the province between 1971 and 1981. Total manufacturing employment fell by almost one-third (55 000 jobs) during this ten year period. Only plants with less than 25 employees experienced a net growth employment (Table 4.10) but it is clear that this growth of 2200 jobs is tiny compared to the 32 300 jobs which were lost

Table 4.10   Net Manufacturing employment change by establishment size in Northern Ireland, 1971–1981

Size range	1971 employment	%	1981 employment	%	Net Change as % of 1971 total employment	
0–24	10801	6.3	13047	11.2	+ 1.3	} + 0.9
25–49	10580	6.2	9885	8.4	− 0.4	
50–99	15698	9.2	12646	10.8	− 1.8	
100–199	23195	13.5	18115	15.5	− 3.0	} − 12.1
200–499	42053	24.5	26385	22.6	− 9.1	
500–999	20441	11.9	11360	9.7	− 5.3	} − 18.8
1000 +	48762	28.4	25520	21.8	− 13.5	
TOTAL	171530	100.0	116958	100.0	− 31.8	

Source: Hart (1985).

in establishments with more than 500 employees. A further analysis produced by Hart (1985) shows that over three-quarters of gross job losses occurred in plants with over 100 employees. One-third of gross job gains were accounted for by establishment openings and the remaining two-thirds by expansions of existing establishments.

4.2.8   Local studies of employment change in the UK

In addition to the national and regional studies discussed above, there have been a number of local 'components of change' analyses conducted throughout the UK. Examples are Dicken and Lloyd (1978) who studied Greater Manchester and Merseyside; a comparative analysis of Clydeside and the West Midlands by Firn and Swales (1978); Howick and Key (1980) on Tower Hamlets, London; and a study of service sector employment change on Merseyside conducted by Hubbard and Nutter (1982). In most cases, however, it is difficult or impossible to discern the contribution of small firms to employment change from these studies. A series of local studies in the West Midlands (Healey 1984a, 1985; Healey and Clark, 1985) do present data on employment changes by firm size, and these are summarised in Table 4.11. Again, it is clear that there is an inverse relationship between establishment size and net employment change. In Coventry and Nuneaton/Bedworth, plants with fewer than 10 employees were the only group to experience net employment growth. In Warwick, all sizes suffered a decline in

Table 4.11   Employment change as a percentage of initial employment within size group – Coventry, Warwick, Nuneaton and Bedworth districts

Size of establishment	Coventry (1974–1982)	Warwick (1974–1983)	Nuneaton and Bedworth (1974–1985)
1–10	16	− 10	32
11–19	− 35 ⎫	− 9	− 3
20–49	− 19 ⎭		
50–99	− 17		
100–199	− 36	− 31	− 30
200–499	− 4		
500–999	− 49 ⎫	− 22	− 66
1000 +	− 54 ⎭		
Total	− 46	− 24	− 32

Sources: Healey and Clark (1985); Healey (1984); Healey (1985).

employment, but the percentage change for the smaller size categories was less than that for larger plants.

4.2.9   Job generation in the UK: synthesis

This section has briefly summarised the results of several studies which have analysed the contribution of different sizes of firms to employment change in the United Kingdom. The studies vary greatly in their sectoral and geographical coverage, the time period covered, and the form of presentation of the results. Despite this heterogeneity, the verdict is almost unanimous. *Small firms have been net creators of jobs in the UK at a time when job losses have occurred in the large firm sector*. Meaningful comparisons with the North American studies discussed in Chapter 3 are difficult because the majority of the UK studies cover the manufacturing sector only and because, in almost every case, there is a net decline in total employment in the UK. This means that the measures of 'percentage of net jobs generated' which are common in the USA cannot sensibly be applied to the UK data. Nonetheless it remains true that, in most cases, small firms appear to be the *only* net generators of jobs in the United Kingdom.

4.3   JOB GENERATION IN EUROPE AND ELSEWHERE

Job generation research is most advanced in the United States, Canada and the United Kingdom. However, several studies have been carried out in some European countries, notably the Federal Republic of Germany, and a recent study has analysed employment change in New Zealand manufacturing industry. This section completes the picture by summarising the results of these studies.

4.3.1   Job generation in the Federal Republic of Germany

There have been four job generation studies conducted in the Federal Republic of Germany which permit the contribution of different sizes of firm to employment change to be calculated. The results are summarised in Table 4.12. Fritsch (1984) studied employment change in a sample of 888 firms which applied for assistance in 1974 and 1981 to the Kreditanstalt fur Wiederaufbau, a publicly-owned financial institution which administers a variety of public financial assistance schemes to firms. The cohort of firms experienced an increase of 2664 jobs (1.9 per

Table 4.12   Job generation studies in the Federal Republic of Germany

Study	Area covered	Annualised percentage change in employment (percentage of total base year employment) Size of Firm/Establishment					
		<20	20–49	50–99	100–499	500+	Total
Fritsch (1984)	Sample of firms throughout FRG – all sectors	+ 0.2	+ 0.2	+ 0.2	+ 0.2	– 0.5	+ 0.3
Hull (1985)	Sample of firms in four regions of FRG – all sectors	+ 0.8	+ 0.7	– 0.0	– 0.2	– 0.5	+ 0.8
Dahremoll-er (1985)	Northrhine-West-falia – manuf. only	– 0.2	– 0.3	– 0.3	– 0.9	– 1.3	– 3.0
Eckhart *et al.* (1986)	Dortmund and Frankfurt – all sectors	+ 1.1	– 0.4	– 0.4	– 0.5	+ 0.5	+ 0.3

Source: Hull (1987)

cent) over the 1974–1981 period, but the performance of different sized firms varied markedly. Firms with over 500 employees in 1974 declined by 5138 jobs (7.2 per cent), whereas those with less than 10 employees in the base year more than doubled their employment from 532 jobs in 1974 to 1795 jobs in 1981. All sizes of firm below 500 employees experienced net increase in employment. If employment change is expressed as a percentage of base year employment in each size band, the performance of very small firms is extremely impressive, and net employment change declines in line with size of firm. However, an examination of the absolute numbers of jobs created shows that firms with up to 200 employees were responsible for the generation of significant numbers of jobs.

Hull (1985) surveyed 458 small independent manufacturing firms in four localities of northern West Germany, with between 10 and 200 employees at the time of the survey. The results are similar to those obtained by Fritsch in that the smallest firms were observed to have extremely rapid rates of employment growth. For instance, employment in firms with less than 10 employees in 1974 had increased two-and-a-half times by 1980. When employment change is expressed as a percentage of *total* base year employment, the performance of the smallest firms is still more impressive than that of firms in the larger size categories, but the percentage change is much smaller. Hull also conducted a series of regression analyses on his data which suggest that the age of a firm is as important as its size in determining net employment performance.

The coverage of the two studies noted above is only partial in the sense that the Fritsch study covers only firms which have survived over the seven-year period of study, thus omitting births and deaths of firms, whereas the Hull study covers a limited size range of firms and omits deaths from the analysis. The study of manufacturing employment change in Northrhine-Westfalia 1978–84 by Dahremoller (1985) using data especially compiled by the Northrhine-Westfalian Statistical Office, includes *all* components of change (births, deaths, *in situ* change) in its analysis. The study shows that, if in-situ change is considered in isolation, the pattern of employment growth by firm size is similar to that noted in the Fritsch and Hull studies. However, if closures are included in the analysis, the picture alters. All size groups experience a net loss of jobs, but the percentage loss in the smaller firms is less than that in large firms, when expressed as a percentage of base year employment by size category. In absolute terms, however, large firm job loss is much greater than that experienced by small firms.

Preliminary results from a study of employment change in Dortmund and Frankfurt 1975–1980 using data from a credit-rating agency, Verin Creditreform, by Eckhart, von Einem and Stahl (1986) are also shown in Table 4.12. This shows that both very small and very large firms experienced net employment growth, with firms between 21 and 500 employees registering a net decline in employment. It is interesting to note that total net employment change is positive in this study, in contrast to the majority of UK and other European studies which give full coverage of employment change (i.e. including deaths). It is also one of the very few studies outside North America in which large firms register a net increase in employment.

4.3.2 French studies of job generation

Guesnier (1987) has produced statistics derived from a database covering manufacturing industry in the Poition-Charentes region of France which illustrate the extent of employment change by enterprise size between 1972 and 1984. Unfortunately, data is not provided on the initial level of employment by size of firm, but it is clear that the pattern of small firm net job creation and large firm net job loss is repeated in this French region. A provisional analysis of the national picture in France, for all sectors presented by Guesnier (1987) reveals a similar pattern. The French results are illustrated in Tables 4.13 and 4.14.

Table 4.13   Employment change by firm size in the Poition-Charentes region of France, 1972–84

Size of firm in initial year	Absolute employment change				
	1972–1975	1975–1978	1978–1981	1981–1984	1972–1984
0	4709	5639	5996	9484	24123
1	246	42	− 35	− 47	629
2	− 69	− 25	− 109	− 101	− 256
3	− 3	− 41	− 14	− 93	− 278
4–5	51	136	− 134	− 159	− 305
6–9	− 126	− 18	− 271	− 394	− 407
10–19	− 100	91	− 334	− 705	− 967
20–49	356	− 533	− 925	− 1742	− 2996
50–99	− 514	− 1363	− 1648	− 2394	− 3438
100–199	− 1157	− 1206	− 1629	− 1185	− 5899
200–499	695	− 1144	− 2752	− 4020	− 6681
500 +	− 132	− 1904	− 4147	− 4632	− 11825
Total	4016	− 326	− 6002	− 5988	− 8300

Source: Guesnier (1987)

Table 4.14   Employment change by firm size in France 1981–1983

Size of firm	Absolute employment change	As percentage of base year employment in size group
0	+ 46354	—
1	+ 2023	
2	+ 483	
3	− 236	+ 0.05
4–5	− 1275	
6–9	− 3862	− 0.37
10–19	− 44973	− 3.25
20–49	− 109700	− 4.66
50–99	− 88419	− 5.04
100–199	− 105534	− 5.93
200–499	− 163231	− 7.10
500 +	− 213025	− 4.78
Total	− 264172	− 1.5

Source: Guesnier (1987)

4.3.3 Manufacturing employment change in Ireland 1973–1980

A detailed analysis of employment change in Irish manufacturing industry between 1973 and 1980 has been undertaken by O'Farrell (1986) using data provided by the Industrial Development Authority (IDA). Table 4.15 illustrates that plants with less than 300 employees were net creators of jobs, whereas larger plants lost a total of over 8000 jobs over the 1973–1980 period. Net employment growth in the smaller plants was, however, sufficient to offset the large plant job loss, resulting in a positive net change in Irish manufacturing employment over this period. It should be noted that these figures are based on establishments rather than enterprises. This distinction is particularly important in a country such as Ireland with a relatively high concentration of branches of multinational enterprises. A further analysis by O'Farrell (1986, p. 90) shows that small indigenous single plant enterprises which were in existence in 1973 had lost 707 jobs by 1981, whereas small branches of multinational enterprises had gained 1454 jobs over the same period. Thus it seems that a significant proportion of the net gain in employment in small establishments is due to large firms rather than small firms.

4.3.4 Job generation in Italy

Contini *et al.* (1984) produced a major report analysing the determinants of productivity and employment in the Italian SME sector, using data

Table 4.15 Manufacturing employment change by establishment size in the Republic of Ireland, 1973–81

Establishment size	Net employment change 1973–81	As percentage of total 1973 employment
0–50	+ 11941	5.5
51–100	+ 5500	2.5
101–200	+ 1156	0.5
201–300	+ 553	0.3
301–500	− 3662	− 1.7
500+	− 4399	− 2.0
Total	+ 11089	5.1

Source: O'Farrell (1986) pp. 32–3.

derived from the records of two Italian statistical agencies, ISTAT (covering manufacturing firms) and INPS (covering all firms with more than one employee). For the purposes of this review, two tables from this study are of particular interest, and their contents are summarised as Tables 4.16(a) and 4.16(b). The first table presents an analysis of jobs gained and lost in births and deaths of firms over the 1978–1981 period. The data is disaggregated by broad industry group, by region and by size of firm. The figures illustrate that jobs gained through births exceed those lost through deaths in the smallest size group (1–5 employees). The picture for the 6–19 size category varies by industry and region. For the largest size group, the net effect of births and deaths on employment is almost always negative. Table 4.16(b) shows the percentage change in employment amongst surviving firms over two separate four-year periods. The broad picture which emerges from this table is that large firms grew more rapidly than small over the 1973–77 period, whereas the reverse appears to be the case between 1977 and 1981, when small firms performed better than large in terms of net employment change.

4.3.5   Job generation in New Zealand manufacturing

Bollard and Harper (1986) used a sample derived from the file known as CARB kept by the New Zealand Department of Labour to investigate employment change in manufacturing industry between 1980 and 1984. This study shows that gross employment growth (births plus expansions) varies approximately inversely with plant size, apart from the largest size category (200+ employees) which exhibited relatively high employment growth rates. Gross employment losses (contractions plus deaths) also varied inversely with establishment size, a result which is in marked contrast to the findings of most of the other studies discussed in this chapter. When gross employment gains and losses are summed to derive net employment change, it is found that establishments with less than 30 employees exhibit a net loss of employment, and those with more than 100 employees exhibit net employment growth (Table 4.17). The experience of New Zealand with regard to firm size and employment change therefore appears to be very different from that of North America and Europe. However Bollard and Harper do point out that the high growth rate of large establishments may be due to the inclusion of several major energy projects which took place between 1980 and 1984, and that different results might have been obtained in a study of an alternative time period.

Table 4.16(a) Job creation and destruction through births and deaths, by firm size, industry and region, Italy, 1978–1981

Sector	Size by number of employees	North West			North-East and West			Central-Southern			Southern Area and Islands		
		created jobs	destroyed jobs	balance	created jobs	destroyed jobs	balance	created jobs	destroyed jobs	balance	created jobs	destroyed jobs	balance
Chemicals & Metals	1–5	1119	991	+337	1664	1249	+135	1116	762	+147	952	761	+135
	6–19	375	403		51	525		197	253		87	97	
	20–500	1111	954		1140	1406		276	427		116	162	
Engineering	1–5	10310	7618	+1662	10245	3816	+6277	4876	2091	+2750	2472	1203	+1224
	6–19	2500	2323		1813	1670		596	479		124	104	
	20–500	2784	3991		3282	3580		319	471		38	103	
Consumer Goods	1–5	16730	10685	+4861	27423	16421	+9448	12177	8182	+3309	6476	5167	+1207
	6–19	1908	2372		3200	4047		928	1402		245	354	
	20–500	1709	2429		2025	2732		414	626		43	36	
Building	1–5	19660	17166	+2239	31905	27571	+3155	16702	13209	+2888	18738	16190	+2056
	6–19	858	1032		1235	2280		865	1300		380	677	
	20–500	100	181		160	295		—	170		—	195	
Others	1–5	7317	4790	+2475	8029	5348	+2534	8623	5397	+3176	4925	3530	+1373
	6–19	47	97		96	237		35	82		16	37	
	20–500	4	5		12	17		—	3		—	—	
Industry Total	All firms	66532	54958	+11574	92741	71192	+21549	47124	34854	+12270	34613	29018	+5595

Source: Contini *et al.* (1984)

Table 4.16 (b) Employment change by firm size, industry and region, Italy, 1973–1981

Sector	Size in terms of employees	North West		North-East and West		Central-Southern		Southern Area and Islands	
		1973–1977	1977–1981	1973–1977	1977–1981	1973–1977	1977–1981	1973–1977	1977–1981
Chemicals & Metals	1–99	−1.48	−1.47	3.19	1.33	3.22	6.15	−0.91	7.54
	100–1500	16.11	−2.72	24.87	3.10	43.70	−3.61	20.97	−5.00
	overall mean	2.20	−1.73	7.07	1.64	10.16	4.48	2.96	5.33
Engineering	1–99	1.75	−1.42	4.67	0.68	5.05	0.84	−8.88	26.41
	100–1500	13.16	−1.42	24.08	2.10	21.93	6.34	33.11	−1.22
	overall mean	4.25	−1.42	9.11	1.00	8.70	2.03	1.62	19.50
Consumer Goods	1–99	2.23	−2.21	1.96	−0.42	3.55	4.70	−3.56	1.58
	100–1500	9.71	−8.38	29.93	−5.25	20.26	−1.37	28.08	−7.04
	overall mean	0.24	−3.49	6.65	−1.23	6.23	3.73	0.98	0.34
Building	1–99	−8.60	−3.19	−6.54	−0.51	18.12	5.02	−3.46	27.93
	100–1500	17.07	−13.98	53.60	−5.60	87.70	−11.93	88.55	−27.39
	overall mean	6.64	−4.01	−2.12	−0.88	24.23	3.53	9.40	20.20

Source: Contini et al. (1984)

Table 4.17 Employment change by establishment size in New Zealand, manufacturing 1980–84

Size of firm	Gross employment growth (%)	Gross employment loss (%)	Net employment change (%)
2–5	10.3	18.0	– 7.9
6–10	11.4	13.1	– 1.9
11–20	8.8	11.7	– 2.9
21–30	7.8	11.2	– 3.7
31–50	7.6	7.3	0.6
51–100	4.3	7.5	– 3.6
101–200	6.3	6.3	0.1
201 +	9.3	6.2	3.4

Source: Bollard and Harper (1986).

4.4 SMALL FIRMS AND JOB GENERATION IN EUROPE – A CRITICAL REVIEW OF THE EVIDENCE

The results of the studies reviewed in this chapter appear to give almost unanimous support to the proposition that small firms are the main creators of jobs in the European economies, and conversely that large firms are net shedders of jobs. Table 4.18 summarises these results, expressing employment change by firm size as a percentage of total base year employment on an annualised basis. It has already been emphasised that comparisons between different studies, particularly across national boundaries, are extremely hazardous and should be treated with the utmost caution. However, it can clearly be seen that, in the vast majority of European studies, net employment change in firms or establishments with more than 100 employees is negative. The only exceptions to this occur in the Federal Republic of Germany, where one study showed positive net employment growth amongst firms with 100–499 workers, and another showed that the largest size category (500+ employees) experienced increased employment.

Conversely, all studies apart from one show that firms with less than 20 employees are net creators of jobs. In the case of Northrhine – Westfalia, small firm employment change is negative, but the rate of decline is lower than that experienced by the large firm sector. The main difference between the various results lies in the point at which net job generation becomes negative. Most UK studies suggest negative, or very weak, net job generation rates in firms with more than 20 employees. The French national results and the FRG regional studies exhibit a

Table 4.18 Job generation studies in Europe

Country/area	Time period	Coverage	Annualised % change in employment (% of total base year employment) size of firm/establishment					
			<20	20–49	50–99	100–499	500+	Total
UNITED KINGDOM								
East Midlands	1968–1975	Manuf.	+0.4	+0.3	+0.2	−0.3	−0.9	−0.3
Northern England	1965–1976	Manuf.	+0.2	+0.1	+0.0	−0.1	−1.0	−0.8
Northern England	1976–1981	Manuf.	+0.2	0.0	−0.2	−1.6	−3.8	−5.4
United Kingdom	1972–1975	Manuf.	0.0	0.0	0.0	0.0	−0.1	−0.1
United Kingdom	1971–1981	All Sectors	+0.8	−0.1	0.0	−0.1	−1.4	−0.7
United Kingdom	1982–1984	All Sectors	+2.0	+0.3	0.0	−1.0	−2.2	−0.9
Northern Ireland	1971–1981	Manuf.	+0.1	0.0	−0.2	−1.2	−1.9	−3.2
F.R. GERMANY								
F.R.G. (sample)	1974–1981	All Sectors	+0.2	+0.2	+0.2	+0.2	−0.5	+0.3
F.R.G. (4 regions)	1974–1980	All Sectors	+0.8	+0.7	0.0	−0.2	−0.5	+0.8
Northrhine-Westfalia	1978–1984	Manuf.	−0.2	−0.3	−0.3	−0.9	−1.3	−3.0
Ruhr & Frankfurt	1975–1980	All Sectors	+1.1	−0.4	−0.4	−0.5	+0.5	+0.3
FRANCE								
France	1981–1983	All Sectors	0.0	−0.1	−0.1	−0.4	−0.4	−1.0
IRELAND								
Ireland	1973–1980	Manuf.	[+0.7]		+0.3	−0.3	−0.2	+0.6

Source: Storey and Johnson (1987a)

similar pattern. In the national (sample) FRG study of 1974–1980 job generation becomes negative at 50 employees, whereas in Ireland and Northern England (1965–76) firms continue to exhibit positive net job generation up to the 100 employee point. It is unclear whether these findings reflect genuine international differences, or whether they are simply due to variations in coverage and methodology between the different studies.

These results might appear as a justification for the introduction of policies to support the small firm sector at local, regional, national and international levels, as this sector is the only one which has been creating new jobs in Europe. Conversely, policies aimed at large firms are likely to have little effect in terms of job generation and/or the reduction of unemployment. However, the issue is not as straightforward as it might initially appear. In this section, several arguments will be put forward which will suggest that the contribution of small firms to employment creation is not as impressive as it appears from Table 4.18. These arguments can be summarised as follows:

(i)   The methodology used in some studies tends to be biased in favour of small firm job creation;

(ii)   Only a small minority of small firms are responsible for the majority of jobs created;

(iii) New firms make only a modest contribution to manufacturing employment over a relatively long period of time;

(iv)   The underlying reasons for the observed patterns are unclear and may vary between different countries and regions;

(v)   No information is given regarding the type of jobs created, hence the impact of small job generation on unemployment is unclear.

Points (iv) and (v) will be analysed in detail in Chapters 5 and 6, and will be covered only briefly in this section, which will concentrate mainly on points (i) to (iii).

4.4.1   Methodological issues

Our analysis of the North American job generation studies in Chapter 3 illustrated that the nature of the data base used, and the method of analysis employed, is of crucial importance in job generation studies. In particular it was argued that the Dun and Bradstreet data base is a biassed sample which means that, to a certain extent, judgements must be made which will stongly influence the final result. This section will focus attention upon the UK studies which have used a similar data base

(Gallagher and Stewart, 1986; Doyle and Gallagher, 1986). It will analyse the data base and the methodology used, in order to arrive at a judgement as to the true significance of small firm employment growth.

It is true to say that all data bases, including those held by Government departments, suffer from weaknesses and omissions, and to some extent the comments which we will be making on the UK Dun and Bradstreet studies apply to some of the other job generation studies reviewed in Sections 4.2 and 4.3. However, we believe that the UK Dun and Bradstreet studies should be subject to particular scrutiny for two major reasons. Firstly, the data base is similar to that used by Birch and Brookings in the US, and has been shown to produce different results depending upon the method of analysis. Secondly, the two published studies have had a strong influence upon the policies of the UK Government. For instance, the results of the 1971–81 study were enthusiastically welcomed by the Small Firms Minister, Mr. David Trippier, who wrote:

I welcome this article which reveals that small firms will continue to increase their share of the labour market (*British Business*, 13 July 1984).

Similarly, the 1982–1984 study (Doyle and Gallagher, 1986) received Ministerial acclaim:

The success of small firms is critical to the success of our economy . . . their record in creating jobs shows that, far from being a fringe activity, they are at the centre of generating employment.   (Lord Young, Employment Secretary, quoted in *Employment Gazette* November 1986, p. 444).

It should be noted that the conclusions of the authors, particularly of the 1971–1981 study, are rather more lukewarm than the above ministerial statements imply:

No one size of firm is responsible for the majority of job creation in the UK. Rather, all size groups make a significant contribution . . . the overwhelming USA result, that most jobs stem from small firms, is not so clear in the UK, although they are important contributors.
(Gallagher and Stewart, 1986, p. 898).

Indeed, one of the authors of the 1971–1981 study, Henry Stewart, has gone so far as to say:

'there is no evidence that the small firm contribution to employment is sufficient to stimulate recovery, let alone lead it, as the Government appears to believe'   (Stewart, 1986).

It can therefore be seen that even the summary results of a complex piece of empirical research can be subject to a wide variety of interpretations. In this section we will argue that, as with the US job generation studies, the summary figures themselves are strongly affected by the methodology used, and should be treated with extreme caution. Our discussion of the UK Dun and Bradstreet studies will be divided into two parts. The first will investigate the 1971–1981 study and illustrate the divergence in the results which emerge from two earlier published versions of the study. The second part will concentrate upon the 1982–1984 study, which received much publicity on its publication. It will be argued that, although a great deal of effort has been made to overcome the shortcomings of the Dun and Bradstreet data base, the final results substantially overstate the small firm contribution to employment growth.

(i) The 1971–81 UK Dun and Bradstreet study

The main emphasis of this section is to examine whether the results obtained by Gallagher and Stewart (1986) can justify even the relatively modest contribution of the small firm sector to job creation which they identify. This depends partly upon the quality of the data used and partly upon the analysis undertaken. There are several reasons why the data used by Gallagher and Stewart in their analysis of employment change between 1971 and 1981 are of dubious quality. First it will be recalled from Chapter 3 that Dun and Bradstreet specialise in credit rating, and the collection of employment data is a secondary purpose. Updating of employment and other information depends primarily upon the frequency with which Dun and Bradstreet are required to give a rating. This is likely to be a function of size, with large companies being credit-rated more frequently than small. Gallagher and Stewart compare the size of structure of their data base with offical UK statistics for the manufacturing sector, as this is the only sector for which comprehensive statistics exist. They find that Dun and Bradstreet coverage is over 75 per cent for firms with 20 or more employees, but is only 25 per cent for those with less than 20 employees. In order to correct for this relative underrepresentation of small firms, this size group is scaled up by a factor of three. All such scalings are to some degree arbitrary since the Gallagher and Stewart data base includes non-manufacturing enterprises where no information is available nationally on the number of enterprises in 1971. The absence of data on the service sector is a matter of considerable concern since this sector is known to have a much higher proportion of small firms than the manufacturing sector. Of greater concern however is whether the small firms which are in the Dun and Bradstreet data base are representative of small firms as a whole in the economy. This has an important bearing on the final result, as we shall demonstrate in our analysis of the 1982–84 study.

A second area for concern is that Gallagher and Stewart, unlike the United States Dun and Bradstreet analysts, do not have actual employment data for each enterprise. Instead employment is classified by ranges so Gallagher and Stewart assume that the gross number of jobs generated or lost by firms in a size category approximates to the number of firms that cross into a different size range multiplied by the difference in the means of the two ranges. Hence firms moving across size boundaries are assumed to reflect real changes in employment in that group, bearing in mind the large number of firms involved. In Gallagher and Stewart (1985) a test is conducted with the Macey (1982) data which shows that the assumption is only partly valid.

Thirdly the UK Dun and Bradstreet data are based on enterprises so that for multi-site enterprises it is not possible to identify the employment in each establishment. This issue is a major cause of the different results obtained by the MIT and Brookings groups on the relative contribution which small firms make to job creation in the United States (see Chapter 3). In the USA, Dun and Bradstreet collect data at *both* an establishment and an enterprise level, but Armington and Odle observed that the summation of the establishment employment was significantly less than the stated enterprise employment for companies. Armington and Odle believe the enterprise figure (adjusted to remove overseas employment) to be the 'true' figure and so they create phantom establishments to 'absorb' this extra employment. On the other hand Birch believes the establishment data to be correct. In the UK, *only* enterprise data are available so Gallagher and Stewart have to use the enterprise employment data even though the major US studies disagree on its relevance.

The US studies noted that Dun and Bradstreet data had a variety of shortcomings including the presence of clerical errors, infrequent updating of some types of records and inadequate coverage of certain sectors. It is fair to say that Gallagher and Stewart have devoted considerable time to cleaning the UK data. They conducted a postal questionnaire survey of a sample of 1000 firms and, in 90 per cent of cases where a reply was received, the firms confirmed the employment classification given in Dun and Bradstreet. Even so, major reservations must remain about the relevance of conducting analyses on a data base where the 1971 coverage is incomplete and where only broad tests of data reliability can be undertaken. Although Gallagher and Stewart state that 180 000 records exist for 1971 it seem that only about 45 000 of these gave *employment* data for that year. The only years for which size structure comparisons are undertaken with the UK population is for 1978, when Dun and Bradstreet coverage was improving. Furthermore the choice of 1971 as the base was not because data coverage was particularly good, but because of the lack of availability of data for any other year. Indeed had data for any other year been available 1971 would almost certainly not have been chosen since it was the first year in which the Dun and Bradstreet file was fully computerised and one therefore likely to have unique problems. This is particularly important since the size breakdown of expansions, contractions and deaths are based upon 1971 classifications.

A final problem with the use of the Dun and Bradstreet data base for analyses of employment change over the 1971–1981 period is concerned with the estimation of the jobs created by births of new firms. It has already been noted in Chapter 3, with reference to the USA Dun and Bradstreet data base, that it takes perhaps seven years for new firms born in any one year to be assimilated into the data base. Thus, the new records which appear in the database in 1981 will only partially cover firms which were born since 1971 and survived to 1981, particularly the more recent births. One consequence of this is that the 'births' which do appear in the data base at an early stage are likely to be exceptional, in that they are likely to have come to the attention of Dun and Bradstreet through a request for a credit-rating, or through appearances in business directories or other sources of business information. It is likely that the more dynamic fast-growing new firms will appear relatively quickly in the data base, whereas the majority of new firms, which either fail within a short period of time or do not experience significant growth, will either not appear in the data base at all, or only appear after a few years. The method of estimating employment in births is therefore of crucial importance, but this is not explained in detail in any of the papers published by Gallagher and Stewart. However, as we showed in discussing the United States analysis in Chapter 3, the final results are extremely sensitive to methods used for calculating births.

It can therefore be seen that the Dun and Bradstreet files for 1971–1981 suffer from a number of problems which mean that 'judgement' is

Table 4.19 Employment change by size of enterprise: Gallagher and Stewart (1984) (1986)

Range		1–19	20–49	50–99	Employment size 100–499	400–999	1000+	Total
Total jobs (Millions)	1984	1.74	0.99	1.00	3.08	1.58	4.76	13.16
	1986	2.05	0.97	0.96	4.28	1.97	7.47	17.70
Expansions	1984	1.93	0.44	0.41	0.79	0.40	0.00	+ 3.97
	1986	0.73	0.20	0.20	0.83	0.41	0.13	+ 2.50
Contractions	1984	0.00	− 0.09	− 0.10	− 0.35	− 0.30	− 0.63	− 1.47
	1986	0.00	− 0.12	− 0.14	− 0.73	− 0.49	− 1.82	− 3.30
Births	1984	0.26	0.37	0.29	0.73	0.32	1.18	+ 3.16
	1986	1.46	0.19	0.26	0.82	0.28	0.55	+ 3.56
Deaths	1984	− 0.93	− 0.40	− 0.38	− 1.15	− 0.54	− 1.61	− 5.00
	1986	− 1.09	− 0.39	− 1.36	− 1.43	− 0.51	− 1.27	− 5.05
Net Change	1984	− 1.27	0.32	0.23	0.02	− 0.13	− 1.06	0.65
Total Jobs	1986	1.10	− 0.12	− 0.04	− 0.51	− 0.31	− 2.41	− 2.29

Source: Gallagher and Stewart (1984); Gallagher and Stewart (1986).

required in the analysis of the data, and so the results should be treated with some caution. This point can be clearly illustrated by a comparison of two sets of results which were published by Gallagher and Stewart using the same data base for this period. Prior to the final published version (Gallagher and Stewart, 1986), two research reports entitled 'Jobs and the Business Life Cycle in the UK' were produced, one in May 1984 and the other in March 1985 (Gallagher and Stewart, 1984; Gallagher and Stewart, 1985). For the most part, the contents of the two reports are identical, but a close examination of the results reveals several significant differences between the 1984 version and the 1986 version. These are illustrated in Tables 4.19 and 4.20.

For instance, it can be seen from Table 4.19 that in the original (1984) version, total net employment change was estimated at + 650 000 jobs, but in the final (1986) version this has been altered to – 2 290 000 jobs – a significant change. The main reason for this difference lies in the figures for expansions and contractions. The 1984 version suggested that expansions of firms with less than 20 employees created 1.93 million jobs, whereas the final version estimated the equivalent figure to be 730 000 jobs. Similarly, job losses from contractions of very large firms (1000+ employees) altered from 630 000 on the original report to 1.82 million in the 1986 article, an increase of almost 200 per cent. Finally, an examination of the 'births' row reveals that the 1986 figure for jobs created in small firm births is over five times that recorded in the original (1984) version. Conversely, births in the 1000+ employee category have been reduced from 1.18 million to 550 000 jobs. The result is that the figure for total jobs created in births is approximately equal in the two versions, but the distribution by firm size is radically different. The net result of these alterations is to significantly change the picture regarding the relative contributions of the different sized firms to employment change. In particular, net employment change in the 20–499 size group is positive in the original version and negative in the 1986 version, and the extent of net job loss in the larger size category is increased by the alterations.

Table 4.20 investigates in a little more detail the differences between the original and revised versions of the Gallagher and Stewart results for an important group of firms – those with less than twenty employees. The 1984 version of the report suggested that 271 firms grew from having less than 20 workers in 1971 to more than 1000 workers in 1981. In the final version this had been reduced to 25 firms. The figures for expansions into all size bands above 50 employees differ significantly between the two sets of results. A detailed analysis of the absolute figures

Table 4.20 1981 employment size group of firms with less than 20 employees in 1971

	1–19	20–49	50–99	*1981 employment* 100–499	500–999	1000+	Total
1984 Figures							
No. of firms	92252	19625	5140	2360	108	271	119757
(% of survivors)	(77)	(16)	(4)	(2)	(0)	(0)	(100)
1985 Figures							
No. of firms	119659	17072	3231	810	22	25	140819
(% of survivors)	(85)	(12)	(2)	(1)	(0)	(0)	(100)

Source: Gallagher and Stewart (1984) figure 6; Gallagher and Stewart (1986) table 6.

for the birth of new firms shows a substantially higher number of small firm births in the final version (295 000 new firms as opposed to 38 000 in the original version). Full details are given in Storey and Johson (1986).

This analysis of the 1971–81 UK job generation studies has revealed that significant differences exist in two versions of the results, derived by the same researchers using the same data base. It is fair to say that Gallagher and Stewart do refer to the discrepancies in their final version:

> The adjustments described above . . . give *slightly* different results to those of our original study (Gallagher and Stewart, 1984), although the overall trend is the same . . . The main difference is that expansions due to small firms are less. This change is because a proportion of the small firms in the initial study undergoing major expansion were found to be in error. Counterbalancing this, the small firm share of job creation due to firm birth is now higher, as the figure for births of *large* firms was also in error. (Gallagher and Stewart, 1986, 893–4, our emphasis).

It thus seems that the Dun and Bradstreet data base overestimated small firm expansions into the largest size category by *over ten times* and underestimated the number of small firm births by *over seven times*. This significant degree of error which appears to be inherent in the data base for 1971 and 1981 suggests that the reliability of the results for this period is questionable.

(ii) The 1982–84 study

Our discussion of the 1971–81 job generation study has illustrated that the problems of the Dun and Bradstreet data base – lack of exact employment data, under–representation of new and small firms, clerical and other errors – mean that considerable caution should be used in interpreting the results derived from this source.

However, the *central issue* which has not so far been addressed in our analysis is that of the *representativeness* of the Dun and Bradstreet data base, and particularly of the very small firms which are included. It is our contention that although the Dun and Bradstreet data base is extremely large by conventional standards, it is a *biased sample* of the population of UK firms, and in particular of small firms. We believe that the small firms which are included in the Dun and Bradstreet data base contain a disproportionate number of dynamic and fast growing firms, and that by scaling up the Dun and Bradstreet sample to represent the small firm population as a whole, Gallagher and Stewart have overestimated the contribution of very small firms to job generation.

The bias is because, it will be recalled, Dun and Bradstreet collect business information in order to provide credit-ratings, and also to provide lists of companies for sales and marketing purposes. For both these areas of business, and particularly for the latter, Dun and Bradstreet need to accurately identify the rapidly growing firms which are likely to be major targets for any marketing or sales strategy. Thus a data base compiled by an organisation such as Dun and Bradstreet *must* of necessity include a disproportionate number of rapidly growing firms. Of course, *some* stagnating or declining firms will be included, but the key point is that *as a proportion of the total population* this group will be much smaller than the expanding group of firms.

The result of this bias is that the scaling up of *all* small firms in the data base by the same proportion to account for the known under–representation of the small firm population, will lead to an exaggeration of the number of expanding firms, and the amount of employment created by these firms. All studies of job generation in the UK and elsewhere have noted the importance of the relatively small number of rapidly expanding firms in creating jobs [see Section 4.4.2 below]. Thus any excessive scaling up of these few firms is likely to grossly inflate the apparent contribution of small firms to job creation.

This latter point is clearly illustrated by reference to the study of job generation in Britain over the 1982–1984 period carried out by Doyle and Gallagher (1986) using the Dun and Bradstreet data base. Table 4.21 shows the transition matrix between size bands of the firms *actually recorded* in the Dun and Bradstreet files. The boxed figures clearly indicate the importance of a small number of rapidly expanding small firms. Of the 128 000 firms in the file which had less than 50 employees in 1982, only 61 (0.05 per cent) employed more than 500 in 1984. It is particularly surprising to note that *eleven* firms grew from less than twenty employees to over 1000 employees within a period of two years. It would seem sensible to carry out an independent check on these extremely fast-growing firms, as was done in the US studies. However, there is no evidence in their paper that Doyle and Gallagher have attempted to corroborate the Dun and Bradstreet data base. This is particularly surprising, given the level of error noted above, in relation to the 1971–81 study.

Doyle and Gallagher note (Figure 4.1) that in 1982 Dun and Bradstreet only captured around 15 per cent of very small firms (less than 20 employees) but had almost complete coverage of firms with over

Table 4.21 Firm size transition matrix between 1982 and 1984 – raw data extracted from the Dun and Bradstreet data base

| | | deaths | 1984 size group | | | | | | Totals (1982) |
			1–19	20–49	50–99	100–499	500–999	1000+	
births			6196	401	80	48	1	3	6729
1–19		6071	73713	2832	283	98	8	11	83016
20–49	1982	2788	1976	25438	1390	175	7	13	31787
50–99	size	1348	174	1306	10056	808	7	15	13714
100–499	group	1355	81	195	898	9942	169	22	12662
500–999		191	9	11	15	283	1216	54	1779
1000+		220	4	4	4	62	182	1529	2005
Total (1984)			82153	30187	12726	11416	1590	1647	151692

Source: Doyle and Gallagher (1986).

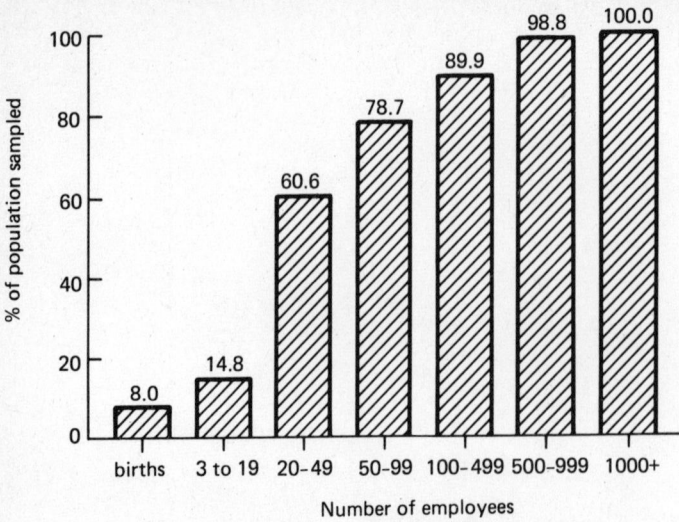

Figure 4.1   Dun and Bradstreet's sampling rates, 1982
Source: Doyle and Gallagher (1986)

500 workers. They adjust the 1982 data by applying the appropriate scaling up factors to the records in each size band. This scaling up factor is applied equally to expanders and non-expanders, with a slightly different correction factor being applied to deaths and births (pp. 4–6). The resulting adjusted transition matrix is shown in Table 4.22. The important point to note from Table 4.22 is that the number of rapidly expanding firms (in the box) has been scaled up by a factor of almost 3 to around 180. The *employment impact* of this scaling up process is considerable. Using the figures for mean employment within each size group presented by Doyle and Gallagher (Table 4.23) it can be calculated that these 180 rapidly growing firms accounted for 274 630 jobs (the method of calculation is described in the Appendix to this chapter). Around two-thirds of these jobs (185 000) have therefore been 'created', simply through the scaling up process. These 'created' jobs represent 20 per cent of all jobs generated through expansions of small (under 100 employees) firms. Expansions of *very small* firms (under 20 employees) are particularly affected by the scaling up procedure. Of the 550 000 jobs created by the expansions of this group, around 100 000 are accounted for by the scaling up of firms expanding into the 1000+ size category.

The arguments presented earlier in this section suggest that such a

Table 4.22 Firm size transition matrix – 'scaled up' version

| | deaths | 1984 size group | | | | | | Total (1982) |
		1–19	20–49	50–99	100–499	500–999	1000+	
births	12 680[1]	67 770	2940	590	520	10	30	84 550
1–19	59 480	491 300	6800	1890	650	50	70	560 250
20–49	4200	3290	42 320	2310	290	10	20	52 440
50–99	1560	220	1670	12 840	1030	10	20	17 360
100–499	1440	90	220	1000	11 020	190	20	13 970
500–999	190	10	10	20	280	1220	50	1780
1000+	210	0	0	0	60	180	1540	2000
Total (1984)	79 770	562 690	53 960	18 640	13 860	1670	1760	647 800

1982 size group (rows 1–19 through 1000+)

[1]This figure refers to the estimated number of firms which are born after 1982 but die before 1984.

Source: Doyle and Gallagher (1986).

Table 4.23   Mean size of firms within size group categories

Size Band	High	Low
3–19	11.05	5.71
20–49	34.55	29.74
50–99	74.56	68.41
100–499	300.49	197.36
500–999	750.07	688.97
1000+	2100.00	2100.00

Note: Firms are assumed to *expand* from the 'high mean' of their 1982 size category to the 'low mean' of their 1984 size category.
Firms are assumed to *contract* from the 'low mean' of their 1982 size category to the 'high mean' of their 1984 size category. e.g. a firm moving from the 20–49 category to the 100–499 category is assumed to have increased its size from 34.55 to 197.36.

Source: Doyle and Gallagher (1986).

major under–representation of rapidly growing small firms in the Dun and Bradstreet data base is unlikely. Moreover, Figure 4.1 shows clearly that, in 1982, the Dun and Bradstreet files included *all* firms in the economy with over 1000 employees. This group presumably includes those firms which had expanded into this category over the previous two years. By the same token, we would expect the 1984 Dun and Bradstreet file to have complete coverage of very large firms (presumably this could be verified by Doyle and Gallagher), but the figures shown in Tables 4.21 and 4.22 imply that Dun and Bradstreet coverage of firms in the 1000+ category in 1984 is only around 93 per cent (1644 firms in the original data base; 1760 in the scaled-up version).[1] Such a discrepancy would be trivial were it not for the relative importance of rapidly expanding firms in job generation. In our view it is equally appropriate to argue that Dun and Bradstreet has complete coverage of these exceptional firms. We may therefore revise Doyle and Gallagher's figures to arrive at the 'revised' figures shown in Table 4.24.[2] These show that it is only the inclusion of births which ensures that net employment change within small firms is positive over the 1982–84 period. The revised figures are also much closer to the results which have been reported in studies of employment change in the UK and elsewhere.

Doyle and Gallagher argue (pp. 20–1) that the deficient coverage of small firms in the Dun and Bradstreet data base is unimportant, because the performance of the small firm sector in terms of net job generation can be inferred from the known changes which have taken place in

Table 4.24 Job creation by firm size 1982–1984: original and revised figures (millions)

1982 size Group	1982 Employment	Births	Expansions Original	Expansions Revised	Contrac- tions	Deaths	1984 Employment Original	1984 Employment Revised	Net Change Original	Net Change Revised
1–19	3.36	0.39	0.55	0.16	−0.00	−0.34	3.96	3.57	0.60	0.21
20–49	1.57	0.09	0.18	0.12	−0.06	−0.12	1.66	1.60	0.09	0.00
50–99	1.20	0.04	0.17	0.16	−0.11	−0.11	1.19	1.18	−0.00	−0.02
100–499	2.84	0.10	0.12	3.10	−0.22	−0.29	2.55	2.53	−0.29	−0.30
500–999	1.25	0.01	0.07	0.07	−0.13	−0.13	1.07	1.07	−0.18	−0.18
1000+	4.55	0.07	0.27	0.27*	−0.38	−0.44	4.07	4.07	−0.48	−0.48
Total	14.77	0.69	1.36	0.88	−0.91	−1.43	14.49	14.02	−0.28	−0.75

* This is a rate which has been assumed by Doyle and Gallagher – no attempt has been made to revise this figure. For method of calculation of revised figures, see Appendix to this chapter.

Source: Doyle and Gallagher (1986).

overall private sector employment and the performance of the medium and large firms in the data base. Thus firms with more than 20 employees in the Dun and Bradstreet data base lost 1.18 million jobs, at a time when private sector employment fell by only 80 000 (Richardson, 1985). Hence small firms *must* have created around one million jobs through new births and expansions.

This argument is fallacious for several reasons. Firstly the ranged nature of the employment data in the Dun and Bradstreet data base means that any calculation of employment change must be an *approximation*. This applies particularly to the largest size bracket (1000 +) where firm size may vary from 1000 employees to perhaps over 100 000, and so considerable changes in employment may take place within this group, which are not reflected in changes of size category. Secondly, lags in the reporting of data to Dun and Bradstreet mean that many records may be out of date by as much as a year. This applies particularly to small firms, but also affects medium sized firms for whom information is not readily available for annual accounts and reports. Thus, the employment recorded in a significant proportion of Dun and Bradstreet records may apply to 1981 and 1983 rather than 1982 and 1984. Employment loss in the private sector between 1981 and 1983 was 481 000. Finally, although our critique has concentrated upon the weaknesses in the small firm data, there is reason to suspect the accuracy of other figures presented by Doyle and Gallagher. In particular, the figures for jobs lost through deaths imply that the closure rate for large firms (1000 +) is the same as that for the 0–20 size category, at around 10 per cent. This is certainly in contradiction to *a priori* reasoning and is inconsistent with results obtained in other job generation studies.[3] Thus we must regard the figures for employment change derived from the Dun and Bradstreet data base as a rough estimate rather than as an exact measure.

To summarise, the most important criticism which can be made of the UK job generation studies using the Dun and Bradstreet data base is that the methodology used to analyse the data has not taken into account the inherent bias of this data base towards fast growing small firms.

4.4.2 The disproportionate contribution of a few firms to job generation

The job generation studies reported in this chapter, and summarised in Table 4.18 are unanimous in concluding that small firms are net creators of jobs. However, this should *not* be taken to imply that *all* small firms create jobs at a uniform rate. The 'transition matrices' presented in the previous section, derived from the 1971–1981 and 1982–1984 Dun and Bradstreet studies of the UK, illustrate quite clearly that only a very small proportion of the small firm population in any one year will grow significantly in terms of employment. For instance, Table 4.22 shows that, of the 560 250 firms estimated to have had less than 20 employees in 1982, 59 480 (10.6 per cent) had ceased trading by 1984, 491 300 (87.7 per cent) still had less than 20 employees in 1984. Hence, less than two per cent of the 1982 population of small firms expanded their employment to such an extent that they employed more than twenty within two years. These 9460 firms, however, created around 550 000 jobs, according to the calculations of Doyle and Gallagher. Of particular importance are the 120 firms which had grown to more than 500 employees by 1984. It can be calculated that these firms, representing 0.12 per cent of the 1982 population of very small firms, created over 275 000 jobs. This represents half of the 550 000 net new jobs which were created by expansions of very small firms, according to the calculations of Doyle and Gallagher. Notwithstanding the methodological problems discussed in Section 4.4.1 above, these figures clearly illustrate that a very small proportion of small firms are responsible for a significant percentage of new jobs created by small firms.

It may be suggested that the short time period covered by the 1982–84 period will bias these results. However, an examination of the 1971–1981 period by Gallagher and Stewart (1986) reveals that, even over a ten-year period, relatively few small firms expand their employment to a significant extent. Table 4.20 shows that, even on the basis of the most 'optimistic' calculations, only 2.3 per cent of firms which had less than 20 employees in 1971 (and survived to 1981) employed more than 100 workers by 1981. The vast majority of survivors remained in the 'very small' category. According to the revised figures, *less than one per cent* of surviving very small firms had grown to become 'large' over a ten year period.

A similar pattern is revealed by the Macey (1982) study of employment change in manufacturing industry between 1972 and 1975. For example, only 5 out of the 10 545 plants which had 11–20 employees in 1972 employed more than 200 in 1975. Indeed, all available studies of job generation by firm size for which the appropriate figures are available show a strikingly similar pattern. Table 4.25 illustrates this point for the 1982–84 UK studies, the two French studies and the O'Farrell study of employment change in the Republic of Ireland.

This finding has important implications for public policy towards the

Table 4.25   Jobs created in expansions of small firms*

	Employment size group at end year						Total employment
	0	*1–19*	*20–49*	*50–99*	*100–499*	*500 +*	
UK 1982–84							
% of Firms	10.6	87.7	1.2	0.3	0.1	0.02	560 250
% of Jobs in							
Expansions	—	0.0	23.1	19.7	22.0	28.3	550 000
France 1981–83							
% of Firms	30.5	64.7	4.5	0.2	0.09	0.005	22 200
% of Jobs in							
Expansions	—	0.0	57.0	16.1	23.5	3.2	15 805
Poition-Charentes 1972–84							
% of Firms	61.9	33.3	4.2	0.5	0.06	0.06	1682
% of Jobs in							
Expansions	—	0.0	47.8	14.5	6.6	31.1	2483
Ireland 1973–80							
% of Firms	25.9	65.5	6.2	1.7	0.7	0.0	1980
% of Jobs in							
Expansions	—	na	na	na	na	na	34 587

*'Small firms' defined as less than 20 employees, apart from Ireland – less than 25 employees.
Source: Storey and Johnson (1987a)

small firm sector, which will be analysed in detail in Chapter 7, where data from North East England will be used to further reinforce the point that *relatively few firms* are responsible for the majority of jobs which are created in the small firm sector.

4.4.3   The impact of new firms on employment generation

It must be recognised that the expansion of existing firms is only one way in which jobs can be created. The formation of new firms will also result in new jobs being created. It must be recognised however that the formation of a new firm may result directly or indirectly in the closure of another firm, through the competitive process. This may be beneficial in terms of economic activity, but in terms of overall job creation, the result may be negligible, or even negative if the new firm is more efficient in the utilisation of labour than the displaced firm. Secondly, it should be noted that many new firms fail within a relatively short period of time. Ganguly (1985) shows that around 20 per cent of firms which register for Value Added Tax (VAT) in year *t* had deregistered by the end of year

$t + 1$, 30 per cent by year $t + 2$ and nearly 40 per cent by year $t + 3$. Hence the contribution of a substantial proportion of new firms to job creation is essentially transient.

An indication of the contribution of new firms to employment change can be given by calculating the proportion of end year employment which is in firms which were started since the base year. For instance, Doyle and Gallagher (1986) estimate that 690 000 jobs in 1984 were in firms which had not existed in 1982. Total 1984 employment is calculated to be 14.49 million. Therefore, employment in new firms constitutes 4.8 per cent of 1984 employment. It should be noted, however, that an estimated 1.43 million jobs were lost in the closure of firms over the same period of time. A similar calculation can be performed on the figures produced by Gallagher and Stewart (1986), which suggest that 3.56 million (23 per cent) of the 15.41 million jobs in existence in 1981 were in firms born since 1971. However 5.05 million jobs were lost over the same period in closures.

The figures produced by the UK Dun and Bradstreet studies, which include the service sector, contrast sharply with both the Macey (1982) study of the UK manufacturing sector and the various local or regional studies which have been carried out, most of which cover only manufacturing. The relevant UK studies for which the appropriate data is available are summarised in Table 4.26. In order to facilitate comparisons, employment in new firms as a percentage of final year employment is standardised to a ten-year figure, using a crude single ratio. The figures show that, for the manufacturing sector, between 1 and 7 per cent of final year employment is likely to be in firms started during the past ten years, a significant but not overwhelming contribution. The Hubbard and Nutter (1982) study of the Merseyside service sector suggests a slightly higher contribution of new firms to employment. As discussed above, the 1971–1981 and 1982–1984 UK Dun and Bradstreet studies suggest that almost one-quarter of final year employment will be in new firms, over a ten-year period.

It seems therefore that there are considerable differences in the contribution of new firms to employment between the manufacturing and service sectors, with the new firm contribution to manufacturing employment being relatively modest over a ten-year period. In the service sector, it appears that there is a higher level of turnover in terms of both numbers of firms and employment. The problem remains, however, that without knowledge of the extent to which new firm employment (or even existing firm expansion) is displacing employment which is consequently lost in closure of firms, it is difficult to precisely identify the contribution of new firms to overall job creation.

Table 4.26   National comparison of new firm formation in the UK

	Author	Time period	% Actual* employment	% Standardised† employment
UK Studies				
UK	Doyle & Gallagher	1982–84	4.8	23.8
UK	Gallagher & Stewart	1971–81	23.1	23.1
UK	Macey	1972–75	0.4	1.3
Regional Studies				
Central Clydeside	Firn	1958–68	1.9	1.9
Birmingham	Firn & Swales	1963–72	1.1	1.2
East Midlands	Fothergill & Gudgin	1968–75	4.2	5.9
Cleveland	Storey	1965–78	2.8	2.2
Durham	Storey	1965–78	4.4	3.4
Tyne & Wear	Storey	1965–78	3.6	2.8
Scotland	Cross	1968–77	2.2	2.6
Manchester	Lloyd & Mason	1966–75	3.8	4.2
Merseyside	Lloyd & Dicken	1966–75	3.7	4.1
South Hampshire	Mason	1971–79	3.5	4.4
Coventry	Healey & Clark	1974–82	1.9	2.3
Cambridgeshire	Gould & Keeble	1971–81	5.2	5.2
Norfolk	Gould & Keeble	1971–81	3.5	3.5
Suffolk	Gould & Keeble	1971–81	3.1	3.1
Durham	Storey	1976–81	3.4	6.8
Cleveland	Storey	1976–81	2.4	4.8
Tyne & Wear	Storey	1976–81	2.2	4.4
Merseyside	Hubbard & Nutter	1971–75	3.3	8.3

Notes:

$$* \% \text{ Actual Employment} = \frac{\text{Total Employment in New Firms in final year}}{\text{Total Employment in base year}}$$

† Standardised Employment relates to a ten year period; a single ratio was used.

4.4.4   The underlying reasons for small firm job creation

The job generation studies which have been reviewed in this book are essentially *descriptive* in nature. The available data are mechanically analysed and presented in tabular form, with little attempt to *explain* the processes which underlie the observed trends. For instance, the fact that small firms are contributing disproportionately to job generation does not necessarily imply that small firms are performing particularly well. It may simply be a reflection of the poor performance of large firms. Small firm job creation and new firm formation may be the result of restructuring within the economy, with tasks which were previously performed in large firms being sub-contracted to smaller firms.

Furthermore a 'job' is not a homogenous entity; jobs vary considerably in terms of the number of hours worked, occupation, skill levels, location, level of wages and other benefits. Job generation studies, however, appear to make little distinction between the different types of jobs which are created. This issue is important, because the overall impact of small firm job creation upon the labour market depends not only upon the number of jobs created, but also upon the types of jobs created. For instance, if a significant proportion of the new jobs are part-time, they are unlikely to be filled by registered unemployed people. Similarly the skills required in the new jobs may not 'match' those offered by the unemployed. Thus small firm job creation may have a differential impact upon the various groups within the labour market. Chapters 5 and 6 explore all these issues in more detail.

4.5 CONCLUSION

This chapter has reviewed the literature regarding job generation and firm size in the United Kingdom, Europe and New Zealand. Almost without exception the studies which have been conducted suggest that *small firms are net creators of jobs, whereas large firms tend to be net losers of jobs.* However, it has been argued that the methodologies used in some studies, particularly the 'scaling up' of samples of small firms, may lead to an overestimate of the role of small firms in the creation of new jobs. Moreover, a detailed analysis of the studies reveals that it is a *relatively small number* of new and expanding small firms which create a substantial proportion of new jobs. Hence it is unwise to conclude that *all* small firms are actual or potential creators of jobs. It has also been suggested that new firms make only a minor contribution to manufacturing employment over a relatively long period of time. The picture for the service sector is less clear, but it appears that a more rapid turnover of firms and employment takes place in this sector, substantially increasing the relative contribution of new firms to employment. Finally, it has been argued that the available studies are essentially *descriptive* in nature with little attempt at explaining the observed trends, and that there is little or no evidence regarding the *type* of jobs created by different sizes of firms. It is to these issues which we now turn our attention.

APPENDIX TO CHAPTER 4

Calculation of revised figures for employment created by expansions of firms with less than 100 employees

Doyle and Gallagher calculate the number of jobs created in expansions by multiplying the number of firms expanding into a particular size category by the *difference* between mean employment in the 1984 size category and mean employment in the 1982 size category (see Table 4.23). For instance, according to Table 4.22, 290 firms moved from the 20–49 category in 1982 to the 100–499 group in 1984. Each firm created an average of 162.81 jobs (197.36 minus 34.55); thus a total of 47 215 jobs were created in these firms (290 × 162.81).

Revised figures for expansions were calculated using the figures for employment means given in Table 4.23 together with a revised transition matrix (Table A1). This matrix is constructed on the basis that the number of expanding firms is scaled up according to the sampling rate for their *end year* (1984) size category rather than their 1982 size category. For example, Figure 4.1 suggests that 89.9 per cent of all firms with 100–499 employees are represented in the data base. It can thus be estimated that 195 firms (i.e. 100/89 × 175) expanded from 20–49 to 100–499 employees, creating 31 748 jobs, rather than the 47 215 jobs estimated by Doyle and Gallagher. This process is repeated for all size categories, and the results are summarised in Table 4.24

Table A1   Firm size transition matrix 1982–84: Revised version

		1984 size group					
		1–19	*20–49*	*50–99*	*100–499*	*500–599*	*1000+*
1–19		491 300	4 673	360	109	8	11
20–49	1982	3 290	42 320	1 766	195	7	13
50–99	size	220	1 670	12 840	1 000	7	15
100–499	group	90	220	1 000	11 020	171	22
500–999		10	10	20	280	1 220	54
1000+		0	0	0	60	180	1 540

Source: Calculated from Doyle and Gallagher (1986).

5 Small Firms and the Process of Economic Development: Explanations and Illustrations from Britain, Italy and the United States

5.1 INTRODUCTION

In Chapter 2 it was shown that the structure of employment units was changing in many OECD countries, and it appeared to be broadly true that since the 1970s a higher proportion of total employment was found in smaller firms. These 'comparative static' pictures were, however, unable to illuminate the dynamic changes taking place at the level of the individual enterprise and so in Chapters 3 and 4 the growth and decline of employment within individual units over a period of time was traced. Broadly Chapter 3 showed that in the United States, and to a lesser extent Canada, small firms were creating jobs faster than large firms but that the techniques for assessment had led some commentators to over estimate that contribution. Chapter 4 showed that outside North America such changes were less clear-cut but it appeared to be the case that the growth of the small firm sector had exceeded that of the large firm sector. Whilst such statistical analysis, with all its uncertainties, does help in quantifying the magnitude of such developments it does not provide an *explanation* of these developments.

It is the purpose of this chapter to begin to provide such an insight into the processes and factors which underpin this shift towards the relative growth of smaller enterprises. Three indicators are frequently used to highlight this shift.

- an increase in the share of small firms in total output and total employment.
- an increase in the rate of new business formation.
- an increase in the stock of businesses.

121

In this chapter it will be argued that there is no single explanation of these changes. Instead there is a complex collection of factors, the relative importance of which varies from one location or one country to another. It is for this reason that we illustrate our description of these developments by reference to three particular locations in which small firms have become relatively more important, but for very different reasons. These are called the three 'models'.

– the Birmingham (UK) model
– the Boston (USA) model
– The Bologna (Italy) model

Whilst description is concentrated upon these three 'models' the purpose is both to highlight common themes within each of these areas and to draw policy relevant conclusions from the analysis.

At this stage a number of *caveats* need to be clearly stated. Firstly although the 'models' apply to particular locations they are to be regarded as illustrative of developments not simply at the specified location but at similar locations. For example the Birmingham (UK) model is designed to illustrate developments in much of the United Kingdom which has had a traditional dependence upon manufacturing industry. Secondly, although the 'model' refers to a single country, its characteristics can be found in a modified form elsewhere. For example the characteristics of the Birmingham model have strong parallels in the Genoa – Turin – Milan area of Italy, in southern Belgium and north west France and in the Cleveland – Detroit area of the United States. Equally there are parallels between the developments described in the Boston (USA) model and those observed in Munich in Germany and in the Cambridge – Bristol corridor of England. Thirdly the word 'model' is used in the sense of being a simplified description of a complex system of change. It is not suggested that a full description of the economy of Bologna, Boston or Birmingham can be provided within these few pages. Instead our focus is upon those factors which affect the size structure of employment units within those localities. Fourthly it is not even suggested that these 'models' encapsulate the full diversity of factors which influence the relative growth of small firms in developed countries. For example in several countries, but most notably in Western Germany, the growth of policies to assist small firms has been closely connected with the increasing influence of middle-class groupings. We do not explicitly include a social class factor in our 'models'.

The models presented here are designed to illustrate general themes and developments, the most important of which is that there is no single explanation for the increasing relative importance of small firms. The nature of the explanation varies according to the industrial and social structure of the area. The 'models' are designed as an antidote to the undue emphasis upon the currently favoured mono-causal explanations.

5.2 THE MONO-CAUSAL EXPLANATIONS

This section examines six 'explanations' of why small firms have become relatively more important as a source of new employment and source of wealth creation over the last ten to fifteen years. These are:

(a) Recession in the world economy leading to a fall in traded goods. Since large firms are more likely to export directly than small firms, then large firms will be disproportionately affected.

(b) The spectacular growth of some newly industrialised countries (NICs), particularly in South East Asia, has meant that many industrialised areas in the developed countries have experienced severe competition in sectors where output was formerly produced in large firms – notably shipbuilding, textiles, electrical goods.

(c) The growth of small firms is often associated with technical changes, particularly the growth of computers, micro processors etc., the effect of which is to reduce the plant level scale economies of the firm.

(d) Structural shifts in the demand for products meant that in most developed economies there has been an increase in the share, if not an absolute gain, in employment, of services at the expense of manufacturing. Plant level scale economies are thought to be less apparent in the service sector and so such sectoral shifts will lead to an increase in the importance of small firms.

(e) It is also argued that the rise in world energy prices in the 1970s meant that since large firms were disproportionately larger users of energy than small firms that this penalised the former and inhibited their rate of growth.

(f) Finally the performance of individuals at work can be of considerable importance. Many individuals increasingly prefer to work in smaller, more personalised units where their own contribution to the enterprise is clearly identified.

Whilst illustrations of each of these 'explanations' may be provided it is equally possible either to cite counter-examples or to demonstrate their irrelevance in particular contexts. For example, as Contini (1984) argues, it is not surprising after more than twenty years of semi-continuous expansion until the early 1970s that a reduction in manufacturing employment should take place. Intuitively it is less obvious why according to explanation (a) recession should necessarily result in an increased share of output and employment in small firms. Indeed it might be suggested that small firms, being marginal producers with higher costs than large firms, would be eliminated first from the market. In principle, therefore, recession might be thought to favour the large rather than the small firm.

Although (b) generally figures prominently amongst explanations for changes in the size structure of enterprises we are unaware of any careful analysis which has attempted to link the loss of overseas or home markets by large firms to changes in overall employment size structure. The argument therefore remains plausible but untested. There are, however, cases, one of which is the Bologna model, where small firms have become *increasingly* important in sectors where the firms themselves were major exporters.

Of all the explanations, the effects of technical change in reducing the comparative advantage of large firms seems to be of widest applicability since its effects cover all sectors of the economy. Nevertheless in the three 'models' which we describe these forms of technical change play a relatively minor direct role in employment creation/loss. Perhaps this reflects the familiar difficulties in identifying and quantifying the contribution of technical change to economic development.

There appears to be only some validity in the view that changes in the size structure of enterprises in economies as a whole over the last fifteen years, merely reflects a structural shift from manufacturing into services. OECD (1985) show, using a shift-share analysis, that at one extreme only 23 per cent of the shift in employment size structure in Austria between 1973 and 1983 could be attributed to structural shift to services. In Belgium, France, and the Netherlands, the figure was under 50 per cent and only in Holland and Japan has this figure exceeded 50 per cent. Even so, there is a causation problem of whether the growth of small firms is due to the expansion of the service sector, or vice versa.

The energy prices explanation (e) has also been questioned by Shutt and Whittington (1984). They argue that although large firms may be larger absolute users of energy, they are less energy-intensive in their productive processes. Hence large firms are likely to have benefited rather than lost from such developments.

Finally explanation (f), which emphasises the benefits of self-employment and small scale units, seems intuitively the least plausible of all. It is difficult to envisage reasons why, out of choice, individuals should wish to take on the additional risks either of working for themselves or in a small firm, unless there are either some compensating advantages in the form of additional income or unless there is no alternative. In either situation the individual is merely responding to economic conditions imposed upon him/her rather than independently changing attitudes. Furthermore unless it is merely a question of 'fashion' it is difficult to see why, if such preferences existed, that the post-war years should have resulted in a declining importance of small firms.

5.3 THE BIRMINGHAM (UK), BOSTON (USA) AND BOLOGNA (ITALY) MODELS

It should now be apparent that whilst each of the mono-causal explanations may have some validity, no single explanation offers a fully satisfactory explanation of this widespread development. Our strategy for the remainder of the chapter is to take three localities in which small firms have become relatively more important, but for reasons which are perceived to be very different. In the Birmingham (UK) model the relative increase in importance of small firms is regarded as undesirable since it stems from a lack of competitiveness of the indigenous economy – particularly of large firms. On the other hand both the Boston (USA) and Bologna (Italy) models stem from an increased competitiveness of the local, small firm sector.

5.4 THE BIRMINGHAM (UK) MODEL: SMALL FIRM GROWTH AS A SYMPTOM OF INDUSTRIAL DECLINE

So far this decade we have created 600 000 self-employed people . . . 140 000 more businesses have started than have closed . . . and we are on our way back to the entrepreneurial society that made us great. (Lord Young, UK Secretary of Statement of Employment, 16 July 1985, *Hansard*, Vol. 466, p. 613).

In less than twenty years the United Kingdom has been transformed from an advanced industrial economy with full employment into a deindustrialised economy with mass, long-term unemployment. Industrial decline has not been matched by an equivalent increase in economic

activity and jobs in other sectors. In the labour market, this transformation has involved a dramatic shift away from fixed, waged employment
(notably in manufacturing industry) towards self-employment,
underemployment and unemployment.

An extreme example of these trends is found in the manufacturing
heartland of United Kingdom – the West Midlands – of which
Birmingham is the main city. Since 1979, unemployment in the West
Midlands County has increased from 5.5 per cent of the workforce (just
below the national average) to 16.5 percent in November 1985 (as
compared to a UK rate of 13.5 per cent). Between 1979 and 1984, the
West Midlands region registered a net decline of 250 000 manufacturing
jobs, a fall of almost 25 per cent in the space of five years. Much of this
decline has been in the Metal Goods, Engineering and Vehicles sector
which has seen its employment in the West Midlands fall from over
600 000 in June 1979 to 436 000 in March 1984. In Birmingham itself, it
has been estimated that manufacturing employment fell by 57 per cent
between 1971 and 1984, as compared with a national decline of 31 per
cent. The national increase of 12 per cent in service sector employment
over the same period has not been repeated in Birmingham, where
service employment declined by 8 per cent (Spencer *et al.*, 1986).

We do not intend here to enter the various debates about the causes of
the UK's industrial decline[1] or that of the relative decline of Birmingham
within the UK context.[2] It is clear that this is the result of a complex
interaction of factors, some specific to the UK economy (decolonisa-
tion, falling industrial competitiveness, growing import penetration)
and some factors common to manufacturing industry as a whole
(introduction of labour-saving technologies, growing internationalisa-
tion of production). It is also clear that these longer-term developments
have not been assisted since 1979 by a combination of government
policies and 'external' events which have affected manufacturing
industry through high interest rates, an overvalued pound, reduced
public expenditure and the export of capital. In general terms, there has
been a decline in UK manufacturing industry over and above that
caused by the world recession, and the perceived shifts in the labour
market, based upon the development of new sectors (services in
particular). Since the West Midlands is more dependent upon manufacturing employment than any other UK region the consequences of
manufacturing decline are clearly visible. Nevertheless it is argued that
the absolute growth of self employment and the relative growth in small
firms in areas such as Birmingham and in the UK as a whole is a
reflection of industrial weakness rather than of renewed strength.

The growth of the UK small firm sector: the evidence

Changes in the size structure of manufacturing industry in Britain can be analysed using the Annual Census of Production conducted by the UK Business Statistics Office. The changes which have taken place since 1968 are summarised in Figures 5.1 (a) and 5.1 (b). In 1968 firms with less than 100 employees accounted for 13.5 per cent of manufacturing employment and 11.5 per cent of net manufacturing output. By 1982 (the latest year for which comprehensive figures are available) these percentages had increased to 21.1 and 17.7 respectively. However an examination of Figure 5.1 (b) shows that the *absolute* level of employment in small manufacturing firms has remained essentially unchanged since 1971, and that the steady increase in the relative size of the small firm sector since 1973 reflects (in statistical terms at least) the massive decline in the absolute level of employment in large firms. It is also worth noting that, despite the stability of total small firm employment, the *number* of small manufacturing firms (i.e. with less than 100 employees) has increased from 55 234 in 1968 (90 per cent of all enterprises) to 80 782 in 1982 (95 per cent of all enterprises). This, of course, has meant a fall in the average size of the small manufacturing firm from nearly 18 employees in 1968 to just over 13 in 1982.

Although it is very difficult as we noted in Chapters 2 and 3 to draw unambiguous inferences from static data, it would appear that the new manufacturing firms are substantially smaller than existing firms and/or that existing small firms have been contracting in terms of employment.

The dynamics underlying the trends for new and small firms in sectors of the UK economy can be discerned to some extent from the data in Table 5.1 on registrations and deregistrations for Value Added Tax, reproduced from Ganguly (1985). The data reveals that there has been a steady increase in the stock of businesses registered for VAT in all years since 1974, with the exception of 1978.

Over the period 1974–82 there has been a slight fall in business birth rates but it has coincided with a more than proportionate fall in business deaths or deregistrations. More recently over the period 1980–1983 there has been a net increase of 108 000 in the number of firms registered for VAT, with gains being recorded in all sectors of the economy apart from the retail sector. It is particularly interesting to note a significant increase in the number of firms in the production sector, although the largest increase in percentage terms occurred in the sector labelled 'all others'.

The VAT statistics have been seen as an encouraging sign by UK

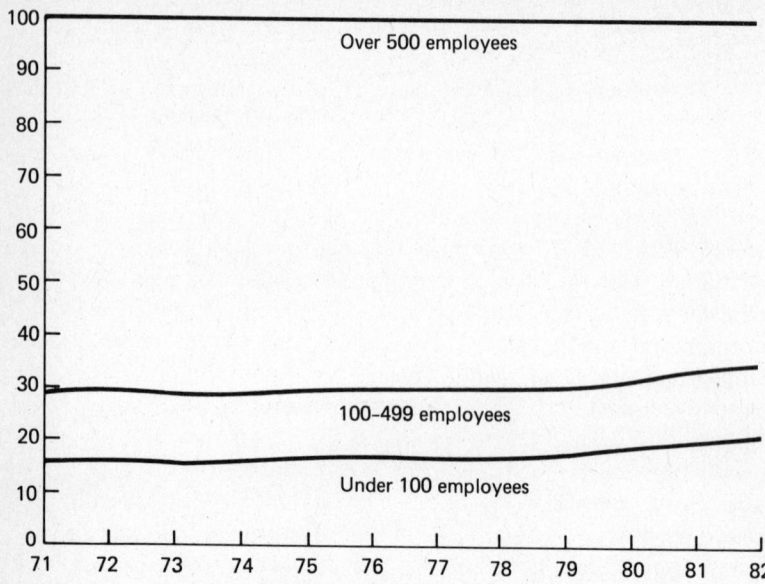

Figure 5.1 (a)   Size distribution of manufacturing employment, UK, 1971–1982 (per cent)

Source: Annual Census of Production.

Table 5.1   UK business registrations and deregistrations for VAT

	Stock of businesses	New Registrations No.	%	Deregistrations No.	%
1974	1 306 034	147 878	11.3	103 337	7.9
1975	1 363 921	161 224	11.8	138 504	10.1
1976	1 394 264	168 847	12.1	145 863	10.5
1977	1 405 495	157 094	11.2	158 101	11.2
1978	1 396 787	149 393	10.7	155 462	11.1
1979	1 412 617	171 292	12.1	124 677	8.8
1980	1 445 036	157 096	10.9	139 969	9.7
1981	1 454 296	149 229	10.3	112 332	7.7
1982	1 480 679	138 715	9.4	104 813	7.1

Source: Ganguly (1985)

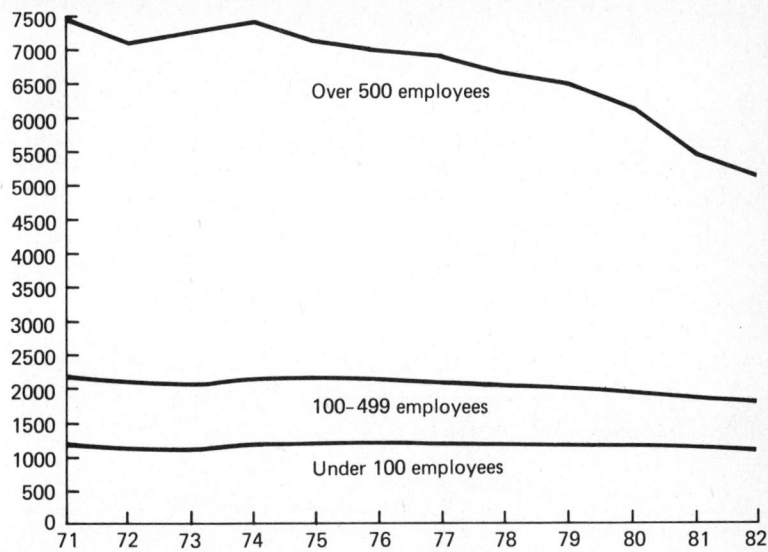

Figure 5.1 (b)   Size distribution of manufacturing employment, UK, 1971–
1982 (thousands)

Source: Annual Census of Production.

Government Ministers, although it has to be remembered that there is a very high mortality rate, particularly amongst young firms: almost half of all new firms fail within four years of starting in business (Ganguly 1985). Research has also shown that most of the firms which do survive fail to grow in terms of employment (Storey, 1985a). Employment growth is, in fact concentrated in very few small, young firms, and it is not clear that the recent increase in the number of firms in existence will lead to an increase in the number of firms with growth potential. We shall return to this argument in due course.

The final piece of evidence which is encouraging to those who believe that small firms embody the desirable characteristics of competitiveness, flexibility and a capacity to create new jobs, is provided by the Department of Employment in its analysis of the numbers of self-employed people in the economy. These figures should be treated with some caution due to the small base upon which estimates are made, and other data problems such as the fact that a proportion of the self-employed population represents workers who may also hold jobs in the formal labour market. None the less it is clear that there has been a dramatic increase in the number of self-employed people in the UK both in absolute terms, and as a percentage of the working population (see Table 5.2). In 1979 the number of self-employed stood at 1.9 million (7.2 per cent of the workforce). By March 1985, this figure had increased to 2.6 million (9.5 per cent of the workforce). This increase occurred in all sectors of the economy excepting agriculture. In the production industries (Groups 1–4, 1980 SIC) the number of waged employees declined from 7.8 million in 1979 to 6.0 million in 1984, whereas self-employment increased from 140 000 to 184 000 over the same time period.

Table 5.2   Trends in self-employment since 1965

Figures for United Kingdom, unadjusted for seasonal variations				
	Working Population (000)	*Self employed (000)*	*% of working Population*	*Un-employed (000)*	*% of working Population*
(June each year)					
1965	25 503	1696	6.7	299	1.2
1966	25 636	1681	6.6	281	1.1
1967	25 495	1762	6.9	503	2.0
1968	25 383	1786	7.0	542	2.1
1969	25 375	1853	7.3	518	2.0
1970	25 308	1902	7.5	555	2.2
1971	25 207	2021	8.0	696	2.8
1972	25 267	1997	7.9	778	3.1
1973	25 614	2032	7.9	557	2.2
1974	25 658	1996	7.8	528	2.1
1975	25 878	1994	7.7	838	3.2
1976	26 093	1949	7.5	1 265	4.8
1977	26 209	1904	7.3	1 359	5.2
1978	26 342	1904	7.2	1 343	5.1
1979	26 610	1903	7.2	1 235	4.6
1980	26 819	2011	7.5	1 513	5.6
1981	26 718	2118	7.9	2 395	9.0
1982	26 757	2190	8.2	2 770	10.4
1983	26 575	2221	8.4	2 984	11.2
1984	27 012	2494	9.2	3 030	11.2
1985 (March)	27 332	2588	9.5	3 268	12.0

Source: *Department of Employment Gazette*

It must be emphasised, however, that the bulk of the self-employed are in the Construction, Distribution, Hotel, Catering, Repairs and Other Services sectors, areas which are generally not considered to be dynamic motors of national economic growth. A sub-sector of the self-employed population which has experienced one of the most dramatic rates of growth in recent years has been females working in the 'other services' sector, the numbers of which have more than doubled from 77 000 in 1979 to 158 000 in 1984.

It is clear then that the figures which tend to be seen as signs that the UK economy is becoming more dynamic and competitive, with small firms providing the seed-bed for major employment growth in the future, are less impressive than they initially appear.[3] Of far greater importance, however, is the need for clarification of the processes which have given rise to the observed trends. We now demonstrate that the developments which are occurring in the UK economy, most notably in the West Midlands area, are a reflection of the ashes rather than the phoenix.

(i) *Mass redundancies*

Since the late 1970s, mass redundancies have become commonplace in the UK (over 2.5 million between 1977 and 1981), while the official level of unemployment has risen dramatically from 1.2 million in 1979 (4.6 per cent of the workforce) to its 1986 level of over 3.3 million (13.7 per cent). Large corporations have played a central role in generating the redundancies in manufacturing: Between 1977 and 1981, 20 corporations alone were responsible for 22.8 per cent (264 200) of all officially recorded manufacturing redundancies. (Townsend and Peck, 1985) This extensive shedding of labour by the large corporations is in part the effect of reducing productive capacity in the UK (often accompanied by the transfer of production overseas), and in part the combined effect of a number of strategies aimed at reducing unit labour costs and raising productivity. Reducing labour demand and reorganising the technical basis for production have involved complex social and occupational changes within production, and it is these changes which have led to new forms of entrepreneurship.

It is, of course, true that the UK has experienced increases in unemployment in the past, but the significant features of the present recession for the purposes of our argument are –

(i)   unemployment is not only affecting the unskilled and semi-skilled workers who, as a group, have tended to suffer during periodic economic downturns, but is also hitting a significant number of skilled workers and middle managers.

(ii) the present rise in unemployment is generally perceived by both manufacturing industry and by workers as being a long-term, or even permanent, feature of the labour market, with little prospect of a significant increase in manufacturing employment, even in the event of a sustained national economic recovery.

These two features of the present recession combine to massively increase the pool of potential 'entrepreneurs', and to increase the *relative* attractiveness of self-employment or new business formation as opposed to formal employment.[4] It should be noted that this increase in the relative attractiveness of self-employment occurs mainly because of a reduction in the expected future returns from formal employment (due to the low probability of re-employment for many workers), rather than an increase in the attractiveness of self-employment *per se*.[5] In fact the relationship between labour shedding and new firm formation is complex. Binks and Jennings (1986) for example show that a number of potentially-conflicting interactions exist between births and deaths of companies. The death of companies, can, for instance, lead to an increase in the formation of new companies partly because workers are 'forced' into entrepreneurship, but also because the realisation of the capital assets of deceased firms provides an attractive source of start up capital for many new firms. In their own survey work in Nottingham, Binks and Jennings found that 70 per cent of new businesses relied to a significant extent upon cheap second-hand plant and machinery to start up in business.

The birth of companies, however, can also lead to the death of existing companies, most especially where markets are finite and localised. Frequently in sectors which are easy to enter and hence attractive to the unemployed such as car repairs, jobbing engineering, retail shops etc., increases in business formation rates may mean the displacement of existing businesses.

Finally deaths of companies can lead to additional corporate deaths since the sale of the stocks of goods of deceased firms at below market price can further lower prices and so undermine businesses which might otherwise have continued to trade. The supply side of the entrepreneurship equation has also been boosted in recent years by the modest redundancy payments received by some displaced workers, by Government schemes such as the Enterprise Allowance Scheme, and generally by a torrent of propaganda from Government and other quarters on the social desirability of being an entrepreneur.

The current role of large firms in spawning the growth of new businesses and of increasing the stock of businesses in the economy can most easily be illustrated with reference to Figure 5.2. It shows the

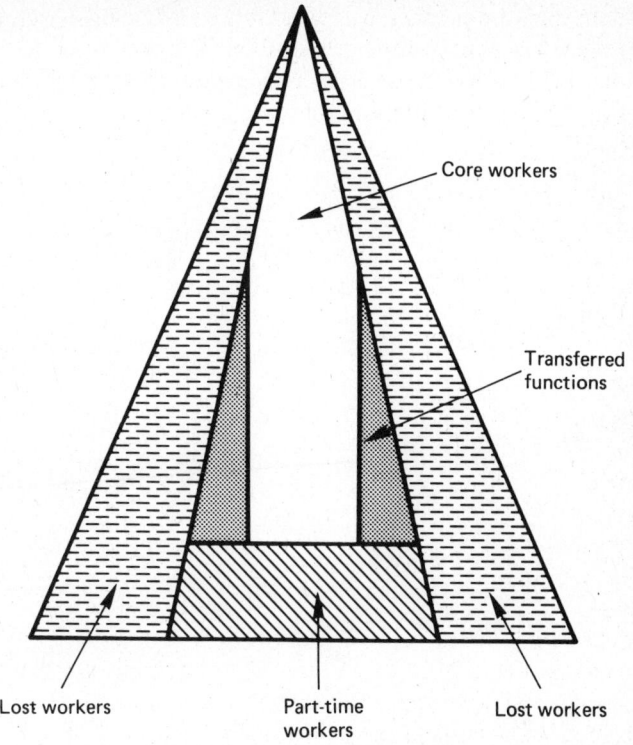

Figure 5.2   Job changes in a contracting company

stripping away of peripheral functions which is taking place in large firms experiencing fierce international competition. By examining each of the groups identified in Figure 5.2, in turn it is possible to explain how the large firm response to increasing international competition can lead to an increased relative importance of small firms in the economy. Four major groupings can be identified.

– Core workers
– Low skill workers replaced by part-time workers
– Lost workers
– Transferred functions

The corporate triangle in Figure 5.2 is therefore shrinking towards the core but, perhaps somewhat perversely, the workers who are fortunate enough to be retained within the core are experiencing major increases in real income. Illustrations of these developments are provided by

Gregory, Lobban and Thomson (1986) who highlight differences in pay experienced by core and non-core workers in large UK companies. They find that in the United Kingdom since 1979 high pay settlements are made to core workers on the basis of tight internal labour markets compared with much lower increases for those outside the core, where the rates are determined primarily by the threat of redundancy. Gregory, Lobban and Thomson feel this illustrates the existence of a dual labour market based on a core of secure, well paid full time employees serviced by a shrinking peripheral group of temporary, less well paid and often part-time workers.

The first group of peripheral workers are the unskilled and semi-skilled, mainly male, workers at the bottom of the corporate hierarchy. This group forms the core group of the long-term unemployed, who have little prospect of re-employment in large manufacturing firms. The evidence presented by Rajan and Pearson (1986) suggests that where firms are increasing the employment of workers at the bottom of the corporate hierarchy, they are often doing so through the use of temporary workers and workers from the secondary sector of the labour market (such as part-time married women). Workers who are displaced by this type of corporate restructuring activity have several 'choices':

  (i)   remain unemployed.
 (ii)   seek formal employment in the small firm sector, usually at lower pay rates and with inferior employment conditions to those in the large corporate sector.
(iii)   become self-employed (i.e. start a business).
(iv)   participate in the informal (or black) economy.

Options (ii) and (iii) will lead to an increasing level of employment in the small firm sector relative to large firms. Small firms are able to obtain labour previously employed in the large corporate sector, at a price which they can afford, which is likely to improve their competitive position. It is also worth noting that unemployment amongst the predominantly male primary labour force may induce 'secondary' workers, (generally the wives of the displaced male workers) to enter the labour market thus providing both the large and the small firm sector with an additional source of cheap, flexible labour which was unavail-able in times of relatively full employment.

In terms of the type of business being started by the displaced unskilled workers, it would seem unlikely that these would be in the industries from which the workers were displaced. On *a priori* grounds we would expect such individuals to enter industries which require very little capital and a minimal level of skill, e.g. small shops, electrical and building repair, car repairs, etc. These frequently have saturated finite local markets, and so any new entrant into the market is likely to either go bankrupt fairly quickly, losing any savings/redundancy money which has been invested, or put an existing firm out of business. The net effect, therefore, is to raise the birth rate of new businesses, but also to raise the death rate, and to have little overall impact on the stock of businesses or the level of employment in the small firm sector.[6]

If we are to explain the net increase in the *stock* of businesses and numbers of self employed in the UK as well as the increase in the business birth rate, we need to further examine the consequences of corporate restructuring. It has already been noted that job losses have affected not only the lower end of the corporate hierarchy, but have to some degree impinged upon the skilled workers and management personnel who have largely been immune in previous periods of increased unemployment. This is partly due to the fact that plant closures tend to affect all levels of the occupational hierarchy at plant level, but also reflects a growing trend within large firms towards what is sometimes referred to as the 'flexible firm' (Atkinson, 1985, CBI, 1985).

Concentrating upon plant closures for the moment, it is possible that some displaced management workers will be re-employed elsewhere within the same company, or will obtain employment within the management labour market. However, there is likely to be a significant number of workers with managerial experience who may be motivated to start their own businesses, rather than, for example, change their location.

We can categorise these workers into two groups. Firstly, there is likely to be a significant number of executives in late middle age who view their prospects of re-employment within the executive labour market as weak. Such individuals frequently start a business, or classify themselves as self-employed, mainly to 'tide themselves over' until retirement. Frequently their children will have left home and their outgoings will be sufficiently reduced to establish a new business which provides a modest level of income. The business itself is treated almost as a hobby and may indeed stem from the former manager's leisure activities. From the point of view of economic development and job creation such businesses are not formed with a view to expansion either in terms of output or in terms of job creation. They are primarily a social activity which is formally classified as a business, but one which again stems from job shedding and large firm lack of competitiveness. These are the British equivalent of the US 'Mom and Pop' Stores.[7]

The second group of management personnel also induced to establish businesses are younger than those discussed above. They may lose their jobs due to plant closures, or may feel that their prospects of promotion are extremely slim, given that large firms are contracting rather than expanding employment at all levels. Such individuals may be motivated by a desire to put into practice ideas which have been formulated whilst employed in the corporate sector, but which have been ignored by the firm. They are likely to enter markets which have some prospect of growth and their businesses are much more likely to grow in terms of output and/or employment than those formed by unskilled workers or older executives. In short, it is these businesses which are most likely to exhibit the rapid employment growth often attributed to small firms in general, and which may begin to alter the structure of the economy away from dependence upon large corporations. It seems likely that labour shedding by large companies may lead to an increase in the number of new businesses started by younger and middle aged former employees. It could also be hypothesised that some highly qualified graduates, who may previously have entered a career in a large firm, may be tempted to start their own businesses. However, it can be argued that there have always existed individuals within large firms who become disillusioned with corporate life, and are motivated by a positive desire for independence and start their own firms. Such individuals do not need the 'motivation' of actual or potential unemployment to enter self-employment. It is also true that many large firms are improving the pay, conditions and job security of 'core' workers who are likely to include young, well qualified managerial staff. Hence, it is possible that corporate restructuring may, in fact, deter the most capable young managers from starting businesses, but induce less suitable individuals to do so.

(ii)   *Management buy-outs*

An alternative course of action for managers and executives facing the threat of redundancy through plant closure is to buy the plant from the parent company and run it as an independent company. The number of 'management buy-outs' of this type has increased rapidly in recent years.[8] Although management buy-outs usually result in some job losses, it is argued that a proportion of the jobs which would have been lost by complete closure, are saved. This is undoubtedly true in some cases, but generally it seems that many large firms are deliberately encouraging management buy-outs as a means of withdrawing from marginal and unprofitable markets, and shifting the burden of risk away from the parent body to the newly formed independent company. Dawkins (1985) suggests that 'many large corporations now feel that they need to pull out of peripheral activities and concentrate on their core businesses after years of expanding through hastily considered acquisitions'. In terms of the observed data, a management buy-out would appear as a new birth, a reduction in large firm employment and an increase in small firm employment. However, in reality, no new jobs would have been created, as there has simply been a transfer of employment and, in all probability some job losses.

(iii)   The 'flexible firm'

Evidence also appears to be growing regarding the increasing trend amongst large corporations towards what has become known as the 'flexible firm'. Not only are firms divesting themselves of peripheral plants and products, but there is a move towards the transfer of peripheral *functions* from within the firm to outside of the corporate hierarchy. Services such as transport, cleaning, catering and security appear to be increasingly sub-contracted by large firms rather than being performed in-house. Often these are being performed by the same personnel, who are now working for small firms (often owned, for instance, by the former manager of the depot or service) rather than the large conglomerates.[9] It is becoming clear that it is not only the more mundane services which are being affected by such restructuring, but also higher level functions such as computer programming and sales are being performed by former employees working on a self-employed basis. The Department of Employment, for instance, has discovered some evidence of a trend towards home-based work, especially by females working with a telephone and a computer terminal (Hakim, 1984).

Additional flexibility for the larger firm is also provided by extensions and developments of the sub-contracting system, a recent review of which may be found in Imrie (1986). For many large British companies such as British Leyland sub-contracting has traditionally been a feature of its operations (Friedman, 1977) but there appears to be evidence, albeit of an anecdotal nature, of an increasing role for sub-contracting. For example Kaplinsky (1983) shows that in electronics the initial development of computer-aided design was undertaken on a sub-contracted basis by small firms as a way of spreading the development risk. Other examples of the growth of sub-contracting occur in the retailing sector where Marks & Spencers have a myriad of suppliers providing goods according to tight specification and equally tight profit margins. In their survey work, Rajan and Pearson (1986) report that 35 per cent of engineering and allied companies had increased the amount of sub-contracting, and only 15 per cent said sub-contracting business had reduced over the 1983–85 period. Rajan and Pearson note this to be particularly true for larger companies who indicate that sub-contracting provides the advantages of scale economies, albeit at one remove, the ability to handle fluctuating demand, the avoidance of skill shortages – particularly in Southern England, and the freedom of sub-contractors to specialise in their own strengths – design, assembly, maintenance, consultancy, etc.

(iv)   Ownership transfer

Within the UK the final factor influencing the increase in the number of businesses and the relative increase in small firms has been the programme of Central and Local Government in transferring functions out of the public sector into the private sector. At a national level the privatisation of British Telecom has led to the formation of many new company suppliers. The effect may have been greater at a local level where there has been a major upsurge in the provision of private contract cleaners in schools, hospitals and other public buildings. Street cleaning contracts have been awarded to private firms, whilst functions such as the provision of school meals are now also increasingly provided by private firms rather than public sector workers (Labour Research, 1986).

(v)   Synthesis

In statistical terms, all such developments will again appear as an increase in new firm formation, in the stock of small businesses (in both the manufacturing and service sectors), as an increase in the relative share of small firm employment and as an increase in the level of self-employment. However, in reality, there is little overall increase in employment. There has simply been a direct transfer of employment from large firms to small firms, or from the public sector to the private sector. Much of the apparent growth of small firms and enterprise can therefore be characterised as a reflection either of the competitive weakness of large firms or of political decisions by government.

The above analysis demonstrates that in an economy, dominated by large firms, which is undergoing a prolonged period of job shedding and corporate restructuring due to declining competitiveness, increases in both the birth rate and the stock of businesses, and the level of self-employment, can occur *without* this necessarily leading to any substantial net increase in employment and output in the economy as a whole. Indeed, the Birmingham (UK) model illustrates that the growth in relative importance of small businesses and self-employment can be the *result* of industrial decline rather than the *cause* of new forms of economic activity and increased employment. The only benefit to the economy is that perhaps without this restructuring decline might be even more rapid. The increased relative importance of small firms may therefore *reflect* decline. There is no necessary reason why decline leads automatically to rebirth.

The Birmingham (UK) model is consistent with the observation of an increased number of small firms struggling against each other (rather than with the larger corporate sector) for a stake in a smaller and low profit segment of the British economy. Such small firms are either tied to the corporate giants or they operate in areas abandoned by them. Such a scenario does not suggest that many are emerging as a force to be reckoned with in the national and international markets. What is noteworthy about their development in recent years is not their alleged injection of dynamism and growth into the British economy, but rather the opposite. They are the visible expression of economic decline and industrial restructuring in the UK; individualistic responses to mass redundancies, mass unemployment and falling job opportunities. This is reflected in the low levels of introduction of new technologies into small firms. Rajan and Pearson (1986) show that less than 10 per cent of small firms felt they had been affected to a large extent by the introduction of new technologies over the 1982–4 period and that more than 75 per cent felt that the effect of new technologies had been negligible.

In conclusion, however, it is worth reiterating that we are not arguing that corporate job shedding and restructuring reflected in the Birmingham (UK) model is the *sole* reason for observed trends in small firm employment in the UK, but rather that it explains the changes which are being experienced in many parts of the United Kingdom. Indeed much of the evidence we quote is for areas outside Birmingham. Of course it is recognised that there exist some areas in Britain where there has been a significant increase in the number of small high-technology firms which do not conform to the above model (Segal Quince and Partners, 1985). However, in *numerical* terms, such firms are relatively insignificant as a proportion of the observed increase in firm formation rates in the UK economy as a whole, and the direct impact of such firms on job creation is very small. Furthermore, there is little clarity about the degree to which many small high-tech firms are really free operators in the market, or whether they owe their existence to protective contracts with other large high-tech firms or with the various institutions attached to the government's defence programme.

We do not wish to argue that this type of firm is always insignificant in *economic* terms. Indeed, the case of Boston in the USA which we now discuss, demonstrates the potential importance of a dynamic export-oriented sector (whether high-tech or not) in generating a *positive* cycle of small firm growth, in contrast to the *negative*, recession-related factors dominating the Birmingham UK model.

5.5   THE BOSTON (USA) MODEL

I would rather look at the United States of America and in particular the State of Massachusetts which contained so many so called 'sunset industries' . . . They brought (unemployment) down from 11 per cent to 3.6 per cent . . . by policies which relied on enterprise and the ability of individuals to go out and create the wealth which the nation requires.   (Lord Young, UK Secretary of State for Employment. Hansard 15 January 1986)

The Birmingham (UK) case where a relative increase in the importance of small firms is attributable to the process of restructuring within large firms contrasts totally with the Boston Model.

It must be understood that the Boston Model is based upon the observation that the New England economy, and that of Boston in particular, has undergone a massive transformation in recent years. Twenty years ago the New England economy was based upon traditional industries such as textiles, footwear and apparel which were in long term decline due to increasing competition from European and Asian producers.

Today the situation is reversed with New England, and Massachusetts in particular, being among the most wealthy and dynamic areas in the United States. The area has created significantly more jobs in recent years than has the whole of Europe.

Employment growth in Massachusetts between 1976 and 1984 is shown in Table 5.3. It shows that, over the period, employment increased by more than half a million jobs, or a cumulative increase of 23 per cent. In fact 80 per cent of this increase was in the non-manufacturing sector, even though the motor for growth was the high technology sector. Table 5.3 shows that over the period, the high technology sector

Table 5.3   Massachusetts employment (in thousands)

	1976	1984	Increase	
Total High Tech.	195.8	328.4	132.6	(68%)
Total Manufacturing	593.6	675.9	82.3	(14%)
Total Non-Manufacturing	1729.9	2175.8	445.9	(26%)
Total Employment	2323.5	2851.7	528.2	(23%)

grew by a remarkable 68 per cent in terms of employment. Much of this growth is clustered around the city of Boston and its 'ring' road Route 128. The effect of these developments have been to transform not only Boston but the surrounding area. For example Flynn (1984) notes that Dr An Wang, founder of Wang Laboratories Inc., having started his own business in a small office above a garage in Boston chose the city of Lowell as the site for his company's headquarters. Lowell is also the location of Apollo Computer and Automatix Inc. The impact of the growth of these firms has been to bring about a radical effect upon unemployment in the Lowell Labour Market. For example in 1971 unemployment in Lowell was nearly 13 per cent compared with a national average of 6 per cent. By 1983 unemployment in Lowell had fallen to $5\frac{1}{2}$ per cent whereas the US average had risen to $9\frac{1}{4}$ per cent. High technology industry in the Boston area has grown on the twin pillars of a localised concentration of high educational expertise and defence spending plans. The educational excellence of the area derived not only from the world-famous universities such as Harvard and MIT, but also from a myriad of other colleges offering degree-level courses.[10]

Therefore there exists a vast student population within which many see the founding of a firm, or working for their former teachers in a local firm, as a way of continuing to live in a sophisticated cultural centre rather than returning to their home areas. In a study of the growth of employment in high technology businesses throughout the United States, Armington, Harris and Odle (1983) showed that the level of education and technical skills in a metropolitan area was closely associated with differences in high technology growth rates, but *not* with those in low technology or 'other' industries.

The US defence budget and its space exploration programme have also contributed towards growth in the New England area. The requirement for the US to maintain a technical lead in space exploration, nuclear technology and conventional arms production has generated major research and development budgets much of which have civilian applications. The concentration of this expenditure in and around the New England area has meant that new high technology firms have been able to grow up in a protected, almost greenhouse, atmosphere. Malecki (1984) shows that more than 70 per cent of US defence contracts, by value, are concentrated in 10–15 states. Subsequent work by Markusen (1986) has shown that the areas benefiting most from these contracts are amongst the most prosperous in the nation.

These firms, although they create relatively few jobs directly, are major creators of wealth. The owners of the high tech firms are extremely wealthy and pay exceptionally high salaries to key personnel, although it must also be admitted that the process workers in many high tech manufacturing companies are non-unionised and relatively poorly paid. Nevertheless the high incomes for significant numbers of workers have a major impact upon the demand for local consumer and business services.[11]

The growth of high technology firms has altered employment patterns for several reasons. First many of the high tech firms, particularly in the software industry are little more than loose confederations of individuals, sometimes husband and wife and sometimes two or three married couples. In many traditional industries the female was included in the company for taxation purposes but her activities were limited perhaps to occasional secretarial and accounting services, whilst the husband ran the company. This is not the case in many of the new computer software companies. Here the female is as well educated and as competent as the male and it is difficult to differentiate, on the basis of gender, the roles undertaken by the partners.

A male/female couple will recognise that there is a considerable loss of family income if the female were to stop working. Many women regard participating in the business as more satisfying than being housewives, so when the couple have children this creates a demand for domestic services such as child minding. It also increases the demand for services such as restaurants because of the reduced home cooking. Other consumer-based services which are boosted include home repair services, gardening etc. which cease to be performed by the family, since by devoting its time to one extra hour of work the couple can earn perhaps five or six times the rate which it would have to pay to a car repairer or to a gardener.[12]

The demands of the high-tech sector are felt not only by the consumer service sector but also by the business service sector. It is unclear in the Boston model whether the venture capital industry is a response to the growth of the high tech industry, or whether it is a factor explaining its growth. What is clear is that the growth of high tech firms has had major consequences for the financial services market. Many individuals who established high tech firms which were subsequently bought out by larger groups have themselves become venture capitalists by taking an equity stake in existing or new small businesses in similar sectors. The circulation of such funding has induced a greater variety of services to be provided by the financial institutions: it has induced the growth of the insurance industry and has led to innovations in a variety of professional services such as advertising, market research, design etc.

The vast majority of the new job creation in small businesses in the Boston model therefore actually occurs in firms and enterprises outside the high-tech sector yet it has been caused by the exceptional growth of the latter sector.

5.6   THE BOLOGNA (ITALY) MODEL

The third model of recent small firm development related to manufacturing is quite different from the other two models we have described. The Boston (USA) model is an example of economic revitalisation led by the recent development of high-tech industry which has generated new employment in small businesses outside of manufacturing. The Birmingham (UK) model is an example of small firm growth being a response to and symptomatic of deindustrialisation and mass unemployment. In contrast the Bologna (Italy) model is virtually a unique example of areas in the advanced industrial economies experiencing relatively high growth rates in manufacturing (in value and employment terms) based upon the production in small firms of so-called low-tech goods (e.g. specialised light engineering, shoes, clothing, furniture, musical instruments, jewellery) which are highly competitive in international markets. That such firms can continue not only to survive, but actually grow in recessionary times, in mature product markets frequently dominated by large corporations which are fiercely competing against each other and against cheaper imports from some Third World countries, comes as quite a challenge to analysts of small firm competitiveness.

5.6.1   The Italian small firm in the 1970s

Before describing the Bologna (Italy) model it should be re-emphasised that there is no suggestion that the model applies throughout Italy or that it numerically represents the most significant form of small firm development in that country. Indeed, one of the striking features about Italy is the existence of a number of types of small firms, reflecting the enormous differences between the social and economic structures of the various regions. For instance, in the South, there is still a noticeable presence of artisans and small (often illegal) firms which manage to survive because of the structure of local demand for their goods and their ability to reduce costs through tax avoidance and minimising unit labour costs (Del Monte and Giannola, 1978).

However the South has also seen the development of small and medium sized firms stimulated by the wave, between 1969 and 1974, of private and public sector investment from the North, in industries such as motor vehicles, mechanical engineering and electronics (Del Monte and Raffa, 1977). The growth of this type of small firm has also been helped by regional policy and other incentives (Del Monte, 1984).

Yet another type of small firm development in Italy resembles, in many respects, the characteristics of the Birmingham model. The increasing use of subcontracting by large firms in Piemonte and Lombardia, as a means of reducing direct labour costs and risks, and rendering the production process more flexible is particularly character-istic of Fiat, Olivetti, and other Northern Italian giants. There are a number of different forms of this type of subcontracting in Italy ranging from the putting-out of various tasks in production to already existing small firms and domestic outworkers, to providing incentives to workers at different levels of the large firm's occupational hierarchy to become entrepreneurs. In other areas of Northern Italy such as Genoa the decline of the shipbuilding industry has also induced 'Birmingham' type characteristics within the economy.

What is most interesting about the small firms in what we have chosen to call the Bologna (Italy) model is that they do not conform to the assumptions made, notably by external observers, about small firm formation in Italy being related to the decentralisation of production by large firms, or to the existence of market niches which do not interest large firms because of insufficient or unstable demand, or to the ready availability of a cheap and flexible workforce drawn from Italy's large secondary labour market. The small firms in the central and North-Eastern regions (Trentino – Alto Adige, Veneto, Friuli, Emila – Romagna, Toscana, Umbria and Marche) are not in general subcon-tractors for large firms, nor is their price competitiveness dependent upon single factors such as low wages or the intensive exploitation of labour.[13]

Indeed, Schiattarella (1984) demonstrates that the strength of small firms in Italy as a whole during the 70s had more to do with increases in productivity related to technical and organisational changes in production, than with the ability of firms to rely upon a 'deregulated' labour market. Firstly, he shows that while the share of national output by firms employing between 20 and 100 workers rose from 31 per cent in 1972 to 34 per cent in 1980, in the group of traditional sectors featuring a high level of small firm activity (textiles, clothing, shoes, leather and fur goods), their share of employment actually dropped marginally from 36.1 per cent in 1972 to 35.8 per cent in 1979. Labour productivity among these small firms in 1972 was only marginally lower than that within firms employing more than 500 workers and rose at the same rate within both groups during the 70s. Interestingly however, productivity remains comparable between the two groups at a time when, owing to higher wage increases among the smaller firms, the differential in the cost of labour between the two is virtually halved from about 40 per cent to 20 per cent in 1980. The competitiveness of these firms therefore does not appear to derive from low wages.

It could of course derive from a higher level of labour utilisation although this does not appear to be confirmed by the evidence on the rates of investment within the two size groups in the sectors mentioned above. The level of per capita investment in tools and machinery among the small firms grew by 59 per cent between 1968 and 1973 and rose dramatically by 169 per cent between 1973 and 1978 whereas among the large firms it grew by 91 per cent in the first period and only by 64 per cent in the second – recessionary – period. Thus while in 1972 the fixed investment per employee ratio in the small firms was 3 per cent lower than the ratio for the large firms, by 1980, it was actually 16 per cent higher. This evidence, in contrast to the traditional view, suggests that the basis for Italian small firm competitiveness during the 70s is modernisation and new investment. Given the enormous variation that exists between small firms, this observation, drawn from aggregate data is of course no substitute for detailed analysis, but it does nevertheless raise certain doubts about small firm survival in the traditional 'low-tech' industries being solely a function of low wages and a deregulated labour market.

5.6.2 Central and North Eastern Italy – the Bologna (Italy) model

The small firms in the central and north eastern regions of Italy are the expression of a quite novel form of growth within the traditional industries. In 1951, agriculture was the principal source of employment in the seven regions in question, but by 1971 manufacturing industry had become the principal source. In the course of the 70s, industrial output in all these regions grew at a higher rate than the national average, well above that of Piemonte, Italy's oldest and most industrialised region (Bagnasco, 1985). In 1971, 37 per cent of the firms and 35 per cent of the employment in Italian secondary manufacturing industry (i.e. excluding energy, mining, chemicals and construction) was located in these regions, rising respectively to 42 per cent and by 38 per cent by 1981. While the stock of firms and employment at the national level in secondary manufacturing grew respectively by 22 per cent and 15 per cent during the 70s, their increase in the seven regions was 38 per cent and 28 per cent respectively. Both in 1971 and in 1981, over 70 per cent of the manufacturing firms in these regions were in the low 'value-added' and 'traditional' sectors such as food, textiles, clothing, shoes, leather goods, furniture, paper, jewellery, musical instruments and toys. Nationally, the number of firms and employment in these traditional sectors (taken as a whole) grew respectively by 13 per cent and 8 per cent, while the rate of increase in these seven regions was significantly higher – 32 per cent and 21 per cent respectively. The majority of the firms in each region (75 per cent in Emilia – Romagna and 85 per cent in 1981 in Tuscany) are tiny, employing less than 10 workers; and between 60 and 70 per cent of total secondary manufacturing employment in each region occurs in firms employing less than 100 workers.

These are startling results confirming that the regions in Italy with the highest growth rates are those dominated by a myriad of very small firms producing traditional sector consumer goods. Moreover the goods are highly competitive in international markets: the share of these products (excluding food industry) in Italy's export of manufactures rose from 20.5 per cent in 1968 to 27.7 per cent in 1977. Clearly not all of the regions have developed along the same lines and not at the same pace, but there are nevertheless three characteristics which have produced a reasonably homogeneous form of small firm development. These characteristics, one exogenous and the other two endogenous, *in combination* isolate the essence of this model.[14]

(i)   Fluctuating markets

The first condition concerns the nature of the market niche for the commodities, which is such that it requires and permits small-scale production. The goods which are produced in central and north eastern Italy are of medium-to-high quality, often trading on a brand-name or even the 'Made in Italy' label which conjures up various images of style or craftsmanship. They are not the cheap, mass produced and standardised goods which usually characterise the traditional consumer industries. On this point it is interesting to observe that Italy's exports in these industries to the OECD countries remained quite stable during the 70s (Onida 1980) despite the onslaught by much cheaper products from the less developed countries (LDCs). For example, between 1968–69 and 1977, the share of the LDCs in OECD imports grew from 22.6 per cent to 29.5 per cent for leather and skin goods, 28.7 per cent to 35.9 per cent for wood manufacturers, 13.7 per cent to 17.0 per cent for textiles, 26.5 per cent to 42.8 per cent for clothing, 21.0 per cent to 45.1 per cent for travel goods and 9.8 per cent to 29.4 per cent for footwear. In the same period, Italy's share in the respective industries changed from 7.7 per cent to 11.4 per cent (leather) 15.1 per cent to 19.1 per cent (wood), 9.1 per cent to 9.3 per cent (textiles) 17.9 per cent to 12.6 per cent (clothing), 18.5 per cent to 23.5 per cent (travel), 42.4 per cent to 36.1 per cent (footwear). The stability of Italian exports without doubt reflects the shift towards the higher quality end of the product market by producers.

The first advantage drawn by the small firms selling in the upper tiers of the market is that because the demand for the product depends less on its price than on its quality, the competitiveness of the firms is not entirely determined by their ability to minimise unit costs. Under these circumstances, small firms with production costs which are marginally higher than those within large firms which are able to exploit scale economies, can nevertheless continue to compete in the market. Of course competition on the basis of price is not eliminated, and in fact the maintenance by the Italian authorities of an undervalued Lira throughout the 70s gave the small firms in question a significant price competitive advantage in export markets. The second advantage which the small firms possess in the market is their ability to meet demand for non-standardised goods – a demand which is erratic and subject to major seasonal fluctuations. This ability derives from possessing, like other small firms, shorter production runs which can cope with short-term demand. But the firms in the Bologna model also possess, as we shall see below, a unique production structure which is highly sensitive to the peculiarities of the market.

(ii) Flexible production and the division of labour between firms

The second condition which explains the economic buoyance of the small firms in central and north eastern Italy concerns the organisation of production on a highly flexible basis. Since the 1970s large-factory production, organised along the Fordist lines of continuous flow and mass integrated production, and along the Taylorist principles of scientific management, has undergone a series of transformations towards achieving more flexibility in the use of labour and machinery. The search by large firms for new economies in production through rationalisation, the introduction of numerically controlled machinery, changes in the internal division of labour (e.g. the putting-out of certain tasks to independent subcontractors and in-house specialisation of other tasks), and changes in the external division of labour (e.g. just-in-time delivery of supplies), have dramatically altered the face of manufacturing industry. In simple terms, this reorganisation of the labour process has sought to eliminate the rigidities of large-scale production which includes restrictive labour practices, management and organisational diseconomies of scale, stockpiling in the event of demand fluctuations, and mismatches in the time and flow of goods between different phases of the production process.

The economies in production by the small firms in the central and north eastern regions closely resemble those related to new forms of flexible production within the large firms. While many of the small firms may originally have begun as subcontractors due to the vertical disintegration of production among the large firms now, owing to the evolution and consolidation of a particular industrial structure in the individual areas, they trade with other local small firms and small merchants. It is this latter development which has enabled the emergence of a form of flexible production which is different from, and not tied up with, the new experiments taking place within large industry.

The distinctive feature of the industrial districts which have developed around the provincial towns of central and north eastern Italy is that each one specialises in the production of a particular commodity (Brusco, 1986). The real strength of the areas however derives from the way in which production is organised within and between the small firms. Clusters of small firms are productively integrated with each other on a subcontracting basis. Strategic entrepreneurs, usually merchants or small businessmen from the provincial cities purchase the finished goods on a contractual basis from a number of small firms which in turn subcontract to several smaller family firms and domestic outworkers.

This system of complex subcontracting allows costs and risks to be spread between a number of firms, but it also allows production to be based upon short-term contracts which can be rapidly adjusted to market requirements by switching between subcontractors when a particular type of good is required or by raising or reducing subcontracting when the level of demand fluctuates.

The producers themselves vary in the degree of autonomy they possess *vis a vis* the subcontracting firms. Very often the domestic outworkers and the small family units carrying out deskilled production tasks are caught in the clutches of one or two buyers, while firms specialising in certain skilled operations will tend to attract many more customers. However common to all the producers is the lack of any real contact with the market mechanism: the purchase and the sale of goods does not occur through the free market but though a series of direct contracts, between the buyer and the seller. The replacement of formal ties with the market, by reciprocal arrangements, introduces a measure of flexibility (quite often forced) in the exchange relations between the entrepreneurs which the market would not normally permit. Direct negotiations on issues related to prices, delivery, payment, credit and even the cost of materials and technologies, ensure, through the principle of reciprocal benefits, the survival of both parties entering into the contract. The flow of goods and information between the production units (the small firm) and the merchants occurs *outside* the open market.

The division of the full production cycle required to make a product into its constituent parts and their separation between producers has generated new economies, reflected in the final price of the finished good. Firstly it eliminates many of the bottlenecks and inelasticities associated with the fully integrated production process in which the production times and the flow of the line in the different stages of production require to be always in consonance with each other. The fragmentation of the labour process into separate units allows each one to set its own pace of work and its own level of output, and in consonance with the immediate market rather than with another phase in the production process. Fragmentation does of course require the efficient circulation of goods and information between the producers. In the Bologna (Italy) model this is guaranteed by the close geographical proximity between the firms as well as the frequent use of microcomputers to communicate information sometimes even to domestic outworkers.

Built into this system of production, there are also strong pressures to reduce costs. In the case of a large firm deciding to fragment its production process, the latter continues to maintain control over and co-ordinate the separate stages in production: the exchange of parts between the different stages is *not* governed by the laws of the market. In the Bologna (Italy) model, there is no overall co-ordinating body and the production of the finished commodity takes place on the basis of competitive exchange between separate entrepreneurs. What may have once been the different parts of one production process are now separate commodities bought and sold on the basis of contractual agreements and competition between separate owners. Each firm therefore seeks to minimise costs either through the use of the most appropriate production technologies (e.g. multi-purpose tools and machinery which can be put to a number of different uses), or through the depression of wage costs and the flexible use of labour (especially within the rural firms and family units at the lower end of the production hierarchy). There is also an important technical factor related to fragmentation which has facilitated the lowering of unit prices. The small firms, through product specialisation and contracts with a number of clients, can achieve scale economies which other small firms cannot normally achieve.

The most interesting aspect about small firm competitiveness in the Bologna (Italy) model is the limited relevance of an explanation based upon the peculiarities of the *individual firm*, such as the way in which labour is recruited, used and remunerated, or the form of the technologies adapted, or the marketing skills of the entrepreneurs. It would be misguided to give emphasis to the economic and the social organisation of production within the individual firms. This is because the firms are not free operators in a free market but one part of a complex and integrated *system* of production, deriving their strength from the economies and the stability achieved by the system as a whole. We are not talking about independent small firms in the traditional sense, nor about subcontractors for large firms, but about the development of an industrial system (almost a corporation) composed of interlinked but independently-owned production units. The uniqueness of the industrial districts derives more from the economics of the vertical disintegration of the production process resulting in a new set of interfirm relationships (Giannola 1985), than from the small firms themselves.

(iii)   *The uniqueness of place*

The third element which characterises the Bologna (Italy) model concerns the nature of the local, social and institutional traditions which have enabled the growth of the industrial systems. These are traditions which are unique and cannot be reproduced elsewhere. This second 'endogenous' factor is related to the establishment of a peculiar but dynamic relationship between the modern market town and the once agricultural countryside (Bagnasco, 1985).[15]

The producers are located in the rural areas which surround the provincial towns of the central and north eastern regions of Italy. These are areas with a long-standing tradition of peasant farming, largely through share cropping. The origins of the new industrial entrepreneurship are located in the dynamics of a recent agricultural history in which a large number of small peasant households were farming not only for subsistence but were also producing cash crops for the market. In other words they are areas with an established petty-bourgeoisie, embracing an entrepreneurial and not a proletarian culture, and accustomed to market transactions. This is the ready mechanism which has generated the new entrepreneurship which in its social organisation of production is virtually identical to the old entrepreneurship: Family units (which may even hire-in or hire-out labour). These are capable of working flexible hours, capable of saving by reducing wage costs and family expenditure, capable of coping with fluctuations in demand for the product because of income derived from other interests, and capable of entering into market transactions. In other words, it is the unique social structure of these areas which has produced this kind of small firm development. Of course the transition from peasants to artisans is not simple, especially in the formation of the appropriate skills. Brusco (1986) has in fact noted that the specialisation of an industrial district in a particular trade originates in most cases from the presence, at some point in time, of a large firm in the same product sector which enabled the diffusion of skills in the area through its workforce, and also acted as a seed-bed for the development of specialist supply firms.

The producers in the countryside have limited marketing outlets of their own, and this is where the towns have played a crucial role. The 'strategic' entrepreneurs of the city are not just the merchants who buy the goods from the direct producers but, like the middle-men of pre-capitalist economies, they constitute the main bridge between town and country, between production and distribution. These individuals co-ordinate production in the small units by supplying them with information on market trends and also orders from the larger merchandising houses. But as merchants from towns which have for centuries been independent trading and financial centres, they are also responsible for marketing the product to an international audience at the frequently held trade fairs.

In the 1980s, each industrial district, in symbolising a single trade, has come to assume a corporate identity which facilitates the reproduction of the system. This is not only because it provides a series of structures and functions suited to local industrial requirements, such as the specialised production goods, machinery and skills. It also, through product specialisation, offers a host of producer, marketing and financial services which facilitate the survival of the small firms.

5.7 CONCLUSION

We noted in Chapter 2 that, contrary to popular wisdom, there is no clear evidence that the share of output or employment produced by small firms in an economy is associated with job creation or unemployment change. Employment performance and the size structure of the economy are either unrelated, or related in a complex multivariate manner.

This chapter has shown that whilst in some countries small firms have become increasingly important over the last decade or so, this can be for very different reasons. To illustrate this point we highlight the three 'models', which demonstrate that the major factor which 'explains' the increasing importance of small firms is the international competitiveness of groups of firms in the economy. In the Birmingham (UK) model, however, the increasing importance of small firms occurs because of the process of restructuring within large firms, whereas in the Boston (USA) and Bologna (Italy) models it occurs because of the increasing competitiveness of very particular types of smaller firms. The Boston and Bologna models differ because in Boston the employment is primarily created indirectly in the service industries which are able to thrive only because of the considerable wealth creating (rather than job creating) competitiveness of the hi-tech sector. In the Bologna model wealth creation and job creation are undertaken *pari passu*.

The key policy question for an economy which approximates more closely to the Birmingham (UK) model is whether it is possible to learn lessons from either of the other two 'successful' models. Several points appear clear. First it is not simply the number of small firms in an economy nor even their relative importance which determines the performance of that economy. Instead it is the quality and nature of these firms and their ability to sell directly or indirectly in international markets which is crucial to their international competitiveness. In Boston, the 1960s and 1970s saw a massive increase in the number of new small high-tech firms which were able to grow from very modest beginnings to major international 'names' relatively quickly. Many such firms have failed, but the Boston area illustrates that it is only a select few firms in an area which have the capacity to transform an economy.

In some respects these points might appear to be contradicted by the Bologna model where there appears to have been a widespread flowering of entrepreneurship in the sense of large numbers of new firms being formed, but these firms remaining small. Further examination, however, illustrates some striking similarities. First in both the Boston and

Bologna cases it is the capacity to sell overseas which is the foremost characteristic. In the case of Boston it is based upon high technology but in the case of Bologna it is based upon high quality in fashion-conscious but essentially low technology industries. Secondly it is a misunderstanding of the Bologna model to regard it as one based upon small *independent* firms. As we noted it is true that production takes place in small units which are legally independent in the sense of being locally owned. However the Bologna model is a production *system*, controlled by relatively few merchants in the major towns and cities of central and North East Italy. It is the merchants who determine the products in response to perceived demand as certainly as if they undertook production themselves. Again this illustrates that, as with the Boston model, it is a relatively small set of key actors or individuals who effectively determine the success of the area.

Another key issue is the extent to which these developments chronicled in the Boston and Bologna 'models' have taken place 'spontaneously' and the extent to which they evolve intentionally or unintentionally from government policy. In the Boston model, whilst it is clear that wealth creation takes place in private sector hi-tech firms and employment creation takes place in private service sector businesses, much of the initial impetus comes from the twin pillars of government defence expenditure and higher education – the bulk of which is publicly financed. The development of a hi-tech sector depends crucially on numbers of graduates of the highest calibre and government research and development and defence orders. It is no coincidence that the three best performing states of the USA are Massachusetts, California and Texas where these motors for growth, defence and higher education expenditure are increasingly concentrated. For a country as dominated by the state as Italy it may appear surprising that government policy has had significantly less effect on the performance of the Bologna model than in the USA. There appears to be some justification for the view that the growth of the North East and central area has taken place in isolation from government policy. Indeed some have argued that it has taken place as a response to an over-regulatory state but we believe this to be an overstatement.

Unfortunately in those parts of the United Kingdom where the Birmingham (UK) model is applicable, current government policy appears to recognise few of the lessons of any of the three models. Currently policy is targetted at increasing the number of small firms in the economy in the belief that more small firms will lead to a stronger economy. Much of the policy is directed towards the creation of an

'Enterprise culture' in which a major objective is to raise the formation rate and stock of new businesses. All three models, however, demonstrate that it is not the absolute number of small businesses in an economy which determine performance but rather the 'quality' of those businesses. Both the Boston and Bologna models also demonstrate that it is relatively few businesses which are the prime determinants of the success of an area. In our view this means a *selective* policy, of assisting the relatively few businesses which have the capacity to transform an economy through their international competitiveness, is to be preferred to one based on encouraging unsuitable individuals to gamble their life savings by starting a highly risky business venture.

Within the UK there also appears to be a reluctance on the part of government to recognise the impact that public expenditure can have upon regional economic development even though this clearly is a key element of the Boston model. For example Boddy and Lovering (1986) point out that regional assistance to Wales in the period 1974/75 to 1977-78 was far outweighed by defence procurement expenditure in the primarily 'non-assisted' neighbouring region of South West England. It is likely that in subsequent years the regional distribution of defence expenditure has become increasingly concentrated in the currently prosperous areas.

Finally it is of paramount importance to recognise which of the models is applicable to the particular economy under policy consideration. We have frequently pointed out that each of the models is merely illustrative of developments, and that the USA economy has elements of the Birmingham (UK) model and the UK has elements of the Boston (USA) model. One of the major purposes of highlighting the models in this way is to demonstrate that the policy prescriptions which flow from the Boston (USA) model, could even be harmful if applied in the Birmingham (UK) model. For example it might reasonably be inferred from the Boston (USA) model that further employment creation could take place by encouraging the formation of new businesses, perhaps by reducing entry barriers by the provision of training, subsidised premises etc. Such a policy could be justified because of the presence in the area of major wealth creating businesses which either directly require services, or where owners or workers require the provision of consumer services. It would therefore be a sensible policy to induce an increase in the number and stock of service sector businesses.

On the other hand such policies would be unwise if the economy approximated more closely to the Birmingham (UK) model. Here the priority has to be the creation of new wealth, and this can only be undertaken by efforts to increase international competitiveness. To devote resources to increasing the number of service sector businesses, in the absence of new wealth creation, will lead to an increase in the death rates of new businesses and of existing firms. Whilst it may lead to an increase in the stock of firms it is much less likely to lead to net increases in employment. It is for these reasons that the catastrophic decline in manufacturing employment and the debate over deindustrialisation is of importance. In the United States there has been a major increase in the share of total employment provided by the service sector. There is no evidence, however, of an absolute reduction in the USA's manufacturing base. As Kutscher and Personick (1986) show it is only in the last cyclical downturn that manufacturing employment fell in the United States. It is upon this relative strength that the US is able to develop its service sector. The contrast with the United Kingdom where manufacturing employment has fallen each year since the mid 1960s and catastrophically since 1979, could not be more stark.

We therefore conclude that an understanding of the reasons for the increasing relative importance of small firms in many economies is of paramount importance. Only then can appropriate policies to increase aggregate employment and output be implemented.

6 The Labour Market Impact of Small Firm Employment Growth

6.1 INTRODUCTION

Our review of the relevant studies in Chapters 2 to 4 of this book has established that:

- in the majority of OECD countries, employment is becoming increasingly concentrated in smaller units;
- many countries are experiencing rapid increases in self-employment, in both absolute and relative terms;
- throughout the developed world, large firms are experiencing major job losses, whereas small firms have been the main source of new jobs.

This chapter considers the implications of these observed trends for the labour market, and for groups within it, particularly the unemployed. The stimulation of new firm formation and self-employment has become a major plank of employment creation policies at national, regional and local levels throughout many OECD and EEC countries, as we will demonstrate in Chapter 7. It is important, therefore, to consider the *type* and *quality* of jobs created by new and small firms, in addition to the *number* of jobs created.

There are strong *a priori* reasons for believing that jobs in small firms may differ in nature from those which exist in the large firm sector. An often-noted characteristic of the small firm is its flexibility – its ability to respond quickly and efficiently to changes in market demand. Unlike most large firms in oligopolistic markets, small firms generally have only a small share of the market and cannot influence the level of market demand through their marketing and advertising strategies. Small firms cannot plan ahead for long periods of time in the same way as many large firms do. Thus small firms may be expected to demand more flexible labour inputs than large firms. It may be expected that part-time and temporary jobs are more prevalent in small than large firms, and that small firms recruit a higher proportion of 'high turnover' employees such as married women and young people, than large firms with more stable levels of demand for labour.

With regard to the skill and occupation structure of employment, two key factors may be noted. Firstly, small firms tend to have a less rigid division of labour than large firms, and thus may be expected to employ a greater proportion of multi-skilled or multi-functional employees. Secondly, small manufacturing firms often specialise in the production of one-off or small batch products as opposed to mass-produced standardised products. The manufacture of customised products such as specialised machine tools involves a higher proportion of skilled labour than large scale mass-production. Thus it may be expected that small firms, particularly in the manufacturing sector, will employ a relatively high proportion of skilled workers and correspondingly fewer unskilled workers.

Finally, it may be expected that wages and conditions of employment will be inferior in small firms to those of larger firms. This is partly because small firms are likely to employ more 'peripheral' workers, and also reflects the relatively low level of trade union membership in small firms. Fixed costs of employment such as National Insurance payments tend to form a significant proportion of small firm labour costs, and thus small firm employers will try to minimise these costs. The result is that small firm employees are likely to receive lower wages and enjoy poorer conditions of employment and fringe benefits than their counterparts in large firms.

This chapter reviews the available evidence regarding the gender and full/part time composition of employment, the occupational structure of employment, and the quality of jobs in small as opposed to large firms. Section 6.2 examines the comprehensive data available from the United States Small Business Administration. Sections 6.3 and 6.4 review the evidence from the UK, and data from other OECD countries are presented in Section 6.5. The broad conclusion to this chapter is that the hypotheses outlined above are largely borne out by the evidence – there are fundamental differences in job quality between small and large firms. Furthermore, the type of jobs which are being created by new and small firms, particularly under the Birmingham (UK) model, are unlikely to remove large numbers of people from the unemployment register. The policy implications of these findings are discussed in Chapter 7.

6.2   FIRM SIZE AND JOB QUALITY IN NORTH AMERICA

6.2.1   The US Small Business Administration study

In March 1984, the United States Small Business Administration (SBA) published a comprehensive review of employment in different sizes of firm in Chapter 4 of *The State of Small Business – A Report of the*

President (US Small Business Administration, 1984). The data used in this review were obtained from the May 1979 Current Population Survey, carried out by the Census Bureau, which included questions regarding the size of the firm/establishment in which the respondents worked. Thus, a great deal of information was collected regarding the demographic characteristics of workers in different sizes of firms, together with information regarding occupation, hours worked, wages and conditions of employment. This study contains the most comprehensive data available regarding the characteristics of employment by firm size.

The results of the US survey are reproduced here in Figures 6.1 to 6.8 and Tables 6.1 to 6.6. The figures and tables are largely self-explanatory, and we shall limit ourselves here to a description of the key results.

Figure 6.1 and Table 6.1 illustrate the *age distribution* of workers in small and large businesses. It is clear that small firms employ a relatively high proportion of both younger and older workers, with large firms

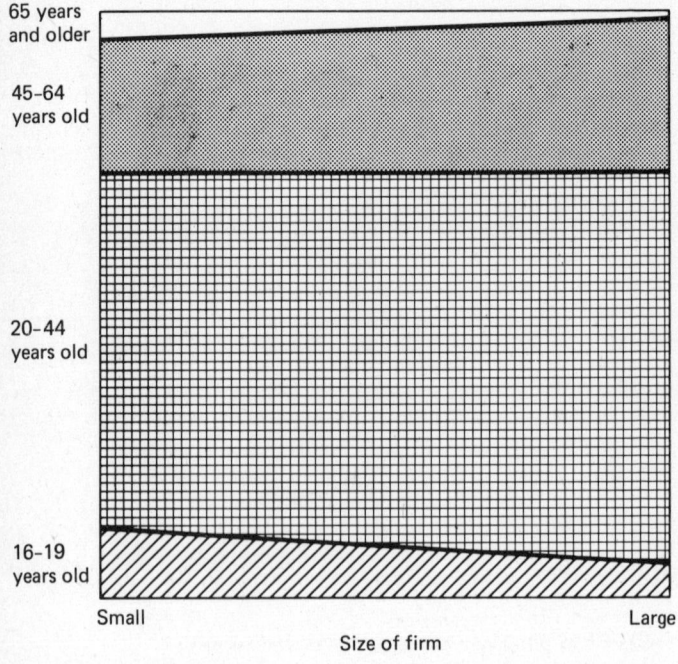

Figure 6.1   Age distribution of employment by firm size, USA, 1979

Source: US Government Small Business Administration, 1984.

Table 6.1   Age distribution of employment by firm size, USA, 1979

Industry	Total All Firms	Employment size of enterprise		
		1–99	*100–499*	*500+*
Total, All Industries				
No. (000s)	33 977	13 972	4287	15 718
Percent	(62.3)	(57.5)	(63.3)	(67.0)
Mining				
No. (000s)	448	76	38	334
Percent	(69.6)	(76.2)	(51.2)	(71.0)
Construction				
No. (000s)	2197	1607	280	309
Percent	(60.0)	(58.9)	(61.1)	(73.2)
Manufacturing Durable Goods				
No. (000s)	6975	1145	854	4976
Percent	(67.9)	(58.3)	(67.8)	(70.6)
Manufacturing Non-Durable Goods				
No. (000s)	3968	834	637	2497
Percent	(66.8)	(55.5)	(64.3)	(72.4)
Transportation, Communications & Public Utilities				
No. (000s)	2931	699	236	1997
Percent	(72.4)	(65.9)	(74.3)	(74.8)
Wholesale Trade				
No. (000s)	2017	980	382	656
Percent	(67.5)	(60.4)	(71.6)	(78.8)
Retail Trade				
No. (000s)	5297	3231	426	1639
Percent	(48.6)	(50.4)	(45.4)	(46.4)
Finance, Insurance & Real Estate				
No. (000s)	2596	1058	322	1215
Percent	(64.6)	(63.7)	(60.7)	(66.7)
Misc. Services				
No. (000s)	7548	4342	1111	2095
Percent	(62.3)	(60.1)	(66.7)	(65.0)

Note: Figures in parentheses are percentages of prime-age workers to total wage and salary workers in each firm size category. Data exclude Agriculture, Forestry and Fishing.

Source: US Government Small Business Administration, 1984.

employing larger numbers of prime age (25 to 54 years old) workers. This is particularly true in the manufacturing, construction, transport and wholesaling industries. In the retail, financial and service industries, there appears to be little or no relationship between firm size and the age distribution of employment.

The *gender* distribution of employment by firm size is shown in Figure 6.2 and Table 6.2. These illustrate that women comprise a larger proportion of the workforce in small as opposed to large firms. However, Table 6.2 shows that there are major variations by industry. In the 'Manufacturing of non-durable goods' industry, the proportion of women employees is clearly higher in small firms. The position is reversed in the retail industry and in the finance, insurance, and real estate sector, women dominate the workforces of the medium sized (100–499) employees.

Figure 6.3 and Table 6.3 show that black workers form a lower proportion of employment in small as opposed to large firms. This is broadly true for all industry groups, apart from Transportation, Communications and Public Utilities.

The *occupational distribution* of employment by firm size in the US is illustrated in Figure 6.4 and Table 6.4. These show that 'service industry workers' are disproportionately represented in smaller firms, with the proportions of blue- and white-collar workers tending to increase with

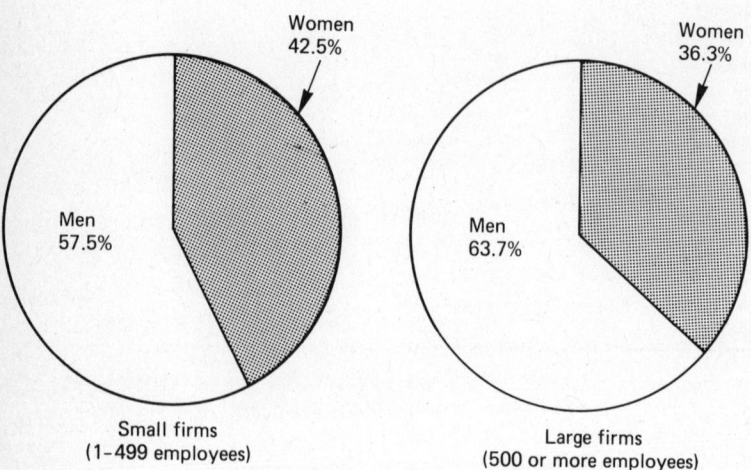

Figure 6.2   Gender distribution of employment by firm size, USA, 1979

Source: US Government Small Business Administration, 1984

Table 6.2   Gender distribution of employment by firm size, USA 1979

Industry	Total All Firms	Employment size of enterprise		
		1–99	*100–499*	*500+*
Total, All Industries				
No. (000s)	21 704	10 316	2881	8507
Percent	(39.8)	(42.4)	(42.5)	(36.3)
Mining				
No. (000s)	50	9	1	40
Percent	(7.7)	(8.7)	(0.5)	(8.6)
Construction				
No. (000s)	315	251	28	36
Percent	(8.6)	(9.0)	(6.1)	(8.5)
Manufacturing Durable Goods				
No. (000s)	2603	401	394	1808
Percent	(25.4)	(20.4)	(31.3)	(25.7)
Manufacturing Non-Durable Goods				
No. (000s)	2188	695	451	1042
Percent	(36.8)	(46.3)	(45.5)	(30.2)
Transportation, Communications & Public Utilities				
No. (000s)	984	254	61	669
Percent	(24.3)	(24.0)	(19.4)	(25.1)
Wholesale Trade				
No. (000s)	816	469	148	199
Percent	(27.3)	(28.9)	(27.8)	(23.9)
Retail Trade				
No. (000s)	5147	2947	364	1836
Percent	(47.3)	(46.0)	(38.8)	(52.0)
Finance, Insurance & Real Estate				
No. (000s)	2375	963	359	1053
Percent	(59.1)	(58.0)	(67.6)	(57.8)
Misc. Services				
No. (000s)	7226	4327	1075	1824
Percent	(59.7)	(59.9)	(64.5)	(56.6)

Note: Figures in parentheses are percentages of female workers in each firm size category. Data exclude Agriculture, Forestry and Fishing.
Source: US Government Small Business Administration, 1984.

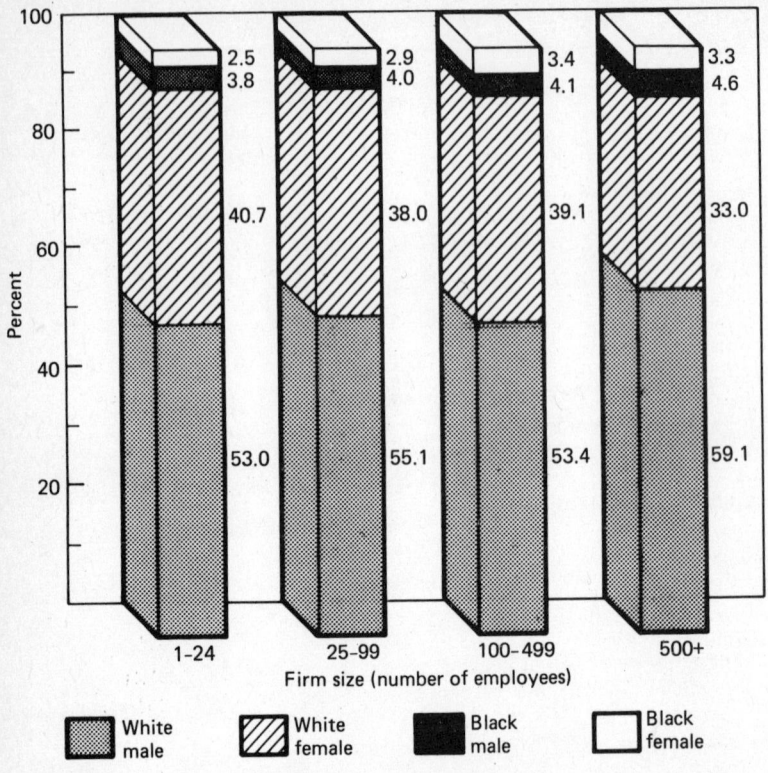

Figure 6.3   Race distribution of employment by firm size, USA 1979

Source: US Government Small Business Administration, 1984.

firm size. The more detailed occupational breakdown given in Table 6.4 shows that small firms employ a relatively high proportion of craftworkers and a low proportion of operatives. Of course, differences in occupational structure by firm size may reflect differences in industrial distribution, with small firms concentrated in the retail and service sectors, hence the high proportion of sales and service industry workers. Unfortunately, the SBA have not published the detailed industry statistics which would enable this to be clarified.

Over one-quarter of the employees of the smallest firms (with less than 25 employees) worked *part-time* in 1978 (Figure 6.5). In contrast, only 10 per cent of workers in firms with over 500 employees were employed part-time. Detailed figures (not shown here) reveal that 15 per cent of

Table 6.3   Race distribution of employment by firm size, USA 1979

Industry	Total All Firms	Employment size of enterprise		
		1–99	*100–499*	*500+*
Total, All Industries				
No. (000s)	3940	1576	508	1856
Percent	(7.2)	(6.5)	(7.5)	(7.9)
Mining				
No. (000s)	27	0	0	27
Percent	(4.2)	(0)	(0)	(5.7)
Construction				
No. (000s)	290	186	62	42
Percent	(8.0)	(6.7)	(13.5)	(10.1)
Manufacturing Durable Goods				
No. (000s)	733	152	65	516
Percent	(7.1)	(7.7)	(5.1)	(7.3)
Manufacturing Non-Durable Goods				
No. (000s)	513	109	75	329
Percent	(8.7)	(7.3)	(7.6)	(9.5)
Transportation, Communications & Public Utilities				
No. (000s)	352	107	11	234
Percent	(8.7)	(10.1)	(3.6)	(8.8)
Wholesale Trade				
No. (000s)	108	41	21	46
Percent	(3.6)	(2.5)	(4.0)	(5.6)
Retail Trade				
No. (000s)	623	352	68	203
Percent	(5.7)	(5.5)	(7.2)	(5.8)
Finance, Insurance & Real Estate				
No. (000s)	245	62	42	141
Percent	(6.1)	(3.7)	(7.9)	(7.8)
Misc. Services				
No. (000s)	1049	567	164	318
Percent	(8.7)	(7.9)	(9.8)	(9.9)

Note: Figures in parentheses are percentages of black workers in each firm size category. Data exclude Agriculture, Forestry and Fishing.

Source: US Government Small Business Administration, 1984.

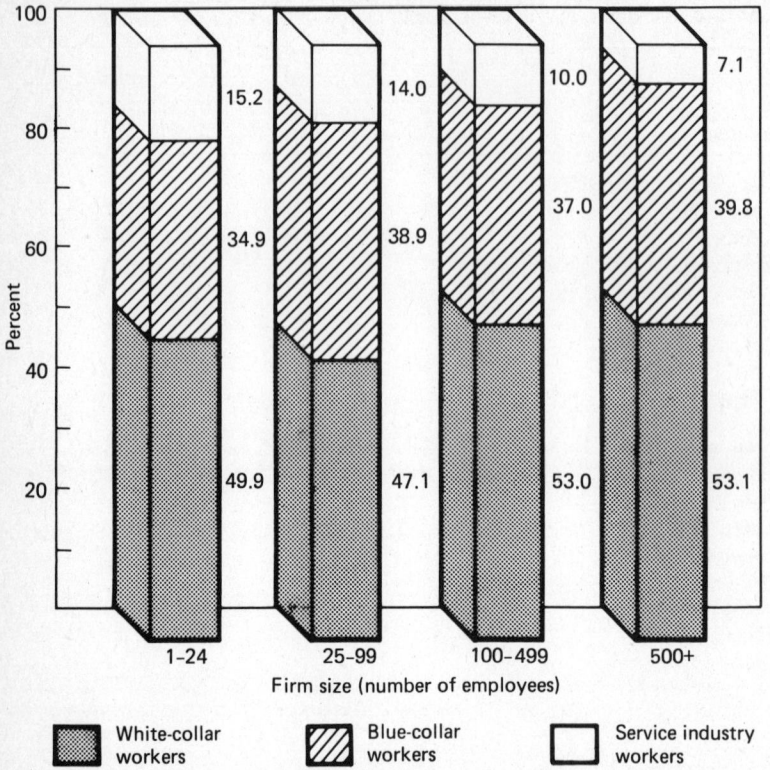

Figure 6.4   Occupational distribution of employment by firm size, USA 1979

Source: US Government Small Business Administration, 1984.

workers in very small firms worked less than 20 hours per week, and that 35 per cent were employed for only part of the year. Table 6.5 shows that the proportion of part-time workers declines with size of firm in all industries apart from retailing and mining.

The final set of figures and tables refer to the *quality* of jobs in firms of different sizes in terms of earnings and fringe benefits. Figure 6.6 clearly shows that the level of *earnings* increases with firm size. Table 6.6 shows that this is broadly true in all industry groups. Only 20 per cent of very small firm employees are covered by *pension* plans, as compared with almost 90 per cent in firms with over 500 employees (Figure 6.7). Finally, Figure 6.8 shows that *union* membership is much lower amongst small firm workers.

Table 6.4 Occupational distribution of employment by firm size, USA 1979

Occupation	Total All Firms	Employment size of enterprise			
		1–24	*25–99*	*100–499*	*500+*
Total, All Occupations					
No. (000s)	54 555	16 226	8093	6771	23 465
Percent	(100.0)	(100.0)	(100.0)	(100.0)	(100.0)
Professional & Technical					
No. (000s)	7073	1509	775	949	3840
Percent	(13.0)	(9.3)	(9.6)	(14.0)	(16.4)
Managers & Administration					
No. (000s)	6329	1990	1077	872	2390
Percent	(11.6)	(12.3)	(13.3)	(12.9)	(10.2)
Sales					
No. (000s)	4002	1594	580	423	1405
Percent	(7.3)	(9.8)	(7.2)	(6.2)	(6.0)
Clerical					
No. (000s)	10 542	3002	1383	1342	4815
Percent	(19.3)	(18.5)	(17.1)	(19.8)	(20.5)
Craftsworkers					
No. (000s)	8532	2795	1316	845	3576
Percent	(15.6)	(17.2)	(16.3)	(12.5)	(15.2)
Operatives (except transportation)					
No. (000s)	7356	1226	1103	1094	3933
Percent	(13.5)	(7.6)	(13.6)	(16.2)	(16.8)
Transportation Operatives					
No. (000s)	2113	716	360	260	777
Percent	(3.9)	(4.4)	(4.4)	(3.8)	(3.3)
Labourers (except farms)					
No. (000s)	2653	927	370	305	1051
Percent	(4.9)	(5.7)	(4.6)	(4.5)	(4.5)
All other service workers					
No. (000s)	5955	2467	1129	681	1678
Percent	(10.9)	(15.2)	(13.9)	(10.1)	(7.1)

Note: Figures in parentheses are percentages of total wage and salary workers.
Source: US Government Small Business Administration, 1984.

This review of the evidence presented by the US Small Business Administration has illustrated that substantial differences exist between large and small firms in terms of the *type* of employment offered. Although there are some variations by industry, it is broadly true to say that small firms employ a disproportionate number of young, female

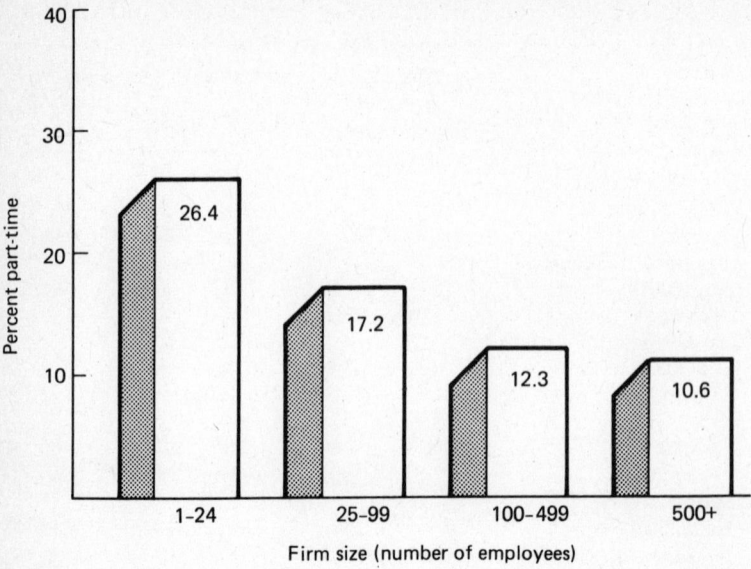

Figure 6.5   Full/part time distribution of employment by firm size, USA 1979

Source: US Government Small Business Administration, 1984.

and part-time employees and that small firm workers earn lower wages and enjoy fewer fringe benefits than do their large firm counterparts.

6.2.2   Small firm employment in Canada

A similar picture of small firm employment emerges from a survey by the Canadian Federation of Independent Business (1984) of 6371 of its members which are considered to be farily representative of the national small firm population. The survey was more limited in scope than the US survey described above, covering only gender, age, full/part time distribution and job tenure.

Table 6.7 shows that Canadian small firms tend to employ a greater proportion of young workers, than firms as a whole in Canada. Moreover, the proportion of young workers declines with size, even within the small firm sector.

Table 6.5 Full/part time distribution of employment by firm size, USA 1979

Industry	Total All Firms	Employment size of enterprise		
		1–99	*100–499*	*500 +*
Total, All Industries				
No (000s)	8202	5113	769	2320
Percent	(16.4)	(23.3)	(12.3)	(10.6)
Mining				
No. (000s)	18	4	6	8
Percent	(3.1)	(4.6)	(9.6)	(1.7)
Construction				
No. (000s)	306	276	23	7
Percent	(9.5)	(11.3)	(5.6)	(1.8)
Manufacturing Durable Goods				
No. (000s)	348	158	32	158
Percent	(6.2)	(8.8)	(2.7)	(2.4)
Manufacturing Non-Durable Goods				
No. (000s)	346	181	65	100
Percent	(8.2)	(12.9)	(6.9)	(3.1)
Transportation, Communications & Public Utilities				
No. (000s)	308	127	29	152
Percent	(8.2)	(13.1)	(9.7)	(6.1)
Wholesale Trade				
No. (000s)	241	176	27	38
Percent	(8.6)	(11.7)	(5.4)	(4.7)
Retail Trade				
No. (000s)	3261	1897	228	1136
Percent	(33.6)	(33.4)	(27.8)	(35.5)
Finance, Insurance & Real Estate				
No. (000s)	496	262	64	170
Percent	(13.4)	(16.9)	(12.9)	(10.3)
Misc. Services				
No. (000s)	2877	2031	295	551
Percent	(26.2)	(31.3)	(19.2)	(18.5)

[1] Worked less than 35 hours per week.
Note: Figures in parentheses are percentages of total wage and salary workers working part-time in each firm size category. Data exclude Agriculture, Forestry and Fishing.
Source: US Government Small Business Administration, 1984.

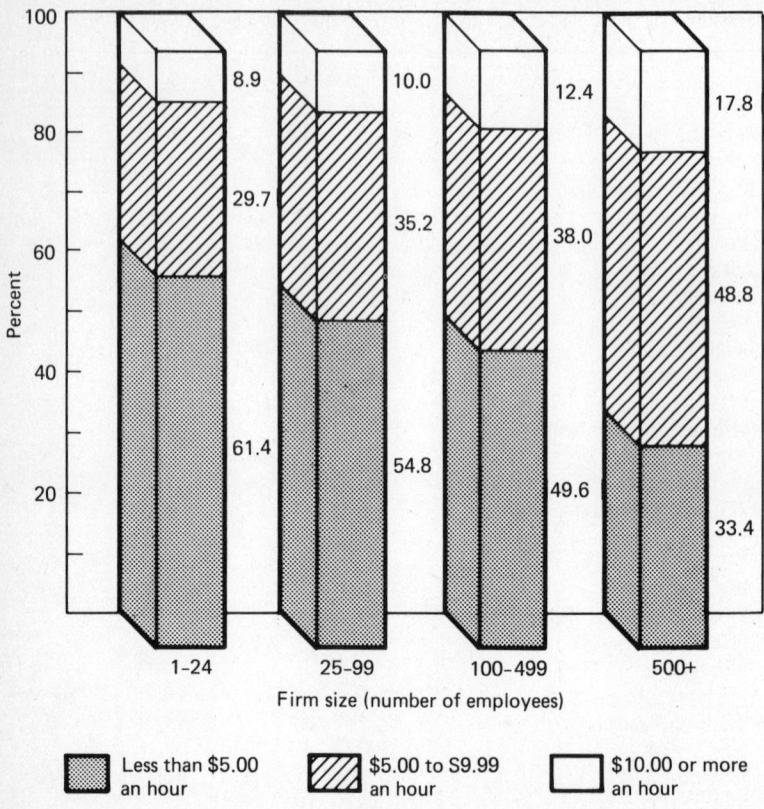

Figure 6.6   Earnings of employees by firm size, USA 1979

Source: US Government Small Business Administration, 1984.

In contrast to the US findings, Table 6.8 shows that Canadian small firms employ a larger percentage of male workers than is the case for the Canadian labour force as a whole. The main discrepancies between small firm employment and employment in the economy as a whole occurs in the service sector where 54 per cent of small firm workers are male as compared with 39 per cent in the labour force as a whole.

With regard to *part time* employment (Table 6.8) the percentage of such employees is similar in the small firm sample and the labour force as a whole, although small firms employ a greater proportion of part-time

Table 6.6   Earnings of employees by firm size, USA 1979

Industry	Total All Firms	Employment size of enterprise		
		1–99	*100–499*	*500 +*
Total, All Industries				
No. (000s)	23 311	12 918	3108	7285
Percent	(46.7)	(59.2)	(49.6)	(33.4)
Mining				
No. (000s)	120	30	24	66
Percent	(20.0)	(32.1)	(35.0)	(15.1)
Construction				
No. (000s)	1212	1050	90	72
Percent	(37.7)	(43.0)	(21.4)	(20.3)
Manufacturing Durable Goods				
No. (000s)	2983	929	534	1520
Percent	(31.0)	(51.8)	(45.2)	(22.8)
Manufacturing Non-Durable Goods				
No. (000s)	2306	823	502	981
Percent	(41.5)	(58.7)	(53.5)	(30.5)
Transportation, Communications & Public Utilities				
No. (000s)	955	502	97	356
Percent	(25.4)	(51.8)	(32.1)	(14.3)
Wholesale Trade				
No. (000s)	975	584	177	214
Percent	(34.9)	(39.3)	(35.6)	(26.5)
Retail Trade				
No. (000s)	6658	4041	528	2089
Percent	(69.0)	(71.8)	(64.4)	(65.3)
Finance, Insurance & Real Estate				
No. (000s)	1781	810	312	659
Percent	(48.3)	(52.5)	(62.9)	(39.9)
Misc. Services				
No. (000s)	6321	4149	844	1328
Percent	(57.6)	(64.1)	(54.8)	(44.7)

Note: Includes only wages and salary workers employed in 1979. Figures in parentheses are percentages of total wage and salary workers earning less than $5 per hour from wages and salaries in each firm size class. Data exclude Agriculture, Forestry and Fishing.

Source: US Government Small Business Administration, 1984.

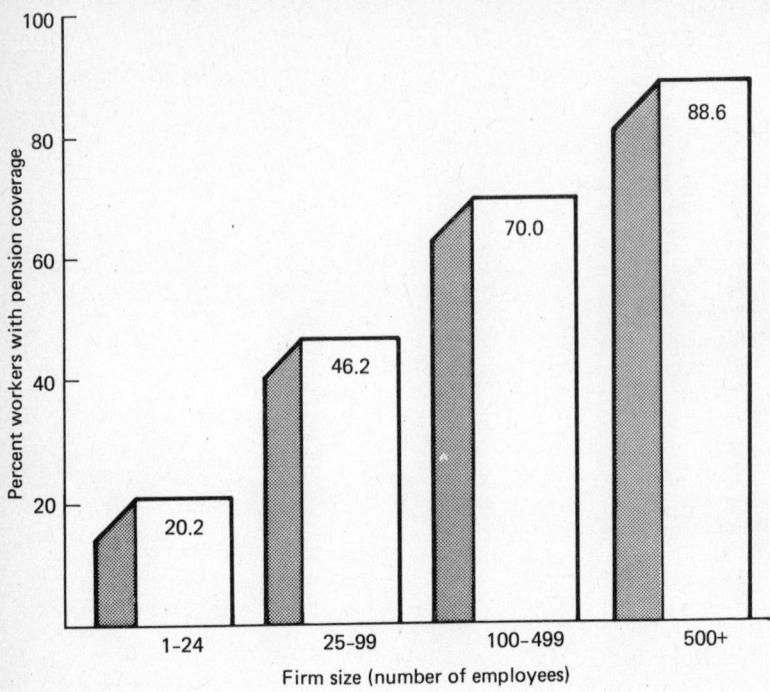

Figure 6.7   Pension coverage of employees by firm size, USA 1979

Source: US Government Small Business Administration, 1984.

Table 6.7   Age distribution of employment by firm size, Canada 1984

| Age of employees | Canada labour force | CFIB Firms (No. employed in firm) | | | | | |
		All firms	Under 10	10–19	20–49	50–99	100 +
Under 25	21.1	26.4	28.7	28.8	25.4	23.3	24.1
25–54	67.1	64.5	61.8	63.2	66.4	66.8	54.9
55–64	10.0	7.4	7.8	6.7	6.7	8.7	7.7
65 +	1.8	1.6	1.7	1.5	1.4	1.2	2.4

Source: Canadian Federation of Independent Business (1984).

Table 6.8 Employment structure – CFIB firms compared with Canadian labour force, 1984

	Male				Female			
	Full-Time		Part-Time		Full-Time		Part-Time	
	Labour force	CFIB firms	Labour force	CFIB firms	Labour force	CFIB firms	Labour force	CFIB firms
Agriculture, Forestry, Fishing	67.1	63.1	7.2	8.9	15.9	19.6	9.5	8.3
Mining	86.5	76.0	—	1.2	12.3	19.5	—	3.3
Construction	86.6	87.1	4.1	3.1	5.8	8.0	3.3	1.8
Manufacturing	70.5	68.9	1.4	2.4	25.8	25.7	2.4	3.0
Transportation and Public Utilities	73.4	66.7	2.8	12.1	19.5	17.3	3.9	4.0
Trade	48.8	52.0	8.2	7.4	25.4	25.9	17.5	14.7
Finance, Insurance and Real Estate	39.3	37.8	2.8	2.4	49.3	49.5	8.7	10.3
Services	33.4	46.3	5.4	7.2	42.3	32.9	18.8	13.7
Other, n.e.c.	—	66.8	—	5.4	—	21.6	—	6.2
Public Administration	61.4	—	2.1	—	31.9	—	4.8	—
All Industries	53.9	59.5	4.5	5.7	30.3	25.5	11.2	9.3

Source: Canadian Federation of Independent Business (1984).

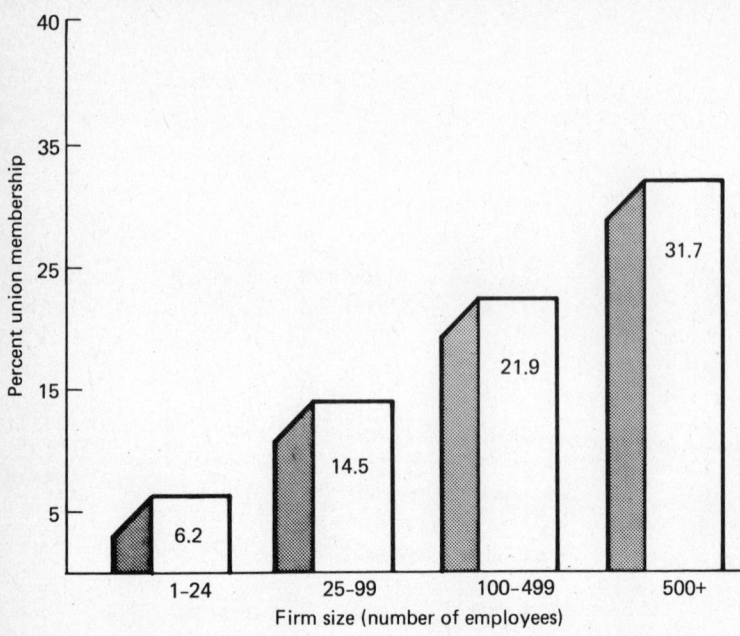

Figure 6.8   Extent of union membership by firm size, USA 1979

Source: US Government Small Business Administration, 1984.

males. Figure 6.9 shows that, within the small firm sector, the percentage of part-time workers is highest in the 0–10 size category and lowest in the 20–49 size group.

6.3   EVIDENCE FROM UNITED KINGDOM OFFICIAL SOURCES

6.3.1   The Annual Census of Production (ACOP)

This is the only UK official survey of industry and/or employment which publishes results broken down by size of firm and/or establishment. Unfortunately the employment information available from ACOP is limited to a breakdown between operatives and administrative, technical and clerical staff (ATC). Figure 6.10 shows that the proportion of ATC staff has been increasing in UK manufacturing industry between 1971 and 1982, and that the proportion of ATC staff increases with the

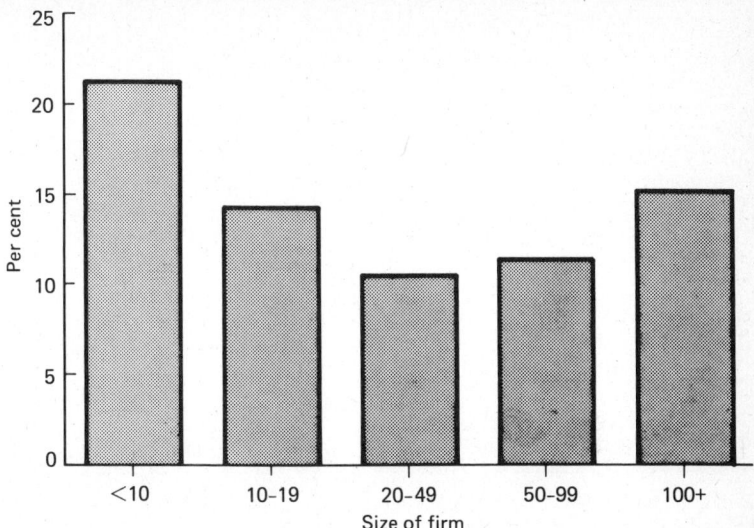

Figure 6.9   Part time employment by firm size, Canada, 1984

Source: Canadian Federation of Independent Business, 1984.

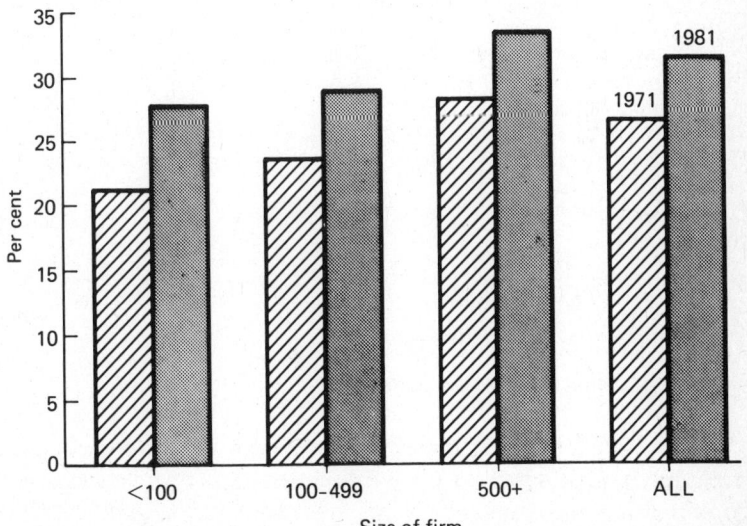

Figure 6.10   Administrative technical and clerical staff as a percentage of total employment by firm size, UK manufacturing, 1971 and 1981

Source: Annual Census of Production.

size of the firm. A more detailed analysis by industry group (Table 6.9) shows that larger firms tend to employ a greater proportion of ATC staff than do small firms. In most industries, the largest size group (1000 + employees) employ the highest percentage of ATC staff, although in metal manufacture, chemicals, mechanical engineering, instrument engineering, and timber and furniture, the proportion of ATC staff 'peaks' at the 500–999 employee level.

Table 6.9   Administrative, technical and managerial staff as a percentage of total employment, by enterprise size and industry, 1983

	Enterprise size (employees)					
	1–99	*100–199*	*200–499*	*500–999*	*1000+*	*ALL*
Metal Manufacture	26.9	28.2	27.3	29.0	28.6	28.3
Manufacture of non-metallic mineral products	24.8	23.9	24.9	25.5	27.1	26.1
Chemicals	44.1	45.4	47.3	47.9	43.0	44.2
Metal goods n.e.s.	24.1	23.7	26.6	26.0	28.1	25.6
Mechanical engineering	32.2	36.1	38.2	43.5	41.0	38.2
Electrical engineering	35.2	35.6	35.3	38.1	42.2	40.2
Motor vehicles	24.6	23.6	25.2	26.5	27.5	27.0
Other transport equipment	23.4	26.4	31.1	32.1	40.4	38.3
Instrument engineering	38.2	39.6	40.0	46.2	39.4	40.0
Food, drink, tobacco	19.7	21.3	22.3	23.2	23.2	22.6
Textiles	18.9	19.1	19.4	19.4	22.6	20.6
Clothing and footwear	16.0	16.4	16.2	17.0	17.4	16.6
Timber and furniture	23.3	25.5	25.3	29.9	26.5	24.7
Paper, printing, publishing	36.6	37.1	37.7	40.6	40.9	39.0
Rubber and plastic	26.4	24.9	30.4	29.4	32.6	29.6
All Manufacturing Industry	27.1	27.9	29.9	31.8	34.4	31.8

Source: Annual Census of Production, 1983.

Without a more detailed analysis of employment type, such as a division into skilled and unskilled categories, it is difficult to draw any firm conclusions from the data presented in this section. Detailed figures in the UK are available only from the results of various surveys which have been carried out, and data bases which have been constructed, often on a local or regional level. The findings of these surveys are summarised in section 6.4 below.

6.3.2   Self-employment in the UK 1981–84

The self-employed represent an important sub-sector of the small firm population. The Department of Employment estimates that approximately 2.7 million people were self-employed in Spring 1985 (*Department of Employment Gazette*, May 1986). Moreover, the self-employed have been a particular target of the UK Government's employment policy, with an increase in the number of self-employed being viewed as an important means of reducing unemployment. The policy issues are discussed in detail in Chapter 7. This section will confine itself to an analysis of the characteristics of the self-employed population and the changes which have occurred over the period 1981 to 1984, using the results of the Labour Force Survey as the basic source.

The term 'self-employment' covers a large number of categories, not all of which may be considered to be part of the small firm population. In particular, a large group of people are 'nominally' self employed in that they describe themselves as self-employed in order to take advantage of favourable tax treatment (Sidaway, 1983). There are considerable advantages to employers in using labour-only subcontractors, particularly in industries such as construction, where most projects are short-term and employers may wish to avoid employment-related costs such as National Insurance contributions and redundancy payments. A crude measure of the extent of nominal self-employment can be derived from the fact that almost two-thirds of the self-employed population do not employ others (Creigh *et al.* 1986). Of course, some of these may be genuine one-person businesses, but it seems that perhaps half of those who describe themselves as self-employed fall into the 'nominal' category. There is some evidence that nominal self-employment is increasing more rapidly than 'genuine' self-employment. Creigh *et al.* (1986) suggest that 78 per cent of the increase in self-employment over the 1981–84 period was accounted for by the self-employed without employees, whilst 'the CBI says much greater sub-contracting of work is taking place throughout British industry. It is the largest cause of the growth of self employment' (Lloyd, 1986).

Table 6.10 compares the age distribution of the self-employed with that of employees in employment in 1984. This shows that the self-employed, and particularly those with employees, are disproportionately concentrated in the 30–49 age category; 54 per cent of the self-employed are in this age group, as compared with 44 per cent of employees. Conversely, one third of employees are less than 30 years of age; for the self-employed this figure is 17 per cent. There are no

Table 6.10 Age distribution of the self-employed and employees in employment, 1984

Age	Employees			Self-employed				
	Male	Female	All	Male	Female	All without employees	All with employees	All
16–19	7.8	9.6	8.6	1.7	1.3	2.2	0.5	1.6
20–24	12.8	14.2	13.4	6.7	5.5	8.5	2.7	6.4
25–29	12.2	10.5	11.4	9.2	10.0	10.7	7.1	9.4
30–34	11.6	9.6	10.8	11.5	14.0	12.2	11.9	12.1
35–39	12.3	12.6	12.4	17.2	17.1	16.9	17.8	17.2
40–44	9.9	11.1	10.4	13.6	13.2	12.5	15.3	13.5
45–49	9.5	10.7	10.0	11.2	10.8	9.9	13.1	11.1
50–54	9.0	9.6	9.3	10.4	9.6	9.5	11.6	10.2
55–59	8.0	7.6	7.8	7.7	8.1	7.1	8.9	7.8
60–64	5.5	3.3	4.6	6.0	5.9	5.6	6.7	6.0
65 and over	1.3	1.2	1.2	4.7	4.5	4.8	4.3	4.6
Total	100	100	100	100	100	100	100	100
Base (thousands)	11 658	8 980	20 638	1 980	638	1 682	937	2 619

Source: Creigh et al. (1986).

significant differences between self-employed males and females with regard to age distribution, but those with employees tend to be older than those without employees, with only 10 per cent of the former being less than 30 years of age.

Table 6.11 suggests that young people (under 25 years old) are increasing as a proportion of the self-employed population, with this group growing by almost 60 per cent over the 1981–84 period, as compared with 21 per cent for the self-employed as a whole. The share of those aged 50 and over is decreasing, with the 25–49 category remaining approximately stable as a proportion of the self-employed. All age groups experienced an absolute increase in self-employment between 1981 and 1984.

Table 6.11   The age distribution of self-employment 1981–1984

Age Group	1981 (000)	%	1984 (000)	%	Change 1981–84 (000)	%
16–19	23	1.1	42	1.6	19	82.6
20–24	110	5.1	168	6.4	58	52.7
25–34	507	23.4	563	21.5	56	11.0
35–49	863	39.9	1095	41.8	232	26.9
50–59	419	19.3	471	18.0	52	12.4
60–64	131	6.1	157	6.0	26	19.8
65 & over	112	5.2	120	4.6	8	7.1
All Ages	2164	100.0	2619	100.0	455	21.0

Sources: Sidaway (1983); Creigh *et al.* (1986)

Table 6.12 shows that the self-employed are heavily concentrated in the construction and service sectors, with only 8 per cent of the self-employed working within the manufacturing sector (as compared with 30 per cent of employees). Over 70 per cent of self-employed females work in distribution, hotel, catering, repairs and other services. The self-employed with employees are concentrated in the distribution, hotel, catering and repairs sector. The analysis of 1981–84 changes in Table 6.13 shows that all sectors apart from agriculture have experienced a net increase in self-employment, with females growing more rapidly than males in all sectors. Overall, female self-employment increased by 40 per cent and male self-employment by 13 per cent, resulting in an increase in the female share of the self-employed from 20 to 24 per cent. Almost all of the rise in female self-employment was accounted for by the service sector, and in particular 'other services' where the number of self-

Table 6.12 Sex and industry distribution of the self-employed and employees in employment, 1984

Industry division	Employees			Self-employed				
	Male	Female	Total	Male	Female	All without employees	All with employees	Total
Agriculture	1.9	0.9	1.4	11.9	6.7	9.9	11.9	10.7
Energy, water supply	5.1	1.2	3.4	0.2	0.1	*	*	0.2
Extraction of minerals	5.3	2.0	3.9	0.5	1.2	1.0	*	0.6
Metal goods, engineering and vehicles	16.9	5.9	12.1	3.1	0.6	2.7	2.1	2.5
Other manufacturing	11.5	9.8	10.8	5.0	6.3	5.5	5.0	5.3
Construction	9.5	1.6	6.0	26.5	1.4	24.6	12.8	20.4
Distribution, hotels, catering and repairs	13.9	25.5	19.0	27.8	41.8	25.2	42.1	27.8
Transport	9.0	3.0	6.4	5.9	1.6	5.5	3.7	3.7
Banking, finance, insurance and business services	7.5	9.6	8.4	9.0	9.8	7.9	11.5	9.2
Other services	19.5	40.5	28.6	10.0	30.5	17.6	10.5	10.0
Total	100.0	100.0	100.0	100.0	100.0	100.0	100.0	100.0
Base (thousands)	11 658	8 979	20 638	1 980	638	1 683	936	2 619

* Indicates not significant

Source: Creigh et al. (1986).

Table 6.13   Self-employed by sex and broad industry group 1981–1984

Industry group		1981 (000)	1984 (000)	Change 1981–84 (000)	% Change
Agriculture	Male	221	221	0	0.0
	Female	28	28	0	0.0
	TOTAL	250	249	−1	−0.4
Manufacturing	Male	123	147	24	19.5
	Female	23	34	11	47.8
	TOTAL	146	181	35	24.0
Construction	Male	382	454	72	18.8
	Female	6	10	4	66.7
	TOTAL	388	464	76	19.6
Services	Male	914	1027	113	12.4
	Female	359	514	155	43.2
	TOTAL	1273	1541	268	21.0
All Industries and services	Male	1640	1850	210	12.8
	Female	417	586	169	40.5
	TOTAL	2057	2435	378	18.4

Source: *Employment Gazette*, May 1986.

employed females increased by 80 000 (nearly 80 per cent) between 1981 and 1984.

The number of hours worked by the self-employed is compared to those worked by employees in Table 6.14. This shows that there is a much greater variation in hours worked amongst the self-employed than amongst employees in employment. A relatively high proportion of the self-employed, and particularly those with employees work more than 60 hours per week. At the other end of the scale, one in six self-employed females worked less than nine hours per week in 1984. The proportion of part-time workers (defined as working less than 30 hours per week) in the self-employed population is increasing, as illustrated by Table 6.15. In particular, the number of women working less than nine hours per week has increased significantly, by nearly 40 000 in 1983–84 alone, according to Creigh *et al.* (1986).

Finally, the occupational distribution of the self-employed in 1984 is shown in Table 6.16. One third of the self-employed fall into the 'managerial' category and over half of those with employees belong to

Table 6.14   Hours worked by the self-employed 1984

Weekly hours worked	Employees			Self-employed				
	Male	Female	All	Male	Female	Without employees	With employees	All
1–8	1.2	7.6	4.0	1.6	16.7	7.4	1.4	5.3
9–16	1.0	13.1	6.3	1.8	13.8	6.1	2.2	4.7
17–24	1.0	14.6	7.0	2.2	10.9	5.1	3.0	4.3
25–30	1.1	8.6	4.4	2.9	10.7	5.9	2.8	4.8
31–40	43.7	43.6	43.6	21.8	16.2	23.6	14.6	20.4
41–60	48.3	11.8	32.4	47.0	19.2	37.2	45.7	40.2
61 and over	3.7	0.7	2.3	22.6	12.6	14.6	30.3	20.2
Total	100	100	100	100	100	100	100	100
Base (thousands)	11 658	8 980	20 638	1980	639	1683	936	2 619

Source: Creigh et al. (1986).

Table 6.15   Self-employment by full/part time status and sex, 1983–1984

	1983		1984		Change 1983–84	
	000	*%*	*000*	*%*	*000*	*% Change*
MALE						
Full Time	1623	70.4	1810	69.1	187	11.5
Part Time	130	5.6	170	6.5	40	30.8
TOTAL	1753	76.1	1980	75.6	227	12.9
FEMALE						
Full Time	265	11.5	306	11.7	41	15.5
Part Time	286	12.4	333	12.7	47	16.4
TOTAL	551	23.9	639	24.4	88	16.0
ALL SELF EMPLOYED						
Full Time	1888	81.9	2116	80.8	228	12.1
Part Time	416	18.1	503	19.2	87	20.9
TOTAL	2304	100.0	2619	100.0	315	13.7

Source: Creigh *et al.* (1986) Note: Part-time is defined to mean working less than 30 hours per week.

this group. Amongst males, the processing, making and repairing of metal and electrical goods and construction, mining and related occupations are important, whilst catering, cleaning, hairdressing and other personal services accounts for 11 per cent of self-employed females. This latter group grew by 95 per cent over the 1981 to 1984 period (Table 6.17). Other occupational groups which grew rapidly in percentage terms include literary, artistic and sports (52 per cent) and clerical and related occupations (40 per cent). The managerial category grew relatively slowly over this period (7 per cent), but still remains the largest single occupational group amongst the self-employed.

This section has demonstrated that the self-employed differ substantially from the employed population in terms of age, gender, industry occupation and hours worked. The trends over the 1981–84 period suggest that females, particularly in the service sector, and in the personal service occupations, are increasing their share of total self-employment, and that part-time workers accounted for a disproportionate share of self-employment growth over this period.

Table 6.16 Self-employment by occupation, 1984

Occupational group	Males	Females	Per cent		
			Without employees	With employees	Total
Professional and related supporting management and administration	6.2	2.9	3.8	8.2	5.4
Professional and related occupations in education, welfare, health	4.4	9.7	5.5	6.0	5.6
Literary, artistic, sports	3.2	5.7	5.2	1.5	3.8
Professional and related in science, engineering, technology etc	3.5	0.8	2.6	3.4	2.9
Managerial	29.4	43.5	22.6	51.2	32.8
Clerical and related	0.7	10.2	3.5	2.1	3.0
Selling	4.8	7.5	6.8	3.0	5.5
Security and protective services	0.1	*	0.1	*	0.1
Catering, cleaning, hairdressing and other personal services	2.1	11.2	5.7	1.8	4.3
Farming, fishing and related	2.7	1.9	3.2	1.3	2.5
Processing, making, repairing and related (excluding metal and electrical)	8.2	4.8	9.1	4.3	7.4
Processing, making repairing and related (metal and electrical)	11.2	0.1	10.1	5.5	8.5
Painting, repetitive assembly, product inspecting, packaging	4.4	0.7	4.5	1.6	3.5
Construction, mining and related not identified elsewhere	13.2	0.1	11.4	7.4	– 10.0
Transport, materials moving and storage	5.7	0.9	5.5	2.7	4.5
Miscellaneous	0.3	0	0.3	0.1	0.2
Total	100	100	100	100	100
Base (thousands)	1 980	638	1 682	937	2 619

Source: Creigh *et al.* (1986).

Table 6.17   Self-employment by occupation 1981–1984

	1981	1984	Change 1981–84	
	(000)	*(000)*	*(000)*	%
Professional and related supporting management and administration	110	141	31	28.1
Professional and related occupations in education, welfare, health	119	147	38	23.5
Literary, artistic, sports	66	100	34	51.5
Professional and related in science, engineering, technology, etc.	66	76	10	15.2
Managerial	806	859	53	6.6
Clerical and related	51	79	28	40.3
Selling	114	144	30	26.3
Security & protective services	—	—	—	—
Catering, cleaning, hairdressing and other personal services	58	113	55	94.8
Farming, fishing and related	52	65	13	25.0
Processing, making, repairing and related (excl. metal & electrical)	149	194	45	30.2
Processing, making, repairing and related (metal and electrical)	177	223	46	26.0
Painting, repetitive assembly, product inspecting, packaging	72	92	20	27.8
Construction, mining & related n.e.s.	219	262	43	19.6
Transport, materials, moving and storage	99	118	19	19.2
Miscellaneous	5	5	0	0.0
TOTAL	2164	2619	455	21.0

Sources: Sidaway (1983); Creigh *et al.* (1986).

6.4   UK EVIDENCE FROM SURVEYS AND DATABASES

The official sources discussed in section 6.3 provide very little information regarding the structure of employment in different sizes of firm. The ACOP data provide only a very crude classification of employees within the manufacturing sector only, whilst the LFS data covers only a sub-group of the small firm sector, namely the self-employed. Detailed information on the characteristics of jobs in large and small firms in the UK is available only from various surveys which have been carried out, some with the specific purpose of analysing employment trends, and others with related objectives such as a study of industrial relations structures and practices.

This section summarises the results of five such studies – a survey of 300 new firms in Cleveland by Storey (1982); a survey of 262 small manufacturing firms in the Belfast Urban Area by Hart (1985); a database of firms in the northern region; a study of employment and occupational trends in 300 small firms throughout the UK (Rajan and Pearson (1986)) and some results from the Workplace Industrial Relations survey (Daniel and Millward (1984)).

6.4.1 New firms in the Cleveland economy

Storey (1982) surveyed 301 firms which were new to the Cleveland area between 1971 and 1977. Many of these firms were subsidiaries of larger firms or branches of multi-plant organisations. Of the total sample, 159 firms (33 per cent) were defined to be wholly new independent single-plant firms.

The survey showed that the 300 firms new to Cleveland (i.e. including parents, branches and subsidiaries) created 7 445 new jobs, over 75 per cent of which were for full-time male workers (Table 6.18). The 63 manufacturing firms in the sample created 3 572 jobs, almost half of all the jobs created. However, over 2 600 of these jobs were created in subsidiary plants as opposed to independent single-plant firms, the group upon which the present discussion is focused. The latter group of firms provided only 22 per cent of the new jobs, despite making up over 50 per cent of the population of firms new to Cleveland.

The type of jobs created by the new firms in terms of their gender and full/part time composition and the distribution of skills are analysed. Findings are reproduced in Tables 6.18 to 6.20. Table 6.18 shows that

Table   6.18   Employment structure of new firms in Cleveland

	MALES		FEMALES		TOTAL		
	Full Time	*Part Time*	*Full Time*	*Part Time*	*Full Time*	*Part Time*	*Total*
Mean	18.8	0.5	4.5	1.1	23.2	1.6	24.8
Total	5 627	155	1 345	318	6 972	473	7 445

Note: Figures are based upon 300 responses. One firm did not know its employment level.
Source: Storey (1982).

Table 6.19 Skill structure of employment in new firms in Cleveland

	Skilled	Semi-Skilled	Unskilled	Professional/Managerial	Clerical	Others	Total
Independent	2.9 (40)	0.8 (11)	1.1 (15)	1.4 (19)	0.9 (12)	0.2 (3)	7.3 (100)
Parent	16.1 (59)	0.4 (2)	0.9 (3)	5.6 (20)	4.1 (15)	0.4 (1)	27.5 (100)
Branch	3.9 (35)	2.1 (18)	1.3 (11)	1.7 (15)	1.9 (17)	0.5 (4)	11.4 (100)
Subsidiary	13.0 (30)	4.9 (11)	14.1 (33)	4.7 (11)	5.7 (13)	0.8 (2)	43.2 (100)
No of jobs	1859 (35)	592 (11)	1327 (25)	744 (14)	708 (13)	118 (2)	5348 (100)

Note: Percentages in parentheses.
Source: Storey (1982).

Table 6.20 Skill structure by industry – new firms in Cleveland

	Skilled	Semi-Skilled	Unskilled	Professional/Managerial	Clerical	Others	Total
Manufacturing	14.8 (31)	5.1 (11)	16.5 (34)	5.0 (10)	5.7 (12)	0.8 (2)	47.9 (100)
Construction	5.8 (47)	1.9 (16)	0.6 (5)	2.1 (17)	1.6 (13)	0.3 (2)	12.3 (100)
Prof. Services	3.1 (39)	0.5 (6)	0.2 (3)	2.0 (25)	1.8 (22)	0.4 (5)	8.0 (100)
Distribution	2.7 (24)	1.4 (13)	2.6 (23)	2.3 (21)	1.7 (15)	0.4 (4)	11.1 (100)
Other	3.7 (45)	0.9 (11)	1.6 (19)	1.1 (13)	0.9 (11)	0.1 (1)	8.3 (100)
No. of jobs	1859 (35)	592 (11)	1327 (25)	744 (14)	708 (13)	118 (2)	5348 (100)

Source: Storey (1982).

the vast majority of new jobs created by the 300 firms were in the category 'Full Time Male' (76 per cent) with 2 per cent being part-time male, 18 per cent full time jobs for women and only four per cent were part time female jobs.

The skill composition of the new jobs is given in Tables 6.19 and 6.20, Table 6.19 shows that 35 per cent of jobs were in the skilled manual category. An interesting point to note is that this percentage increases to 40 per cent for independent firms and 59 per cent in the parent firms. Conversely, the larger subsidiary firms tend to employ a higher proportion of unskilled manual workers than do the smaller independent firms. There is little variation by firm type in the employment of semi-skilled manual workers and clerical workers, apart from the fact that parents appear to employ few semi-skilled workers. Independent firms employ a higher proportion of professional and managerial staff than do branches and subsidiaries.

Table 6.20 shows the skill composition of employment by industrial group. This reveals clear industrial variations in the structure of employment. Over three-quarters of manufacturing employees are manual workers, whereas less than half of the workers in the professional service firms can be described as such (with the vast majority being in the 'skilled' category). Skilled manual workers also dominate the Construction and 'other' sectors, whereas managerial professional and clerical workers are important in the Professional Service and Distribution Sectors.

The Cleveland results reveal clear variations in the structure and skill composition of employment in new firms by type of firm and by industry. Broadly speaking, large manufacturing firms tend to employ high proportions of unskilled manual workers, construction firms a high proportion of skilled manual workers, and service firms employ relatively large numbers of professional managerial and clerical staff.

6.4.2 Small manufacturing firms in Belfast

A survey of 262 new and small (under 50 employees) manufacturing firms in the Belfast Urban Area was carried out by Hart (1985). Just over half (153) of the surveyed firms were new to the BUA between 1970 and 1980, and 82 per cent of respondents were classified as wholly independent single plant firms. The surveyed firms employed a total of 5379 workers, with a mean size of 20.6.

The relevant results of the Belfast survey are summarised in Tables

6.21 and 6.22. These show that small manufacturing firms tend to employ a lower proportion of full-time males and a higher proportion of part-time workers (both male and female) than manufacturing firms as a whole in Belfast. This applies particularly to new firms – 60 per cent of new firm workers are full-time males, compared with 70 per cent in the manufacturing sector as a whole. Full-time females account for a relatively high proportion of new firm employees. With regard to the skill structure of employment, skilled manual workers form the biggest group, with 57 per cent of the workforce (Table 6.22). New firms employ a smaller percentage of unskilled manual workers and a larger percentage of clerical, professional and managerial staff than small firms as a whole.

6.4.3   Employment structure in Northern England manufacturing firms

The data base of manufacturing establishments in Northern England described in Storey (1985a) and Storey, Keasey, Watson and Wynarczyk (1987) can also be used to analyse the gender and full/part time composition of employment, for the period 1971 to 1981.

Table 6.21   Employment structure in new and small manufacturing firms in Belfast

	All man. firms %	Surveyed firms %	New firms[1] %	Established firms[2] %
MALE				
Full Time	69.7	64.4	59.5	67.4
Part Time	0.6	1.5	1.7	1.3
TOTAL	70.3	65.9	61.2	68.7
FEMALE				
Full Time	26.2	26.8	30.6	23.4
Part Time	3.5	7.3	7.5	7.5
TOTAL	29.7	34.1	38.1	30.9
TOTAL EMPLOYMENT	100.0	100.0	100.0	100.0

[1]Firms new to the Belfast Urban Area between 1970 and 1980.
[2]Firms which were established prior to 1970 and were still in existence in 1980.
Source: Hart (1985).

Table 6.22   Skill structure of employment in new and small manufacturing firms in Belfast

	Surveyed small firms %	New firms[1] %	Established firms[2] %
Skilled Manual	57.2	56.9	57.4
Unskilled Manual	19.3	16.4	21.4
Clerical	20.1	21.6	19.1
Professional/Managerial[3]	3.4	5.1	2.1
TOTAL EMPLOYMENT	100.0	100.0	100.0

[1]Firms new to the Belfast Urban Area between 1970 and 1980
[2]Firms which were established prior to 1970 and were still in existence in 1980
[3]Excluding small firm owner-managers
Source: Hart (1985)

Table 6.23 shows the composition of employment by plant size in 1981. This table clearly illustrates that the proportion of part-time workers (male and female) is negatively related to plant size. 22 per cent of workers in plants with less than 5 employees work part time, compared with only 4 per cent of workers in the largest size category (100 + employees). Part-time females are a particularly important group in the very smallest plants, accounting for 19 per cent of the workforce. Conversely, the proportion of full time males tends to increase with plant size, although there are exceptions. The 50–99 size group has a relatively low proportion of male employees.

Table 6.24 traces the employment changes which occurred in single plant manufacturing firms (the vast majority of which are small firms) in the Northern region between 1971 and 1981. This shows that the composition of jobs lost through closure is similar to that of employment as a whole in 1971. However, firms which existed through the 1971–1981 period decreased their share of full-time male workers, and increased that of the other groups. This trend away from full-time male employment is reinforced by the employment structure of new firms, which employ a relatively high proportion (11 per cent) of part-time workers. The net result of these changes is that, although total employment in single plant independent firms increased slightly over this period, there was a decrease in the level of full-time male employment. Full-time females and part-time males and females all grew in both absolute and relative terms between 1971 and 1981.

Table 6.23 Employment structure in manufacturing plants in the North East of England, by size of plant, 1981

Size of plant (No. of employees)		Full-time male	Part-time male	Full-time female	Part-time female	Total employment	No. of firms
1–4	No.	1338	63	247 *16*	393	2041	(909)
	%	65.6	3.1	12.1	19.3	100.0	
5–9	No.	2823	115	566 *17*	457	3974	(581)
	%	71.3	2.9	14.3	11.5	100.0	
10–24	No.	7248	191	1703	834	9976	(636)
	%	72.7	1.9	17.0	8.4	100.0	
25–49	No.	8390	204	2490	637	11721	(333)
	%	71.6	1.7	21.2	5.4	100.0	
50–99	No.	9782	147	3843	670	14442	(207)
	%	67.7	1.0	26.6	4.6	100.0	
100+	No.	151234	324	39540 *21*	6855	197953	(400)
	%	76.4	0.2	20.0	3.5	100.0	
ALL FIRMS	No.	180815	1044	48389	9846	240094	(3066)
	%	75.3	0.4	20.1	4.1	(100.0)	

Source: Northern England Data base

Table 6.24   Employment structure in single plant manufacturing firms in the Northern region 1971–1981

	All firms in 1971		Failures[1]		Survivors[2]		New firms[3]		All firms in 1981	
	No	%	No	%	No	%	No	%	No	%
No of Firms	446	—	165	—	281	—	649	—	930	—
MALE										
Full Time	12947	73.3	4909	73.1	7249	69.8	5149	67.1	12398	68.6
Part Time	105	0.6	21	0.3	115	1.1	173	2.3	288	1.6
TOTAL	13052	73.9	4930	73.4	7364	70.9	5322	69.4	12686	70.2
FEMALE										
Full Time	3755	21.3	1449	21.6	2402	23.1	1665	21.7	4067	22.5
Part Time	846	4.8	333	5.0	626	6.0	683	8.9	1309	7.2
TOTAL	4601	26.1	1782	26.6	3028	29.1	2348	30.6	5376	29.7
TOTAL EMPLOYMENT	17653	100.0	6712	100.0	10392	100.0	7670	100.0	18062	100.0

[1]Firms in existence in 1971, but not in 1981
[2]Firms in existence in 1971 and 1981
[3]Firms starting in business after 1971 and surviving to 1981
Source: Northern England Data base

6.4.4 Employment and occupations in small firms to 1990 – the OSG study

In 1985 a major employer-based study of trends in employment and occupations throughout the United Kingdom was carried out for the Occupations Study Group (OSG) by the Institute of Manpower Studies (IMS). The report (Rajan and Pearson, 1986) summarises the changes which have taken place over the past five years in employment levels and structures, and their expected trends to 1990. As part of the OSG study, a survey of nearly 300 small independent firms in six different areas of the UK was conducted by the current authors (Johnson and Storey 1987). This survey yielded much valuable information regarding the structure of employment in small firms, its evolution between 1980 and 1985, expected future trends and the key factors which influence employment change in small firms. The results of the survey are summarised in Rajan (1987) and this section considers the changing composition of small firm employment in terms of gender and full/part time status.

(i) *Employment structure in 1985*

Tables 6.25 and 6.26 summarise the employment and occupational structure of the surveyed firms in 1985. The 298 firms employed a total of 1932 workers (an additional 137 workers were indirectly employed), of whom almost 60 per cent were male and 40 per cent female. The majority of males were full-time workers, whereas the females were divided equally between full- and part-time employees. There are significant differences in employment structure between industry groups. The manufacturing and traditional services (construction, transport and motor trade) sectors are dominated by male and full-time employees. In the retail and wholesale industries, over half of the employees are female, and 35 per cent work part time. The professional and personal ' services sector is interesting as it is the sector which experienced the most rapid growth in terms of employment, self-employment and numbers of businesses between 1980 and 1985. Less than 30 per cent of small firm employees in this sector are full-time males (compared with 69 per cent in manufacturing) and one-third of workers are part time females. Indeed females make up almost two-thirds of the workforce in this sector. Table 6.26 illustrates that managerial and professional employees are the largest occupational group within the surveyed small firms. Thirty per cent of workers fall into this category. However, it should be noted that the employment figures include the

Table 6.25   Employment structure by industry group in small independent firms, 1985

	Manu-facturing %	Prof. & personal services[1] %	Traditional services[2] %	Retail & wholesale %	All industries %
MALE					
Full Time	68.6	29.0	87.1	40.6	53.9
Part Time	2.9	6.3	2.0	7.4	4.7
TOTAL	71.5	35.3	89.1	48.0	58.6
FEMALE					
Full Time	16.8	31.4	7.7	24.8	21.3
Part Time	11.8	33.3	3.0	27.2	20.0
TOTAL	28.6	64.7	10.7	52.0	41.3
TOTAL EMPLOYMENT	601	573	335	423	1932
No. of Firms	53	89	50	106	298

[1] Professional Services and Other Services
[2] Construction, road transport and motor trade

Source: IMS/OSG Small Firms Survey (Johnson and Storey, 1987)

owner-manager of the firm who by definition is a 'manager', although he/she is unlikely to be a professional manager by training. Indeed, the flexible nature of many small firms makes it extremely difficult to classify employees into pre-defined occupational categories. At any one time an individual, and particularly the owner-manager, may be performing several functions – management, craft work and sales, for instance. However, the data presented in Table 6.26 gives a broad picture of the occupational structure of small firms. Again, there are significant variations by industry. Small manufacturing firms employ a comparatively large number of craftsmen and operatives, and a small number of managerial and service personnel. In contrast, almost half of the workers in the professional and personal service industries fall into the 'support and personal service' category, with the majority of the remainder being managerial and professional employees.

(ii)   Employment change in surviving firms 1980–85

Of the 298 firms surveyed, 189 had been in existence in 1980, of which 178 provided employment details for that year. Employment change in

Table 6.26 Occupational structure by industry group in small independent firms, 1985

	Manu-facturing %	Prof. & personal services %	Traditional services %	Retail & wholesale %	All industries %
Managerial, prof. technical and administrative	22.7	31.6	32.3	36.3	30.1
Craftsmen	37.1	1.3	41.4	5.5	20.1
Operatives	31.5	11.7	19.4	32.9	24.1
Support & Personal Services	4.6	49.6	4.3	19.7	21.0
Others	4.1	5.7	2.6	5.8	4.7
TOTAL EMPLOYMENT	410	383	232	325	1350
No. of Firms	36	64	42	82	224

See notes to table 6.25
Source: IMS/OSG Small Firms Survey (Johnson and Storey, 1987)

these firms between 1980 and 1985 broken down by gender and full/part time distribution is summarised in Table 6.27. The 178 firms employed a total of 985 workers directly in 1980 (an additional 44 indirect workers were employed, but these are excluded from subsequent analysis); 72 of the firms expanded their employment between 1980 and 1985, creating 236 new jobs; 53 jobs were lost in the 29 firms which reduced their employment level, and employment in the other 77 firms remained unchanged.

The most interesting feature of Table 6.27 is the clear shift which is observed away from full-time male employment towards part-time female employment in the sample of firms. Almost one-third of new jobs created in expanding firms were part-time female, despite this group accounting for only 16 per cent of 1980 employment. In contrast, a disproportionately high number of jobs lost in contracting firms were full-time male positions. Unfortunately, this type of 'survivor' analysis does not allow us to examine the structure of jobs lost in firms which closed between 1980 and 1985, but the figures for contractions suggest that full-time male jobs are likely to have been disproportionately affected by closure.

Table 6.27   Employment change in surviving small firms 1980–1985

| | 1980 Employment | | 1980–1985 Expansions | | 1980–1985 Contractions | | 1985 Employment | |
	No.	%	No.	%	No.	%	No.	%
No. of Firms	178	—	72	—	29	—	178	—
Full-time Male	576	58.5	109	46.2	− 35	66.0	650	55.7
Part-time Male	44	4.5	3	1.3	− 1	1.9	46	3.9
Full-time Female	205	20.8	49	20.8	− 10	18.9	244	20.9
Part-time Female	160	16.2	75	31.8	− 7	13.2	228	19.5
Total Employment	985	100.0	236	100.0	− 53	100.0	1168	100.0

Source: IMS/OSG Small Firms Survey (Johnson and Storey, 1987)

A sectoral breakdown of employment change (not presented here) reveals that this pattern is repeated in the manufacturing, service and retail sectors, with part-time females increasing their share of employment in all industries. The trend is particularly strong in the catering industry.

(iii)   Employment structure in new firms

A total of 108 of the sampled firms were born between 1980 and 1985, with the creation of 493 jobs by 1985; their 1985 employment structure is summarised in Table 6.28. These figure again illustrate a shift towards part-time female employment, apart from in manufacturing industry where full-time males comprised over 80 per cent of jobs in new firms. Over half of the jobs in new service and retail firms were filled by females with around half of these being part-time jobs. The combined effects of changes within existing firms and the employment structure of new firms means that the part-time female share of employment has increased whilst the percentage of jobs filled by full-time males has fallen in small firms.

(iv)   Projected employment to 1990

All 298 respondents were asked to give an indication of the level of employment which they expected to prevail in their firm in 1990, and its full/part time breakdown. The high degree of uncertainty which faces

Table 6.28   Employment structure in new firms

	Manufacturing		Services		Retail and Wholesale		All Industries	
	No.	%	No.	%	No.	%	No.	%
No. of Firms	19	—	48	—	41	—	108	—
Full-time Male	118	81.4	82	38.3	48	35.8	248	50.3
Part-time Male	7	4.8	23	10.7	11	8.2	42	8.5
Full-time Female	13	9.0	55	25.7	35	26.1	103	20.9
Part-time Female	7	4.8	53	24.8	40	29.8	100	20.3
Total Employment	145	100.0	214	100.0	134	100.0	493	100.0

Source: IMS/OSG Small Firms Survey (Johnson and Storey, 1987)

small firms can be gauged by the fact that only 176 respondents felt able to hazard a guess as to their employment level in five years' time. The responses of these firms are summarised in Table 6.29.

Table 6.29   Predicted employment in 1990

	1985 Employment		1990 Employment (predicted)*	
	No.	%	No.	%
Full-time Male	529	51.2	690	53.4
Part-time Male	56	5.4	63	4.9
Full-time Female	209	20.2	272	21.1
Part-time Female	239	23.1	267	20.7
Total Employment	1033	100.0	1291	100.0

* Respondents only supplied a full/part time breakdown. The gender distribution of full and part time jobs has been assumed to be unchanged for the purposes of this projection

Source: IMS/OSG Small Firms Survey (Johnson and Storey, 1987)

Several important points emerge from an analysis of the firms' predictions. Firstly, firms predicted a more rapid employment growth over the 1985–90 period (25 per cent) than had been experienced by firms which had survived through the 1980–85 period (18 per cent).

Secondly, the responding firms predicted that the majority of new jobs (86.5 per cent) would be full time, whereas 38 per cent of new jobs over the 1980–85 period had been part time. Finally, the youngest firms in the sample were both the most uncertain (48 per cent could not predict 1990 employment) and the most optimistic – those which gave a prediction envisaged a 42 per cent increase in employment, compared with around 20 per cent for older firms.

These factors must be taken into account when attempting to predict the overall structure of small firm employment in 1990. It is well known (Ganguly, 1985) that young firms are the most likely to fail within a short period of time; any overall projection must be tempered by this fact. It should also be noted that a considerable number of new firms will come into existence before 1990, and these must be taken into account in projections of employment. Finally, the changing sectoral distribution of employment must be considered.

An overall projection of the level and structure of employment in small firms in the UK has been produced using the detailed figures provided by the survey, together with the data presented by Ganguly (1985) on births, deaths and lifespan of firms by sector. The methods used are described fully in Johnson and Storey (1987).

Two projections are presented in Table 6.30. The first (Projection 1) uses the respondents' own predictions as reported in Table 6.29 as its basis. On the assumption that these predictions are realised, total employment in the UK small firms sector will grow by 1.1 million, or 22

Table 6.30   Projected employment in UK small firms – 1990 (thousands)

	1985 Employment		1990 Employment Projection[1*]		1990 Employment Projection[2***]	
	No.	*%*	*No.*	*%*	*No.*	*%*
Full-time Male	2679.4	53.4	3250.2	53.1	2964.7	52.1
Part-time Male	351.9	7.0	448.4	7.3	452.4	8.0
Full-time Female	1076.2	21.5	1286.8	21.0	1163.5	20.5
Part-time Female	911.0	18.2	1138.6	18.6	1115.2	19.6
Total Employment	5018.3	100.0	6120.7	100.0	5690.0	100.0

* Projection 1: based on respondent's predictions to 1990
** Projection 2: based upon past trends
Source: IMS/OGS Small Firms Survey (Johnson and Storey, 1987)

per cent, with the structure in terms of gender and full/part time remaining essentially unchanged. The discrepancies between *predicted* 1985–90 performance, and *actual* 1980–1985 changes are so great that is seems reasonable to include a second projection (Projection 2) which assumes that past trends will continue. This method of forecasting suggests that there will be a lower (but still significant) rate of job generation in small firms of 670 000 or 13 per cent. Most importantly for present purposes, a continuation of past trends will produce a further shift towards part time female employment in small firms. Forty-five per cent of new jobs will be part time, of which the majority (if past trends continue) will be filled by females. In contrast, only 42 per cent of new jobs will be filled by full-time males, who accounted for 53 per cent of employment in 1985.

A substantial proportion (between 30 and 45 per cent) of the new jobs which are likely to be created in small firms in the future will be part-time jobs, and therefore unlikely to be filled directly by the registered unemployed. As an indication, if we assume that all full-time male jobs and half of the full-time female jobs are filled by the registered unemployed, small firm employment growth will remove 675 600 from the unemployment register over the next five years according to the most optimistic projection, and 328 000 on the basis of Projection 2.

6.4.5 Evidence from the 1980 Workplace Industrial Relations Survey

In 1980, a survey of workplace industrial relations in Britain was carried out by researchers from the Policy Studies Institute (PSI) and Department of Employment (DOE) covering over 2000 workplaces in Britain. (Daniel and Millward, 1983). Although the survey was conducted on the basis of workplaces (i.e. establishments) and covered only establishments with 25 or more employees, the survey report contains some valuable information regarding the relationship between size of unit and variables such as trade union organisation and pay levels.

The survey reveals that small establishments are less likely to recognise manual trade unions than are large ones; 40 per cent of plants with 20–99 employees recognised manual trade unions, compared with 93 per cent of establishments with 1000 or more workers. Table 6.31 shows that this is particularly true for independent establishments as opposed to plants which are part of larger firms. Amongst those establishments which did not recognise manual unions, smaller plants were less likely to have union representatives such as shop stewards or convenors. 69 per cent of plants with more than 1000 manual workers had at least one full-

Table 6.31   Recognition of manual trade unions by size of establishment and independence

	Total	Number of manual workers employed				
		1–24	*25–49*	*50–99*	*100–199*	*200 +*
All establishments	50	25	43	63	78	91
Independent establishments	31	16	24	50	(66)[1]	(67)
Establishments that were part of a group	58	28	55	68	81	92

[1] Figures in parentheses are based on a small sample and should be treated with caution.

Source: Daniel and Millward (1983)

time convenor, whereas the incidence of full-time union officials in small plants (below 100 manual workers) was minimal. Union representatives in small plants took less time off work for union duties and training than their large plant counterparts, and had less access to facilities such as offices, telephones and secretarial assistance.

The extent of the closed shop (where all workers are required to be union members) amongst manual workers is positively related to firm size, as was the incidence of consultative committees and other formal channels for employee involvement in decision making. Industrial relations procedures tend to be less formalised in small plants than in larger establishments. For instance, less than half of establishments with 20–49 employees used formal procedures to deal with pay and conditions disputes as compared with 90 per cent of very large plants (1000 + employees). Industrial action was less prevalent in small plants, even amongst those with a high level of union membership.

Table 6.32 shows that, in line with the findings in the United States, earnings levels are lower in small than in large plants for comparable groups of employees. Earnings in the smallest size group are consistently lower than the average for all establishments, and represent between 75 and 82 per cent of earnings of workers in the 2000 + size category. Further investigation reveals that earnings differences between size groups remain even where allowances are made for other factors such as the proportion of female workers or degree of unionisation. The fact remains that earnings in large firms are up to one-third higher than the earnings of comparable workers in smaller units.

Table 6.32 Level of earnings by employee type and establishment size

Pounds per week	All establishments	Number employed at establishment						
		25–49	50–99	100–199	200–499	500–999	1000–1999	2000 +
Semi-skilled manual workers								
Lower decile	under 50	under 50	under 50	51	54	63	62	67
Mean	74	67	76	75	80	83	85	88
Upper decile	100	91	105	100	109	105	110	122
Skilled manual workers								
Lower decile	59	57	67	66	76	77	84	85
Mean	96	90	97	95	103	104	107	110
Upper decile	125	118	128	124	134	135	138	140
Clerical workers								
Lower decile	51	under 50	52	55	57	57	59	66
Mean	72	69	72	73	75	75	75	84
Upper decile	93	89	95	94	95	92	96	104
Middle management								
Lower decile	89	83	90	90	94	103	105	114
Mean	121	117	121	121	125	132	135	143
Upper decile	160 or more	160 or more	160 or more	160 or more	160 or more	160 or more	160 or more	160 or more

Source: Daniel and Millward (1983)

6.5   EVIDENCE FROM OTHER OECD COUNTRIES

A recent study by the OECD (1985) confirms that the positive association between firm size and average wages suggested by the US and British studies is repeated throughout the OECD countries (Table 6.33). The earnings gap between small and large enterprises is greatest in the United States and least in Denmark. OECD also review the evidence on the provision of fringe benefits by firm size in the United States and Japan (Table 6.34) and conclude that 'in certain important respects, jobs in small firms are not of the same quality as positions in larger enterprises'. Generally, small firm employees are paid lower wages and receive poorer fringe benefits than their large firm counterparts.

The hypothesis that there are significant variations in employment type by firm size is confirmed by analysis of French data produced by Guesnier (1987) and Choeffel *et al.* (1985). These studies suggest that

Table 6.33   Average wages by firm size

		Enterprise/establishment size (number of persons employed)		
		10–99	*100–499*	*500 +*
Belgium[b]	1978	78.1	85.7	100.0
Denmark[c]	1978	93.2	97.3	100.0
France[b]	1978	82.9	86.3	100.0
Germany[c]	1978	89.7	92.2	100.0
Italy[c]	1978	85.4	92.7	100.0
Japan[d]	1982	77.1	82.9[e]	100.0[f]
Luxembourg[c]	1978	74.5	78.7	100.0
United States[g]	1983	57.0[h]	73.8	100.0

[a] For Denmark, Germany, Italy and Luxembourg, the data are by *establishment* size, while for Belgium, France, Japan and the United States, they are by *enterprise* size.
[b] Hourly pay for manual workers in manufacturing.
[c] Hourly pay for male manual workers in manufacturing.
[d] Monthly scheduled earnings for regular employees in the private sector (excluding agriculture).
[e] 100–999.
[f] 1000 –.
[g] Usual weekly earnings for wage and salary earners in the private sector (excluding agriculture)
[h] 1–99.
Source: OECD (1985).

Table 6.34 Firm size and job quality in the United States and Japan

		Enterprise size (number of persons employed)				
United States		1–24	25–99	100–499	500–999	1000 +
Health insurance coverage (%)	1983	35.4	64.9	75.1	79.1	86.3
Pension or retirement plan coverage (%)	1983	17.3	40.7	63.9	74.3	87.9
Average years of tenure with current employer (years)	1983	4.5	5.2	6.0	6.8	9.0
Part-time employment [proportion of employment in each size group (%)]	1983	31.8	16.6	15.8	14.1	12.2

		1–29	30–99	100–299	300–999	1000–4999	5000 +
Japan							
Average cost per regular employee of obligatory welfare services[a](%)	1982	—	70.5	71.8	81.2	92.6	100.0
Average cost per regular employee of non-obligatory welfare services[b](%)	1982	—	28.7	30.4	41.6	60.5	100.0
Retirement allowance at mandatory retirement (%)	1982	—	22.1	[—— 46.7 ——]		[—— 100.0 ——]	
Average years of tenure with current employers (years)	1982	[—— 7.9[c] ——]		[—— 9.1 ——]		[—— 12.2 ——]	
Part-time employment [proportion of employment in each size group (%)]	1983	15.1	8.8	7.5[d]	7.4[e]	[—— 8.4 ——]	

[a] Employer payments for pension scheme, health insurance etc.
[b] Company housing, canteens, recreational facilities, etc.
[c] 10–99. [d] 100–499. [e] 500–999.

Source: OECD (1985)

earnings are higher in large as opposed to small enterprises, although this gap has narrowed between 1968 and 1976. Small firms in France employ a relatively high proportion of part-time employees, but the difference between small and large firms in this respect has also narrowed over recent years. The occupational structure of the work-force also varies with firm size; large firms employ a relatively high proportion of unskilled manual workers, whereas small firms tend to employ white-collar and service staff (skilled and unskilled). White-collar and service staff comprised 52 per cent of employment in firms with 10–49 employees in 1983, compared with 35 per cent in the 500 + size category. Amongst manual workers, the unskilled represented 41 per cent of the total in the largest size group and 33 per cent in the 10–49 category. Finally, the investigations of Choeffel *et al.* (1985) have revealed that jobs in smaller enterprises are less permanent than those within large enterprises. An analysis of employee turnover between 1976 and 1980 reveals that small firms have much higher turnover rates than do large firms. Only 20 per cent of workers employed in firms with less than 5 employees at the end of 1980 had held the same job since 1976. The comparable figure for firms with over 2000 employees is 46 per cent. These findings suggest the existence of a dual labour market in France, with the large firm sector providing relatively secure, well paid jobs, and small firms providing short term, insecure and poorly paid employment.

A study of employment characteristics by firm size in the Netherlands by Van Ginnekin (1985) also suggests that small firms have higher rates of turnover and a shorter duration of employment than large firms. Small firms employ a relatively low proportion of unskilled labour and tend to carry out less on-the-job training than large firms. Small and medium firms employ a greater proportion of women (29 per cent) than do large firms (26 per cent). 37 per cent of employees in firms with less than 10 employees are female. Most of the gender differences in employment are explained by sectoral variations in the size distribution of firms (i.e. more small firms in retailing and personal services), however small manufacturing firms have twice the share of female employment (26 per cent) when compared to large firms (13 per cent). Small firms employ a disproportionate number of young people and students, but a study of employment changes between 1980 and 1981 reveals that large firms took on more school leavers than small and medium enterprises. Finally, small firms employ a relatively high proportion of part-time workers, but this is entirely explained by the fact that small firms are over-represented in the retail and restaurant sectors, which employ a high proportion of part-time staff (De Jong 1987).

Finally, a study of the Federal Republic of Germany by Weiner (1983) shows that small manufacturing firms employ a higher proportion of skilled workers than do larger manufacturing enterprises. Annual gross remuneration increases with firm size for all sub-categories of employment type of gender and status. A separate study by Buchtemann and Schupp (1986) shows that, in line with other studies described in this chapter, female and part-time employees are concentrated in smaller firms.

6.6 CONCLUSION

There are relatively few studies available which systematically analyse the characteristics of existing employment by firm size. There are even fewer which examine the types of jobs *created* by small and large firms. However, those studies which do exist are surprisingly consistent in their findings across different countries, regions, sectors and time periods. Small firm employment is *not* equivalent to large firm employment in terms of skills required, hours worked, gender composition, remuneration and other measures of job quality. The causal factors underlying these findings are, however, unclear. The evidence presented in this chapter has implicitly assumed that *demand* factors are predominant. It is recognised that there may be important labour *supply* factors which influence the structure of employment in small firms, in that there may be certain groups within the labour market – professionals in the service sector or married women, for example – who wish to work in small firms. Furthermore, many of the characteristics of the labour force of small firms are inter-related, such as low pay, low levels of unionisation and a predominantly part-time and female workforce. What is less clear is the extent to which, for example, part-time females receive lower rates of pay in small firms than in 'comparable' large firms. Notwithstanding these comments, the finding that small firm jobs differ substantially from large firm jobs has important implications for policy in two key respects.

Firstly, governments may wish to specifically take into account the quality of the jobs which are being created as a result of policy. It may be desirable to compare, for instance, the social benefits of the creation of large numbers of unstable, part time and low paid jobs with the creation of a smaller number of secure, full-time and well-paid jobs.

Secondly, as the reduction of registered unemployment is often an explicit policy objective, the extent to which the jobs created by new and small firms 'filter through' to the unemployed must be an important consideration. The evidence presented in this chapter suggests that a policy which creates jobs primarily in the new and small firm sector is likely to result in a lower reduction of registered unemployment than one which creates the same number of jobs in larger enterprises, regardless of displacement effects.

7 Public Policy Towards Small Firms

7.1 INTRODUCTION

In this chapter we assess the implications of our analysis for public policy, with particular reference to small firms. We begin in Section 7.2 by examining whether or not there should be public policies to promote the small business sector. We conclude that whether or not such policies can be justified, since they in fact exist in almost every developed country, it is appropriate to evaluate their effectiveness and suggest improvements.

The key point of this book is that whilst small firms have become relatively more important in most developed countries since the mid-1970s, this has occurred for very different reasons – characterised by the Birmingham, Boston and Bologna models. Only through a clear understanding of the mechanisms of small firm development can appropriate policies be devised. The policy implications for an economy which closely approximates to the Birmingham model are very different from those which are appropriate for one which is closer to the Boston or to the Bologna models. For present purposes we shall concentrate upon policies which might be appropriate in the case of the Birmingham model.

In order to assess the effectiveness of policy it is necessary to be clear about objectives, so that even if the criteria for success or failure are not necessarily measurable they must be capable of identification. These are set out in Section 7.3 and hence Section 7.4 presents a collection of 'typical' policy measures which are currently in existence in many developed countries – particularly in parts of those countries exhibiting the characteristics of the Birmingham model.

Section 7.5 then presents a series of criticisms of the typical battery of SME policies, many of which are related to the fact that they are not addressing themselves towards an understanding of the problems of creating new firms and facilitating small firm growth in the Birmingham model.

Given the objectives specified in Section 7.3, and the criticisms levelled in Section 7.5, the remainder of the chapter is devoted to a preferred policy strategy which, at its most simple, may be called 'selectivity'. An assessment of the merits of a selective policy are discussed in Section 7.6

and in Section 7.7 each of the most frequent criticisms are addressed in turn. Section 7.8 then takes a practical example of the operations of a selective policy.

7.2 JUSTIFICATIONS FOR SMALL FIRM POLICIES

During the 1960s, and for much of the 1970s, most countries had no policies for the growth and development of small firms. Small firms were seen as a symbol of backwardness and inefficiency rather than of wealth creation and technical change. In the last few years, however, this has changed completely and most countries have now developed policies to promote the development of the small firm sector. Nevertheless it is still appropriate to ask whether there is a need for such policies.

It is one of the quirks of the small firm sector that the two groups which are most strongly opposed to small firm policies are the two extremes of the political spectrum. Those involved in the liberal traditions of economics oppose State involvement on ideological grounds. They argue that the small firm embodies the characteristics of firms in perfect competition which is a necessary, but not sufficient condition, for Pareto optimality in an economy. For some (see Rowley and Peacock, 1975) even the presence of clear market failure is *not* sufficient to justify the involvement of the state. For such groups the state itself, through its intervention, can induce inefficiencies, and so it is necessary to demonstrate in advance that such intervention leads to an overall improvement in welfare. Such liberals would generally oppose state policies to promote and develop small businesses on the grounds that small firms are an expression of spontaneity and creativity in the economy and that state involvement is likely to dampen these character-istics. Small firms, perhaps above all other groups of firms, should be 'allowed' to develop without state involvement.

At the opposite end of the political spectrum others would argue that a state policy to promote small businesses should be rejected since the sector itself is unworthy of state support. The small businessman is the embodiment of capitalism to which the Left is opposed (Rainnie, 1985). The small businessman rarely employs unionised labour, often provides low rates of pay and poor working conditions. For these reasons the small businessman is seen to be the enemy of the Left and hence not worthy of support.

Whilst these reasons are given for not offering support to the small business sector, there are two main arguments which favour the existence of a public small-business policy. The first is that small business is at a comparative disadvantage to large business. Without state assistance to offset this disadvantage, the sector would either decline or grow less rapidly, with attendant losses to the consumer and society in general. Bannock (1981) presents this argument clearly when he says that small firms are discriminated against by finance houses since they have to pay higher interest rates than large firms because they borrow smaller sums of money. Similarly small firms can be disproportionately affected by having only a very small managerial staff (normally the owner) and yet in some instances have to comply with the same government legislation and bureaucratic demands as a large firm. Bannock (1986), for example, argues that normalised compliance costs with Value Added Tax (VAT) are forty times higher for very small firms than for the largest size of firm. Hence it is necessary to ensure that, at a minimum, public policies do not discriminate against small firms.

Bannock, however, does not advocate a policy of positive discrimination in favour of small firms. Instead he believes that the role of government is to ensure that the small firm is able to compete with other small firms and with larger firms on the basis of equality. This is a somewhat different perspective from that adopted both by many national governments in Europe and also by the European Economic Community Task Force on Small and Medium Sized Enterprises, established in 1986. Their starting point is that much of Europe is currently experiencing high rates of unemployment. Furthermore, in comparison with the United States, European rates of new job creation are low, with most new jobs in the US being created by smaller firms. Hence it is essential for Europe to have a policy which stimulates the growth of small firms as a way of reducing unemployment. We have noted throughout this volume the limitations of this perspective, but the fact remains that most European countries have a collection of policies designed to promote the small business sector, as a way of reducing unemployment. These arguments are much more influential in justifying public small firm policies than the desirability of small firms per se, or that small firms prevent market inefficiencies through reducing industrial concentration. Currently even the 'infant industry argument' is of secondary importance compared with the expectation that small firm policies will lead to job creation.

The remainder of this chapter therefore takes an agnostic stance to the question of whether or not it is appropriate to have a small-business policy. Instead it will adopt the pragmatic view, that since such policies exist, it is appropriate to comment upon and assess them with a view to making recommendations on new directions and developments.

7.3   THE OBJECTIVES OF SMALL FIRM POLICIES

In an ideal world it would be possible, using a general equilibrium model to estimate the impact of small firm policies upon major economic aggregates such as investment, output, income and employment. To our knowledge, however, no models exist which would undertake such sophisticated simulations and so assessments are only in partial equilibrium terms.

Even so, there appears to be a reluctance on the part of governments to specify the objectives of small firm policies in a way which facilitates quantification and assessment. In most cases reference is made to creating a climate in which small firms can develop and in most cases reference is made not simply to employment creation but also to other objectives. For example the small firm sector is thought to be more flexible and responsive to change than the large firm sector and so, where it is perceived that flexibility is a desirable objective in itself, this is used to justify support for small firms. Secondly the small firm sector frequently acts as a major supplier to larger firms and so, by becoming more efficient, this may also enable the large firm to become more competitive. Thirdly the small firm is thought to be an important vehicle for the introduction of technical change, so that support for small firms can lead to faster rates of invention and innovation within the economy as a whole.

The main focus of policy towards small firms, however, continues to be on the creation of employment, even though the relationship between the provision of public assistance and job creation within the small firm is rarely made explicit. Perhaps the nearest to an explanation of such a mechanism is provided by the UK Government in its paper *Burdens on Business* (HMSO, 1985). It suggests that policy changes in the form of assistance to small firms will lead to increased employment in the following way:

> reductions in compliance costs would be likely to feed through into profits and prices; the end result being a higher level of employment in the whole economy.

Given this widespread reluctance of governments to specify the objectives of policies we propose to identify objectives and assess individual policy instruments according to these objectives. In our view there could be seven employment-related objectives for small firm policies:

- Direct job creation
- Secondary job creation

- Well paid jobs
- Low displacement
- Low deadweight
- Interesting jobs with career prospects
- Employment for disadvantaged workers – unemployed, disabled, unskilled, ethnic minorities, etc.

Direct job creation By this measure we estimate the total number of new jobs created *within the small firm* as a result of its being in receipt of policy assistance. Whilst this is relatively easy to identify in theory there are major practical problems in such analysis since it requires an estimate of how the firm would have changed in the absence of policy (Wren, 1987).

Indirect job creation The provision of policy assistance to a small firm may have consequences beyond the small firm itself. For example it may enable the small firm to provide a better (cheaper) product to a large firm customer, so enabling the latter to compete more effectively in international markets. Alternatively the small firm itself may not take on additional workers but it could lead to additional wealth being created and spent in the local community so leading to additional jobs in the service sector.

Well paid jobs One major effect of policies to promote small firms could be that they lead to no more workers being employed but rather to existing workers having higher wages, which again could lead to additional local spending and perhaps additional employment.

Low displacement Most small firms sell the majority of their product locally. For example 70 per cent of the sales of new firms are to customers in their own county (Storey, 1982), and most small firms are found in sectors where local demand is fixed or semi-fixed, e.g. retailing, repair activities etc. Hence new firms entering these sectors are likely to lead to others being put out of business or 'displaced'. Where displacement takes place as a result of a new, different and/or cheaper product being made available there may be benefits to the customer. Where, however, the new firm is merely able to under-cut existing firms simply by being in receipt of policy assistance then the benefits of the policy to the wider community are less clear.

Low deadweight In any economy firms are established and close on a regular basis. This turnover of firms is the result of new demands arising from consumers and supply changes from producers. For this reason it is difficult to estimate the extent to which a firm is established or grows *as a result of being in receipt of assistance*. Nevertheless an estimate of this is essential since public money may merely be used to encourage an individual or business to take actions which it would have taken without the subsidy. In that case there would be strong pressures for the subsidy to be put to an alternative use.

Interesting jobs with career prospects   As we noted in Chapter 6 it is legitimate for policy makers to consider not only the number of jobs created but also their quality. This is a complex matter since some may view the quality of a job in terms of criteria such as job satisfaction expressed by the workforce, the presence of team-spirit and a sense of belonging. Others, however, might view job quality in terms of wage rates, facilities provided at the workplace, security, etc. Whatever measure(s) are used, it is necessary to recognise that the quality of jobs is an important criterion for assessment.

Employment opportunities for the disadvantaged   A final factor might be whether the jobs created are particularly appropriate for disadvantaged groups in society. For example we have emphasised that many of the jobs created in small firms are not necessarily those most likely to be filled by the unemployed since the jobs being created are either part-time jobs or skilled, whereas the unemployed have an above-average number of unskilled males seeking full time employment.

7.4   SMALL FIRM POLICIES IN PRACTICE

A detailed description of the full range of policies which have been implemented in developed countries to encourage employment creation in Small and Medium Sized Enterprises (SMEs) comprises a full book in itself. A review of policies in the EEC is provided in Storey and Johnson (1987a) which shows that almost every country has introduced a large variety of measures which differ in scope and detail. In addition to national policies, local and regional authorities have been active in the promotion of SMEs, whilst private and voluntary sector initiatives are also found in several countries. Here we provide only a brief overview of the type of policies which have been introduced, together with some specific country examples. The various small firms policies will be discussed under the following headings:

(i) Financial assistance for business start-ups;
(ii) Financial assistance for investment and expansion;
(iii) Advice, consultancy and training;
(iv) Support for innovation and technology transfer;
(v) Assistance with premises;
(vi) Locally-based initiatives;
(vii) Private sector and voluntary initiatives.

(i) *Support for business start-ups*

The promotion of new firm formation and self-employment, particularly amongst the unemployed population, is now a significant element within the employment policies of many European countries. Various financial support schemes have been devised to encourage this process. In both the UK and Ireland, an Enterprise Allowance Scheme is in operation, whereby unemployed people wishing to start their own businesses receive a fixed allowance over a period of one year. A similar scheme operates in France, with the unemployed having the additional option of capitalising future benefits in order to provide sufficient capital to start a business. In other countries, such as the Federal Republic of Germany, the Netherlands and Belgium, soft loans are available to suitable people wishing to start a business. A scheme operates in Germany whereby savings which are made by people with a view to business start-up are subsidised from central government funds.

(ii) *Financial assistance for investment and expansion*

Many countries offer some form of grant or subsidy towards capital investment, often under the auspices of regional development policy. Examples of this approach include the Small Industry Programme of the Irish Industrial Development Authority, the 'Sabatini Law' in Italy and Law 1262/82 in Greece. In addition, various credit guarantee schemes aimed at small businesses are found in several countries. In the UK the Loan Guarantee Scheme provides a guarantee of 70 per cent of funds lent by banks to small businesses. A similar Credit Guarantee Scheme operates in the Netherlands. Equity investment in small businesses is encouraged through schemes operated in the UK and FRG. Finally, the Belgian authorities operate various schemes designed to encourage small firms to take on extra staff in specified groups such as the disabled or young unemployed. Employment and wage subsidies also operate at a regional and local level in some countries.

(iii) *Advice, consultancy and training*

Advice, consultancy and training support for small firms is also found in many countries. Two categories of support can be distinguished – direct provision of free advice (UK Small Firm Centres, local EOMMEX in Greece and regional advice centres in the Netherlands) and the subsidisation of consultancy and training obtained from independent bodies by small businesses. The latter approach appears to be favoured in Germany and Denmark, where small firms are refunded a proportion of the costs involved. The UK government is also involved in supporting various small business training schemes such as 'Skills into Business' and the Graduate Enterprise Programme.

(iv) *Support for innovation*

This type of support appears to be attracting growing attention. Grants to support the development of new products and processes are available in the UK, Italy, Netherlands, Belgium, Greece and Denmark. Several countries are experimenting with the introduction of Science Parks (UK, France, Netherlands, Italy) or Innovation Centres (Ireland) in order to facilitate the transfer of technology between universities and research institutes and SMEs. The Federal Republic of Germany is moving away from the direct provision of Research and Development support (thought to benefit large firms) towards indirect support through grants and loans which will be beneficial to SMEs. The German Federal government also operates a scheme whereby the costs to SMEs of recruiting R & D personnel are partly offset.

(v) *Assistance with premises*

This aspect of small firms policy is mainly implemented by national government but on a local level. For example the UK government supports English Estates, which is responsible for ensuring an adequate supply of premises, particularly in depressed areas, and the Danish government subsidises the building of Community Industrial Houses which provide small starter premises with central office facilities.

(vi) *Locally-based initiatives*

In addition to the national schemes outlined above, local and regional authorities have become increasingly involved in attempting to create jobs in the local economy. Their approach has been almost exclusively aimed at small and medium sized firms, which are seen as sources of new jobs likely to remain in the local area, rather than move elsewhere. The provision of suitable premises has been an important aspect of local intervention, but local authorities also provide grants and subsidies over and above those available through national schemes. Hence many UK local authorities provide wage subsidies to employers taking on local unemployed workers. Local advice and support centres are now common in many countries, and many local authorities are keen to support co-operatives and community business ventures and businesses started by members of the ethnic minorities. Finally, an increasing number of local authorities, particularly in the UK, are investing directly in local firms with a view to encouraging expansion and job creation in the local area.

(vii) *Private sector and voluntary initiatives*

Large companies have become involved in support for small businesses in various ways. In industries undergoing substantial job losses in depressed areas of the UK (Iron and Steel, Coal Mining) the firms have set up their own companies designed to help create jobs for redundant workers through grants, subsidies, advice and retraining. Similar ventures have been attempted in Italy through IRI, the government holding company as well as 'private' initiatives undertaken by Montedison or Olivetti. In the Netherlands, the Philips company has set up a small business centre in The Hague in association with Job Creation Limited, a private sector company.

Private companies have been involved in providing support for various initiatives in the UK which go under the umbrella title of 'Enterprise Agencies'. These are organisations supported by private, voluntary and public sector sources, which provide advice and training to people wishing to set up businesses, or businesses wishing to expand. Enterprise Agencies have undergone an enormous growth over the past five years in the UK, and similar movements exist in France and the Netherlands.

7.5 SOME CRITICISMS OF SMALL FIRM POLICIES

Whilst in no single country or locality are the policies to promote the small firm sector identical, the broad thrust is similar. In the majority of countries and localities the objective of policy is either to encourage more individuals to start a business or to reduce the cost of operations of that business below those which existed prior to the policy initiative. The reduction in cost is clear where a direct financial subsidy is paid, but the effect is the same in the case of provision of free or subsidised information. Here, since uncertainty is costly and firms are willing to pay to reduce business uncertainty, information can be treated in the same way as any other imput to the production process. A lowering of the price of the input, *ceteris paribus*, will lead to higher trading profits.

Several criticisms can be levelled against current policies, and policy directions:

(a) Policies may have conflicting objectives.
(b) Policies do not seem based upon a clear understanding of the mechanism of job creation within smaller firms.
(c) SME policies administered nationally are regionally divisive.
(d) SME policies do not tackle the central problem of a lack of international competitiveness.
(e) Assistance to SME's is insufficiently targetted or focused upon those small firms which might benefit from assistance.

(a) *Policies may have conflicting objectives*

In its review of policy instruments to facilitate the creation of small and medium sized companies *Empirica* (1986) notes that policies may have three different objectives.

– Improvement in business climate.
– Profitability.
– Reducing the shortage of entrepreneurs.

In this context *Empirica* define a good business climate to be one in which the entrepreneur has a high social stake, where bureaucratic regulations do not unduly hinder entrepreneurs, and where tax systems and regulations favour the entrepreneur. *Empirica* define profitability in conventional economic terms and treat high profits as an index of the factors which attract or 'pull' entrepreneurs into business. However they also note that there can be a 'shortage' of entrepreneurs because of the limitations of education, on-the-job training, cultural traditions etc.

Policies to promote the growth of new and small businesses may have a much greater impact upon some objectives than upon others. Empirica illustrate this with a table reproduced here as Table 7.1. Reading down the columns it shows that, in their view, the main impact of policy is upon the profitability criteria where a total of eleven X's were obtained, compared with ten for the shortage of entrepreneurs objective and nine

Table 7.1   Types of strategies or fundamental assumptions of policy strategies

	Objectives		
Type of instrument	*Business climate*	*Profit-ability*	*Shortage of entrepreneurs*

1. Deregulation
   to create wage flexibility
   to create flexibility of
   work contracts
   to create favourable tax
   systems
   to simplify the institutional
   framework
	X	X	X

2. Demand management
   to secure a general economic
   equilibrium			

3. Cost reduction by
   low interest loans
   low cost premises
   tax exemption
   other types of subsidies
	X	XXX	X

4. Risk reduction	XX	XX	XX

5. Services in kind to decrease costs of
   starting a new business, to decrease
   time efforts within the process of new
   business starts, to improve
   information and knowledge and
   institutional framework
	XX	X	XX

6. Education and training	XX	X	XXX

X = weak influence
XX = strong influence
XXX = very strong influence
Source: *Empirica* (1986)

for the Business Climate objective. Secondly Table 7.1 also illustrates that, reading across the rows, the different types of policy instruments have a different impact on each objective. For example Education and Training has a very strong impact upon the 'shortage of entrepreneurs' objective, a strong impact upon 'business climate' and a weak influence on 'profitability'. On the other hand some policies have a uniformly weak impact on all three objectives (e.g. Deregulation) whilst others such as Risk reduction (through information provision) appear to affect all three criteria rather more strongly.

   The views presented in Table 7.1 are the well-informed but nevertheless subjective opinions of the *Empirica* authors. Their views are influenced by the nature of small business problems faced in different countries and different Regions in Europe. For example in Table 7.1 education and training are shown to have a relatively weak impact upon the profitability objective and yet, according to the Boston model, education is central to small firm economic development in that city. In a country where the education system is weak or where there is a shortage of key skills education is likely to be a major factor affecting profitability. On the other hand in the German system where an individual can be almost 30 years of age by the time he or she has fully qualified and is able to start a business, there may be some advantage to be gained by reducing formal education and training.

In short, the impact of policies upon objectives may vary considerably from one economy to another. An optimal mix of policies appropriate for local circumstances has to be found.

(b)   The mechanism of job creation

We have noted that the thrust of much government policy towards small business is to reduce the costs faced by small firms with a view to this leading to increased profits, lower prices and ultimately to increased employment.

The precise mechanisms by which such changes occur are, however, not specified but it is our interpretation that the reduction in costs will result in an increase in trading profits (gross profit margins). Depending on the nature of the market in which the firm operates, some or all of this increased profitability may disappear depending upon whether or not new firms decide to enter this market. The new employment created could be either in, as yet, not established firms, or it could be in existing firms choosing to expand their output and employment. It is therefore of considerable importance to be able to gauge the response of existing small firms to an increase in trading profit, although it is recognised that this is only of the two sources of new employment which could flow from government small firm policies.

To examine the relationship between profitability and employment we now briefly report the results of a study of 636 single plant independent manufacturing companies in Northern England, the full study results being available in Storey, Keasey, Watson and Wynarczyk (1987).

The study takes employment change in small companies between 1974 and 1978 and between 1978 and 1981, and examines whether, amongst those companies that increased their employment, there is evidence of this being related to changes in either trading profit or retained profit. The study notes that age of company, which is also closely correlated with size, can also be of importance so it is also explicitly included as a variable in the regression model. Some results are shown in Table 7.2.

Table 7.2   Employment change and profitability

1974–78				
$\Delta E =$	0.377	$- 0.005A$	$+ 0.516 \Delta RP$	$R^2 = 0.152$ $N = 96$
	(8.794)	(2.894)**	(2.661)**	
$\Delta E =$	0.349	$- 0.0006A$	$+ 0.142 \Delta TP$	$R^2 = 0.087$ $N = 96$
	(7.009)	(0.242)	(2.067)*	
1978–81				
$\Delta E =$	0.291	$- 0.004A$	$+ 0.711 \Delta RP$	$R^2 = 0.092$ $N = 78$
	(9.328)	(1.712)	(2.611)**	
$\Delta E =$	0.350	$- 0.003A$	$+ 0.702 \Delta TP$	$R^2 = 0.074$ $N = 78$
	(6.861)	(1.653)	(1.788)	

ΔE = Change in employment
ΔTP = Change in trading profit
ΔRP = Change in retained profit
A = Age of company (in years)
't' values in parenthesis
* denotes significant at 5% level
** denotes significant at 1% level.

These results show that whilst changes in the level of trading profit are significantly positively related to increased employment, the relationship is weaker than that between changes in retained profit and increased employment. Further evidence is also provided in Storey *et al.* (1987) in a study of the characteristics of fast growth (in terms of employment) young companies. It shows that there is little difference in the rate of gross trading profits obtained by fast growth and non-fast growth companies. The *real* difference occurs between levels of retained profits, where fast growth companies have much higher levels of retentions than non-fast growth companies. In essence it shows that the non-fast growers, which constitute the vast bulk of small businesses, responded to an increase in trading profits by increasing Directors' Fees and reducing both Directors' loans and external borrowing. On the other hand the fast growers used this additional profitability to finance further growth in assets and employment.

These results suggest that whilst policies designed to reduce the costs to small businesses are likely to increase trading profits in the assisted companies, it is far from clear how this will 'feed through' into increased employment. If government wishes to more directly affect the level of employment within existing small business, policies should impact upon retained rather than trading profit, which may mean providing fiscal incentives to retain resources within the business.

(c) SME policies administered nationally are regionally divisive:

In 1980 one of the current authors wrote:

> Unfortunately policies to assist small firms are not, at present regionally differentiated . . . Until incentives are greater in the Assisted Areas small firms policy risks being Regionally divisive in the sense that the responsiveness, or take up, will be greater in the South than in the North i.e. in areas which 'need' the employment least.   (Storey, 1980b).

To demonstrate that real variations in entrepreneurship existed within UK Regions, Storey (1982) produced an index of Regional entrepreneurship based upon the factors identified in Table 7.3. The index is derived by ranking the UK standard regions according to their performance in each measure of the table, and the composite index is derived from an unweighted summation of scores for each measure. If the hypothesis of regional divisiveness of small firms policy is correct

Table 7.3   Factors associated with high levels of entrepreneurship

Factors	High entrepreneurship	Index
1. Size of 'incubator' firm	Small Firms	% of small firms in the region
2. Occupational experience	Managerial Experience	% of population in managerial groupings
3. Education	High levels	% of population with degrees
4. Access to capital	Easy access	Savings per head of population House owning population House price values
5. Entry into markets	Low entry barriers	% of population in low entry barrier industries
6. Markets	Wealthy local markets	Regional income distribution

Source: Storey (1982)

then it would be expected that policies to create employment in small firms would have a larger impact (take-up) in the high entrepreneurship regions (as defined by the index) and least impact in the low entrepreneurship regions.

In the UK the four major financial initiatives have been the Loan Guarantee Scheme (LGS), the Business Expansion Scheme (BES), Small Engineering Firms Investment Scheme (SEFIS) and the Enterprise Allowance Scheme (EAS). Regional take-up of these schemes is reported by Mason and Harrison (1986). Table 7.4 presents those data in the form of Location Quotients which indicate the extent to which a region is obtaining its 'fair share' of each particular policy. A location quotient exceeding unity implies that a region is benefiting disproportionately from the policy in question; vice versa for a location quotient of less than one. Table 7.4 also presents the numerical results of the Regional Entrepreneurship index.

When the location quotients for the four schemes are combined to form a composite 'Take-up Index', the Entrepreneurship index proves a good predictor of the regional take-up of policy. Four take-up indices are calculated as the simple means of the location quotients for the four policy instruments. TU1 and TU2 are based on the *numbers* of guarantees issued or firms/individuals participating, whereas TU3 and TU4 are based upon the *value* of the assistance offered under each scheme.

Table 7.5 shows that all four take-up indices are positively correlated with the Entrepreneurship Index, with a significance level of 1 per cent or better (apart from the Spearman Correlation Coefficient with TU4 which is significant only at the 5 per cent level). Full results of this analysis are presented in Storey and Johnson (1987b).

These results suggest that whilst there are local or regional factors influencing the take-up rates of individual schemes designed to assist small firms, the overwhelming regional impact is entirely as predicted prior to their introduction, with the existing prosperous areas being the prime beneficiaries of policy.

(d) *SME policies and competitiveness*

The key element which distinguishes small firms in the Boston/Bologna models from those in the Birmingham model is the greater international competitiveness of the former group. In the Birmingham model the growth in small firms essentially occurs because of the poor international competitiveness of *large* firms. Furthermore the new and small firms being formed will not reverse the downward trend of that

Table 7.4 Regional index of entrepreneurship and location quotients for four small firms policy instruments

Region	Entrepreneurship Index	Loan Guarantee Scheme (LGS) (1) 1981–1984		(2) 1984–1985		Business Expansion Scheme (BES)		Enterprise Allowance Scheme (EAS) Participation Rate	Small Engineering Firms Investment Scheme (SEFIS)	
		No. of Guarantees	Value of Loans	No. of Guarantees	Value of Loans	No. of Companies	Amount of finance		No. of Firms	Value of Finance
	ENT	LGS1N	LGS1V	LGS2N	LGS2V	BESN	BESV	EAS	SEFISN	SEFISV
South East/East Anglia	8.05	1.04	1.14	1.06	1.18	1.30	1.69	1.05	1.13	1.02
South West	7.54	0.95	0.91	1.11	0.91	1.05	0.65	1.22	1.82	1.88
West Midlands	5.18	1.00	0.97	0.90	0.88	0.97	0.93	1.13	0.90	0.97
East Midlands	6.09	0.93	0.95	0.83	0.77	1.24	0.74	1.13	0.97	0.98
Yorkshire and Humberside	4.64	1.02	0.88	0.85	0.73	0.72	0.71	0.97	0.78	0.84
North West	6.64	1.36	1.28	1.04	0.98	0.72	0.49	1.38	0.73	0.82
North	3.45	1.06	0.96	0.99	1.16	0.37	0.07	0.72	0.97	1.10
Wales	3.70	0.85	0.78	0.61	0.57	0.70	0.94	1.12	0.68	0.68
Scotland	5.11	0.95	0.83	1.51	1.39	1.17	0.67	0.75	0.83	0.89
Northern Ireland	4.44	0.32	0.38	0.70	0.76	0.12	0.06	0.92	2.11	2.22

Note: The Location Quotients are calculated as follows:

LGS1N, LGS1V, LGS2N, LGS2V, BESN, BESV : LQ = Regional share of number of loans/companies/value

SEFISN, SEFISV : = Regional share of firms receiving SEFIS grant/amount of grant
Regional share of UK stock of VAT registered businesses
Regional share of manufacturing units with less than 100 employees in Division 3 of the 1980 S.I.C.

EAS : LQ = Participation rate per 1000 unemployed in November 1984
U.K. average participation rate per 1000 unemployed in November 1984

Sources: Storey (1982); Mason and Harrison (1986)

Table 7.5   Correlation coefficients with entrepreneurship index

	Pearson correlation coefficient	Spearman rank correlation coefficient
TU1	0.94**	0.98**
TU2	0.86**	0.87**
TU3	0.89**	0.85**
TU4	0.85**	0.70*

* Significant at 5% level   ]
** Significant at 1% level   ] one tail test.
Source: Storey and Johnson (1987b)

economy. Few, if any, of these firms export their output directly and most are directly competing for business with other small firms in the locality. For these reasons the displacement rates of policies to stimulate the establishment of new businesses are likely to be high.

Given that a lack of international competitiveness is identified as central to the differing performance of Boston, Bologna and Birmingham it seems a clear direction of policy in Birmingham to enhance the competitiveness of all its firms. The objective of public policy should be to stimulate the development and growth of internationally competitive firms. Such policies could take the form of promoting research and development, provision of better information on exporting, encouraging entrepreneurs to attend trade fairs overseas, promoting improvements in design, encouraging technical links with institutions of higher education etc.

In our view, however, whilst these initiatives are worthwhile, very few small firms will take advantage of them and, as a result, alter their behaviour. For example surveys of a random sample of small firms in all sectors in the United Kingdom indicated that 94 per cent did not export any of their output and only 4 per cent exported more than 10 per cent of their output (Johnson and Storey 1987a). Nevertheless it is also clear that the small firms which are selling internationally are those which are both more likely to experience growth themselves and less likely to displace existing local firms. For example in a study of high technology firms, Storey, Wynarczyk and Johnson (1986) found that 40 per cent of this group exported more than 10 per cent of their output compared with only 4 per cent of small firms in the random sample above. On the other hand the high technology firms were expecting increases in employment at approximately four times the rates expected by the random sample.

Hence it seems clear that export performance is related to employment and wealth creation. Firms which are exporting successfully are more likely to be displacing overseas competition than other local firms. They are likely to stimulate other local suppliers and create wealth which is spent in the local community, so generating a more active consumer service economy. It has to be emphasised that whilst the business which exports is not necessarily in the manufacturing sector – although most are – it is essential to recognise the role of international competitiveness in explaining both why economies suffer from the Birmingham problem, and how the problem may be overcome. Clearly it is not likely to be rectified by encouragement to individuals to start businesses in highly competitive sectors which exhibit high rates of local displacement. Such a strategy does nothing to overcome the problems of lack of competitiveness which are at the core of the Birmingham model.

(e)   *Lack of targeting of assistance to small firms*

The most important characteristic of new and small businesses is their high rate of failure. For example Ganguly (1985) shows that for the United Kingdom approximately 40 per cent of firms founded in year t will have ceased to trade by year $t + 3$. Hence public policy which identifies this group as the target for policy initiatives has to expect high rates of failure. Secondly a substantial proportion of job creation within new firms takes place in relatively few firms. This point was illustrated in Chapter 4 in our review of the work of Gallagher and colleagues. Further support for the disproportionate contribution to job creation made by a few firms is shown in Table 7.6. It shows that in the three UK

Table 7.6   New manufacturing firms in Durham, Cleveland and Tyne and Wear

---

1991 businesses started
1258 were trading in 1981
1187 were trading and continued to be independent
Total employment in 1981 in these businesses was 13 313
But:
    34 businesses employ 3439 workers: i.e. 1.7 per cent of starts provide 26 per cent of jobs
    118 businesses employ 6320 workers: i.e. 5.9 per cent of starts provide 47 per cent of jobs

---

Sources: Cleveland County Council (1985), Durham County Council (1986), Tyne and Wear County Council (1986)

Counties of Durham, Cleveland and Tyne and Wear, 1991 manufacturing businesses were established after 1965 and could be classed as independent and locally owned. In total these businesses employed 13 313 workers in 1981 but significantly 34 of the businesses provided jobs for 3439 workers, or 26 per cent of all jobs in new businesses. (Cleveland County Council, 1985; Durham County Council, 1986; and Tyne & Wear County Council, 1986).

The table illustrates a useful rule of thumb that over a lengthy period such as 16 years, more than one quarter of the jobs created are in less than 2 per cent of the businesses which started, and virtually one half the jobs are in 6 per cent of the businesses which start. Because of underenumeration of short life businesses within these data bases it is likely that half the manufacturing jobs are created in about 4 per cent of starting manufacturing businesses. These results are similar to the studies of Gallagher and his colleagues who found that, in *all* sectors, half the new jobs in births of firms over a decade were in only 2 per cent of those which started.

The most important characteristic of new and small firms is that many cease to trade in their early years and failure rates remain high throughout their lifetime. From the viewpoint of policy, however, it is essential to recognise that if the objective is high levels of job creation in the medium term, it is relatively few new firms which create the majority of these jobs. It is because the performance of the small firm sector is so diverse and varied that there is a requirement for public policy to become more clearly targeted at the relatively small number of firms with the capacity, and capability to grow.

It is our argument that the current small businesses policy thrust, in areas suffering symptoms of the Birmingham model, is not directed at specific firms or specific groups of firms. Instead it is directed at small firms in general. For example information services are provided to *all* small firms either directly through Public Sector Agencies or indirectly through public financing of private sector bodies such as Enterprise Agencies or Boutiques de Gestion. We also noted that government's efforts to reduce red tape, bureaucracy and other 'unfair' impediments to small firms will benefit *all* firms, not simply those wishing to expand. The Enterprise Allowance Scheme or its equivalent can be used by *any* registered unemployed worker who is capable of assembling £1000 to indicate his or her serious intention to start a business. Even the Loan Guarantee Scheme is responsive in the sense that the bank will generally await a request from a customer. If anything, loans are tailored towards the less successful firms, which are unlikely to be in the 4 per cent which will succeed in creating significant new employment.

The major lesson to be learned from observing and tracking the growth and development of small firms, is that the relatively poor performance of a national or regional economy, if it is related at all to the performance of the small firm sector, is not related to *numbers* of small firms. If any such relationship exists the key is the *quality* of the small firm sector.

Public policy towards small firms in much of Europe appears to have attempted to respond to the problems of unemployment with a philosophy that increases in numbers of firms automatically lead to reductions in unemployment. A frequently trumpeted indicator of policy success is the current simultaneous increase in the *number* of businesses created (birth rates) *and* the increase in the stock of businesses. As has been consistently demonstrated in these pages we do not believe either of these to be necessarily a measure of success. Rather we believe the fundamental problem of economies suffering the symptoms of the Birmingham model to be one of a lack of *quality* rather than *quantity* of small businesses.

Stated simply, the problem in the Birmingham model is that there are too few small businesses which are willing and capable of growing into large businesses, and that current policy is insufficiently directed towards such businesses. Indeed it could be that current policies designed to increase the supply of entrepreneurs could even inhibit the growth of these potentially rapid-growth firms, since this will result in cut-throat competition for businesses at an early, and vulnerable, stage in their life cycle. This is separate from, and additional to, the questionable morality of encouraging redundant workers to risk their life savings and redundancy money in starting a business where the risks are known to be high, and where the individual has been inadequately trained. The current levels of unemployment mean that there is no shortage of potential entrepreneurs and, if at all possible, it should be the objective of policy to *reduce* and *discourage* those who are clearly unsuitable for entrepreneurship. Since figures on the numbers of business starts include both the 'suitable' and 'unsuitable' these should not be used as an indication of the success of small firm policies. There is a case, in some countries such as the UK, for raising, rather than lowering, the barriers to business formation.

In short, an economy suffering symptoms of the Birmingham model should view small firms as a key element in strengthening and widening its industrial base. It is initially through the growth of a relatively small number of such firms that the remainder of the economy can be galvanised into action leading subsequently to the creation of significant numbers of new jobs in the longer term.

7.6   SELECTIVITY: THE ARGUMENTS

The argument so far has been that a small proportion of new and small firms contribute disproportionately to job creation and that policies to maximise the number of business 'starts' could even inhibit the fast growth businesses which are the main source of job creation. Since only a few of these firms 'matter' they should be the target for policy. Several arguments against a strategy of 'selectivity' are, however, normally advanced.

(a)   If firms are fast-growers they will succeed without public assistance, which should be directed elsewhere.

(b)   The public sector has a bad record in implementing selective policies and should leave this to private market forces.

(c)   Since it is easier to increase the number of business starts this policy should be pursued since more 'starts' will lead to more fast growers.

(d)   It is both inequitable and administratively complex to provide assistance to some types of small business and not to others.

Each of these and associated arguments will be discussed in turn.

(a)   'Fast growers will succeed without public assistance'

It is argued that if these small firms are fast growers then they should be left alone since they will succeed anyway and public resources would be better devoted to alternative groups of firms. Survey evidence, both from the UK and from Germany (Storey, 1985b; Geiser, 1981) demonstrates the fallacy of this argument, since it is clear that rapid growth firms have many more problems or at least different types of problems than slow-growth firms. For example fast-growth firms are more likely than slow growth firms to want new premises. They are more likely to be amenable to advice on organising their existing work space better in order to maximise output. Fast growth firms are more likely to require more skilled labour than firms maintaining their employment levels. Fast growth firms, because by definition they are exceptional, are more likely to be perceived as 'risky' by commercial financial institutions and therefore have their growth constrained. For example, using conventional univariate financial ratio analysis it is *not* possible to distinguish between young fast growing firms and firms of a similar age which are likely to fail. (Storey, Keasey, Watson and Wynarczyk, 1987). Since univariate tests are generally favoured by local bank managers lending to small firms, it is not surprising that some fast-growth firms are restricted in their growth by what they, in some cases, quite correctly perceive to be 'conservative' bankers.

Fast growth businesses are also more likely to require information on exports, new technologies etc. This is because, as noted earlier, exporting and the adoption of new technologies are only undertaken by a minority of small firms. For example Johnson and Storey (1987a) found that only 6 per cent of UK small businesses exported any of their product and only 4 per cent of business exported more than 10 per cent of their output. It was also found that more than 70 per cent of small firms reported little change in technology over the two year period 1982–4. For example 76 per cent of respondents thought there had been negligible introductions of new technologies in office functions and 72 per cent thought changes to production processes were negligible. In short it is clear that only a small minority of firms are likely to be inhibited in their growth by such constraints. It is also clear that if these constraints could however be 'relaxed' for the minority then this could lead to significant extra growth.

To be able to provide the type of assistance which could lead to increased employment in the small firm, many small firm Agencies require a much closer relationship with their clients than is currently the case. The types of assistance described in the above paragraph can only perhaps be identified after working with the firm for several months, since each firm has very different problems, and indeed many not even fully understand its own problems. Effectively therefore it is suggested that each Agency, instead of having hundreds of clients to whom it provides a superficial service, has a portfolio of clients with no 'case officer' dealing with more than 10 businesses, and preferably with only three of four at any one time. Assistance and advice would then be fully provided in a 'hands on' situation. We recognise that these developments are now becoming more normal in the more forward looking Enterprise Agencies but the reorientation is still too slow.

(b)   *'The public sector is unable to implement selective policies'*

The above statement combines a number of quite separate arguments. The first group of arguments against a selective policy is that the public sector has a bad record and so whilst it may be a sensible policy in theory, it is impossible in practice. Essentially this is a technical argument which says that identifying fast growth firms is impossible. A second and more political argument is that even if selectivity could be demonstrated to be technically possible, assistance should be provided by the private sector, and public funds could be used for other purposes. Finally it is argued that even if fast growth firms can be identified they may not wish to be 'assisted'. We shall discuss each of these arguments in turn.

It is true that the public sector has a bad record in identifying fast growth firms, and perhaps an even poorer record of avoiding providing support for failing firms. It is also true that a selective strategy is particularly difficult in the small firm sector where, as noted earlier, more than 30 per cent of new businesses cease to trade in their first two years of life, and only one in every two hundred businesses have 100 employees within 10 years of start-up. The problems even of highly experienced venture capital organisations indicate that failure rates are high even when detailed appraisals are undertaken. Nevertheless the growth of venture capitalists suggests that it is possible to eliminate a substantial number of bad risks by sophisticated screening procedures.

To some extent these lessons can be learnt by the public sector. Storey, Keasey, Watson and Wynarczyk (1987) examined whether it is possible to identify failed and non-failed companies three years prior to failure. Using the statistical technique of Multiple Discriminant Analysis upon the Profit and Loss Accounts and Balance Sheets of a sample of 485 failed and non-failed companies, a Z-score was derived for those companies providing data three years prior to failure for the failed companies and for 1979 for the non-failed companies. The function derived was then tested on a 'hold-out' sample, i.e. a totally separate collection of 151 failed and non-failed companies and overall 75 per cent of companies in each group were correctly identified. We do not suggest that this, in itself, is a justification for a selective small firms policy, or even that the success rate of 75 per cent is outstandingly good. Nevertheless it is a potentially efficient way of identifying businesses which are 'at risk' and might merit further investigation. Similar levels of predictive success were obtained when more qualitative factors were used, such as the background and numbers on the Board of the Company, the accounting policies, the speed with which accounts were lodged, etc., all suggesting that it is possible to obtain some warning signs from companies three years prior to their demise. It also suggests that whilst some small companies do collapse 'overnight' due to deaths, Acts of God etc., many such collapses have their seeds sown in earlier years.

This form of analysis can only be undertaken satisfactorily when the business has a track record. In principle at least three years of financial accounts are required before a fully informed judgement can be made and before a Z-score can be calculated. The technique *cannot* therefore be applied to start-up businesses and is a further reason for directing assistance towards relatively well-established businesses, rather than towards start-ups.

Whilst it may be possible, amongst firms that are currently trading, to identify those which fail within the next three years, this is not necessarily the same as being able to identify fast growth companies at an early stage in their life. However our preliminary work in this matter suggests that even this identification is possible once the business has been established for two or three years. Storey, Keasey, Watson and Wynarczyk (1987) show that the median fast growth company (i.e. one which reaches 50 employees within five years of start-up) is on average twice as large in its second year of life, both in terms of employment and assets as the median two year old non-fast growth company. Whilst it is difficult to identify the fast growth company at start up, such businesses identify themselves, once they are more than two years old. Furthermore subsequent failure rates of fast growth new businesses are substantially lower than those of average businesses of the same age.

From a technical viewpoint, therefore, it is possible for public institutions to distinguish failure from non-failure and distinguish fast growth from non-fast growth, by using the same techniques of analysis used in the private sector. Clearly there will be businesses which perform in an unpredictable manner but as a technical exercise selective policies are possible.

There is a second and essentially political objection to the adoption of selective policies to assist small businesses. In several European countries public agencies concerned with industrial policy such as the UK Industrial Reorganisation Corporation have had political pressure exerted upon them to assist large companies with poor commercial prospects. More recently the UK National Enterprise Board was subjected to considerable political pressure to include businesses within its portfolio which had no prospects of becoming commercially viable even in the medium term. Similar strategies have been adopted in Italy by GEPI which has acted as a publicly funded 'hospital' for large ailing businesses. Here there have been relatively few businesses resold to the private sector after treatment, essentially because many were 'terminal' cases. It is because of this perceived poor record of the public sector in promoting economic development on a selective basis in the large firm sector that selective policies for small firms tend to be rejected

Political pressures to assist individual small firms are however, significantly less than those which can be marshalled to support individual large firms. In the case of large firms which are likely to be liquidated or closed there is clearly considerable pressure on local politicians to use their influence to prevent the closure, especially if the locality currently suffers from high employment. Similar pressures cannot be exerted upon a public agency to select a small firm for eligibility for assistance because the firm is small and so has fewer interest groups to support it. This means that public agency judgements on small firms are more likely to be based upon expected performance and existing track record than political influence.

The third associated argument is that if there are potential fast growth firms in the economy it is more appropriate for them to be assisted by the existing private'sector financial institutions such as banks, accountants, and venture capitalists than by the public sector. Essentially this argument suggests that it is in the interests of private financiers to seek out fast growing businesses and provide them with an appropriate financial package, or other appropriate business services. Clearly there are objections which may be made on political grounds to this argument but, even when these are set aside, there is the key problem that the public and private support agencies may have differing objectives. For example the venture capitalists or the accountants will be interested in small firms that are likely to exhibit growth either in terms of profitability or assets. The venture capitalists are particularly concerned with the valuation of the business and the implied or actual value of the shares. The accountancy practices are interested in not only the standard audit fees which it charges the business (which are broadly related to its profit and turnover) but also to its ability to sell to the business a range of specialist services. Clearly the rapidly growing businesses are more likely to purchase such services than those showing more sluggish growth. The commercial banks, in the UK, may have a slightly different interest, in the sense that direct equity participation is rare, but they do have a clear interest in solvency since this determines the ability of the firm to repay a loan.

The objectives of the public sector assistance agencies, however, may be more closely related to the creation of employment rather than financial growth in terms either of assets or profitability. It is shown by Storey *et al.* (1987) that fast growing small companies in terms of profitability or assets are not always those which are experiencing fast growth in terms of employment. This reflects the ability of some businesses to grow rapidly in terms of profitability, sometimes by shedding labour. Even so it is the case that changes in profitability (particularly retained profit) in small firms are significantly correlated with changes in employment. It is therefore broadly true that fast growing companies in terms of assets and profitability will be the focus of attention from the private sector institutions. Nevertheless businesses growing rapidly in terms of employment may not necessarily appear as attractive to those providing commercial business and financial services, and so may be 'constrained' in their employment growth. Hence some relaxation of these constraints by the public sector agencies could lead to faster employment growth. Furthermore in taking such action the public sector would not be 'crowding out' the private sector since the overlap of clients in each group would be small because the private sector would be less interested in small businesses which are performing relatively poorly in financial terms, even though they have the potential to increase employment.

Finally amongst this group of arguments it was pointed out that even if some firms are identified as suitable targets for public policies they may be unwilling to take advantage or collaborate with public agencies. Some firms may be unwilling to participate through a fear that 'the state' or any outsider would become too knowledgeable about their business. They may for example fear that information would be communicated to the taxation authorities or that the adviser would become so knowledgeable that he would be able to set up a business in direct competition with the firm which he is supposed to assist. Some such fears may be valid, at least in the minds of the business owners, whilst businessmen may have strong ideological objections to any form of state assistance. This in no way, however, undermines the merits of a selective approach. Even under present policies, there are numerous public agencies whose function is to assist small firms, and yet a majority of firms claim never to have visited any such agency (Storey, Wynarczyk and Johnson, 1986). The potentially low take-up of any scheme should not therefore be a source of concern, since this is characteristic of most policies to assist small firms. In our view, however, the most familiar criticism by businessmen of publicly provided assistance services is either that they were unaware of them, or that those providing the service appeared unaware of the particular problems which the businessman faced. Such a divide can only be overcome by much closer links between those providing the service and the businesses, but because a more intensive and 'personalised' service cannot be offered to all, a mechanism has to be devised to assist some firms and exclude many more. In essence we are arguing that policy delivery can only be improved through greater selectivity.

(c)   *'More start-ups lead to more high flyers'*

The third argument against selectivity is that since it is acknowledged that identification of fast growth businesses is imperfect, and that it is easier to increase the number of businesses which start, then the latter may still be the more efficient way of increasing the number of fast growth businesses in total. Crudely if there are four 'winners' in every 100 business starts, surely it is better to increase the number of business starts than to increase the jobs created by those 4 'winners'?

However this argument is also flawed since it assumes there is a fixed relationship between the number of 'starts' and the number of 'winners'. Although such a 'fixed' relationship was shown to exist when small firm policies were weak it is unlikely to continue when recession is combined with policies to artificially increase the number of business start-ups. This is illustrated by the fact that entrepreneurs from the higher socio-economic groupings with higher levels of education and previous managerial experience tend to create businesses with a somewhat lower likelihood of failure and a higher probability of growth. It also appears that individuals who are 'pushed' into entrepreneurship either by unemployment of the threat of unemployment tend to establish businesses with lower growth potential than those established by individuals 'attracted' to entrepreneurship (Storey 1982). Not surprisingly, since the late 1970s with the rise in unemployment there has been a sharp increase in the number of 'pushed' entrepreneurs (Mason, 1986; Binks and Jennings, 1986), with the businesses which they establish having a short life, yet perhaps during that short life helping to displace existing established firms. This suggests that the *proportion* of fast growth firms is likely to have fallen even further in recent years, although some survey evidence suggests that during that time the number of 'forced' entrepreneurs may have reduced from their peak levels in the late 1970s and early 1980s (Johnson and Storey, 1987a).

We therefore do not accept that maximising the number of business starts is an efficient or cost-effective way of creating jobs in the small business sector. It risks stimulating unsuitable individuals to start businesses without aspirations for growth. It means that their subsidised presence in the market place can undermine the prospects for existing non-subsidised businesses established with the objective of growth. The Germans are clearly aware of this danger since their 1953 Basic Law on Skilled Crafts and Trades required new entrants to a trade to hold proficiency certificates before they were allowed to practice. Clearly there is some danger, as Sauer (1984) points out, of having centrally regulated proficiency standards but it does prevent, during periods of high unemployment, unqualified and poorly trained newcomers to a sector from entering, lowering prices and standards of product/service and causing some well qualified businesses to fail. It is a function of the state to decide to what extent such entry is in the interest of the consumer in the form of diversified products, lower prices etc. and the extent to which easy entry merely leads to lower standards of service to the consumer and drives out well qualified individuals. Currently some German commentators are suggesting that their governments have gone too far in requiring training and proficiency certificates for those in business (*Empirica*, 1986). Nevertheless it is equally clear that a major lowering of entry barriers to business start-ups may have considerable drawbacks.[1]

(d) *'Selective policies are inequitable and administratively clumsy'*

The final argument against a 'selective' policy to promote small business is that it is both inequitable and administratively clumsy. It is argued that it is unfair to target assistance towards only a few new and small firms whilst leaving the remainder to progress without assistance. The operations of a selective policy also require judgements to be exercised by bureaucrats who would have to decide between firms, perhaps on the basis of incomplete information.

These arguments are very powerful and, in many respects, the most difficult to counter. Indeed the inequality of treatment between firms is central to a selective policy. In essence, however, we believe that selectivity brings considerably greater benefits than costs and that it can therefore be partly justified on these grounds. For example not only will a selective policy create more jobs in the assisted firms but it should lead to lower rates of local displacement than with current policies, because fast growth firms sells a much higher proportion of output to customers outside the Region and outside the country. Hence their growth displaces foreign competition rather than local companies and is likely to lead to an increased demand for local suppliers by generating positive multiplier effects rather than negative displacement. There is also some evidence that the types of jobs created in more established firms are also likely to be of a higher 'quality' than those provided in short life companies. Watson (1984), for example, noted that wages per employee were actually lower in failed small companies than in otherwise similar non-failed small companies.

We recognise that a selective policy imposes additional administrative burdens since it requires judgements to be made upon the firms which will receive assistance and those which are to be excluded. This can cause a sense of grievance amongst firms which are excluded and it also is significantly more expensive to administer than automatic assistance. Any sense of grievance is likely to be heightened when failures occur, as they will, amongst assisted firms. Nevertheless it is increasingly recognised (Robinson *et al.* 1987) that selective economic policies are more cost-effective in terms of job creation than across-the-board assistance, and a cadre of expertise in implementing such policies is gradually being assembled in the public sector

7.7   SELECTIVITY: IN PRACTICE

In this section the practicalities of implementing a selective policy towards small businesses are described. It draws heavily upon our understanding of the operations of the National Development Council (NDC), located in Washington DC, USA. NDC's prime targets are businesses wishing to expand but which are unable to do so because of a shortage of some form of finance. It is NDC's experience that the owners of such businesses are likely to be so busy with day-to-day problems that they do not take the time to fully search all potential sources of finance and are unaware of the many forms of public financial assistance available to a small business. Because the owners are concerned with mitigating the intense day-to-day pressures of running a successful business they generally are not members of small business organisations and so are removed from many sources of information. They can generally only be contacted by the agencies coming to them, rather than by the agency waiting for the owner of the firm to walk through its door.

NDC's expertise is to negotiate on behalf of the entrepreneur an optimal financial package with the appropriate combination of private and public funding and the appropriate combination of equity and loan. This is called loan packaging but there is no reason, in principle, why the NDC model cannot be applied to other forms of small business assistance and advice. Nevertheless for expositional purposes here we will assume that the Agency function is to provide assistance on loan packaging.

NDC staff are either ex-bankers or have a strong banking/financial background. To this is allied a clear understanding of all forms of public financial assistance available to a small business in an area. In the UK context for example this would include any central government assistance available from the Departments of Trade and Industry, Environment and Employment or from the Manpower Services Commission. It would involve a knowledge of all financial assistance schemes such as loans, grants, or low rent premises available from the Local Authorities, together with finance from all other public agencies such as NCB Enterprises, BSC Industry, English Estates, New Town

Development Corporations, together with other forms of finance from the European Economic Community (ERDF, ESF, EIB, ECSC). NDC officials also have a thorough understanding of private sector sources of finance. This would obviously include contact with the Clearing Banks, and their subsidiaries but it would also include a knowledge of Venture Capital Funds, Pension Fund Managers, Property Company Finance, Stockbrokers, Merchant Banks and possibly of wealthy individuals who might be prepared to invest directly in a business.

The unique feature which NDC claims to offer in this field is that it identifies, from lists of established firms made available to it, those which have exhibited growth in the past and which might wish to undergo further expansion. *It then visits all firms which it considers worthwhile*, having studied any publicly available information on the business in advance.

In many cases the owner of the business may indicate no wish for further expansion or that he/she feels able to assemble a financial package themselves. In some cases, however, the business owner may wish to expand but be constrained by what is believed to be an overly cautious bank manager. If the business owner wishes to expand, a business plan is then required by the NDC official *together with three years of audited accounts*. The firm may be assisted by NDC in the production of a business plan, but this will only occur if the NDC officer is satisfied, after a preliminary examination of the accounts, that the business is 'bankable'.

If the business has a satisfactory track record, and the business plan is thought to be viable by the NDC official, then the next stage is to assemble the best possible financial package. This will involve the NDC official, on behalf of the business, presenting the track record and the business plan to different financial institutions initially in the private sector. During these interviews no attempt is made to underestimate the level of risk to the financial institution. Instead a full account is presented in the most objective manner possible, with all potentially interested financial institutions being visited.

During these visits the NDC official will be aware of the sources of public sector finance for which the business is eligible. In the case of automatic grants there is little problem in identifying eligibility but in the case of discretionary grants, loans, etc., NDC officials again act on behalf of the company in such negotiations.

This description should demonstrate that where there are several public and private sources of finance available to the small firm such negotiations can be both complex and time consuming. They are not of great interest, in themselves, to the business owner and indeed he may well find them frustrating and tend to opt for the first, but perhaps not the best deal, which can be completed. The NDC official effectively acts as the owner's nominee in these matters by bringing superior knowledge of public and private finance to the assistance of the entrepreneur although, of course, the final decision on the appropriate package lies with the business owner.

The NDC official is financed by the public sector, usually the State or municipality in the USA, to ensure that no projects which are commercially viable, albeit only with some public sector contribution, are constrained by a shortage of finance. The packaging of a deal can be extremely time consuming, with the NDC official needing a full understanding of the technical, financial and market prospects of the business which he is representing. It means that the number of cases which any individual officer is capable of handling at any one time is limited which, in turn, means that NDC needs to be highly selective about those businesses which it helps.

The NDC's work in the area of loan packaging illustrates several important characteristics of any selective small firms policy. First the reluctance to deal with start-ups which are perceived to be too risky and uncertain. Second the detailed involvement in the business by the NDC officials, in order for them to present the best possible case to financial institutions. Thirdly a concentration upon businesses which have a strong track-record and are wishing to expand. It does *not* attempt to encourage expansion – it merely facilitates a wish to expand on the part of the entrepreneur, who may feel constrained by a shortage of time and expertise in negotiating the appropriate financial package. Fourthly only a very limited number of cases are handled at any one time in order to ensure that NDC officials are fully able to represent the interests of their clients. These lessons are applicable to countries other than the United States and to other forms of small firm assistance.

7.8 CONCLUSION

This book has raised several fundamental questions over small firm policies as currently operated in Europe, by arguing that the mechanism of job creation within small firms is inadequately understood.

It argues that policies designed to increase the rate of new firm formation, without taking account of the *types* of firm, are unlikely to lead to self-sustaining economic growth based on dynamic young businesses. Too many unsuitable individuals are entering the world of business with only very modest prospects of success, and by so doing may reduce the viability of existing businesses.

A second criticism is that many small firm initiatives are designed to improve the competitive position of small firms, in general, through measures such as reducing the burdens of 'red tape', provision of free assistance and advice. It is assumed that reductions in compliance costs will lead to higher profits amongst small firms leading to additional employment. Our research however suggests that for only a relatively few firms will increased trading profits lead to increased employment. Instead a more effective strategy for creating additional employment in small firms would be to provide an incentive for profit retention within the company.

Thirdly we demonstrate that, at least in the UK, the major financial initiatives designed to assist small firms are regionally divisive, as was predicted prior to their introduction. The biggest impact of policy has been in the most prosperous areas and the least impact has been in the least prosperous areas. If small firm policies have a specific job creation/ unemployment reduction objective then an explicit regional dimension is required.

Fourthly there appears to be a risk that the jobs created in new and small businesses may not match, or even filter through to, those who are registered as unemployed, and particularly to those who are amongst the long term unemployed. Many of the jobs are for skilled males whilst a substantial proportion of the remainder are for part time females. Furthermore, as we noted above, the geographical areas where job creation is occurring in small firms may be beyond the travelling distance of the unemployed worker. Expectations that small business policies will lead to clear reductions in unemployment should not be high.

From an examination of the contribution of new and small firms to employment change, however, one important lesson emerges. It is that within the small firm sector there are major variations in firm performance. For example it appears to be broadly true that out of 100 new businesses, 40 will cease to trade within three years of start up and that a further 20 will cease to trade over the following seven years. After ten years half of the employment in those 40 surviving firms will be in the four most successful firms. In short, if the objective of policy is the creation of employment within small firms, only a very few firms matter.

It is for this reason that the following five policy recommendations, essentially the same as those made to the Select Committee on Welsh

Affairs in 1984, are repeated. They represent the key elements of a public policy to promote small business on a selective basis.

(a)   No public assistance would be provided to start up businesses, although individuals wishing to start a business should not be discriminated against.

(b)   A comprehensive public package of assistance would be available only to those businesses with worthwhile employment growth prospects. Assistance could include finance, advice, and marketing assistance, using a 'hands-on' approach.

(c)   Only existing businesses would be selected, i.e. those which could demonstrate a track record of both satisfactory financial performance and an above average growth in employment.

(d)   To be selected for assistance a business would need to demonstrate that it was not merely displacing other local businesses. It would have to show a capacity to sell outside the region and preferably outside its own country.

(e)   Each Agency Officer should have to deal with no more than ten firms but for those firms a 'total' service should be offered.

An economy with the characteristics of the Birmingham model will not revive on the basis of small firm policies. Even over a timescale of two decades employment creation by the small firm sector, in these circumstances, is likely to be modest. More selective small firm public policies, however, will lead to a better return in terms of job creation than the present non-discriminatory policies.

Notes

3 Job Generation in North America

1. For the most part, the figures produced in the SBA publications are derived from work done under contract to the SBA by the Brookings Institution.
2. Although it is not clear from the paper, it would seem that this figure also includes the contribution of new firms, which by definition have an age of zero.
3. The Brookings analysis of 1976–80 (Armington, 1983) suggests that Mining had a lower than average growth rate of employment. There appears to be no convincing explanation for this major difference in results for similar time periods.
4. (Birch, 1979, p. 2).
5. For a more detailed explanation of this process of creating proxy branches, see Armington and Odle (1981).
6. It is important in this context to understand the distinction between the Brookings USEEM and USELM files. The USEEM (US Enterprise and Establishment Micro-data) are cross-sectional files developed from each year's DMI files. The USELM file is the longitudinal file developed by linking each years' USEEM files. As about 50 per cent of the USEEM records are unusable for longitudinal analysis (because of reporting errors and non-updated records) the Brookings team developed a complex weighting system to ensure that USELM is representative of the data contained in the USEEM files. This weighting system is described in more detail in the text.
7. Although foreign employment was included in the earlier Brookings estimates for 1978–80, later tabulations for the 1976–80 and 1976–82 periods excluded foreign employment from growth analysis (Armington and Odle 1984). For the 1976–80 period, it was estimated that small firms accounted for 51 per cent of net employment growth, suggesting that the removal of foreign employment from the files may have had the effect of increasing the small firm share of job growth (Armington, 1983).
8. It is possible that Eckhart, von Einem and Stahl are referring to subsidiaries rather than branches.
9. It would be particularly useful to examine how such problems affected the results of the widely-quoted Birch study of the 1969–76 period (Birch, 1979). However, at present, insufficient information is available with which to carry out such an analysis.
10. The weighting system is described more fully in Armington, Odle and Harris (1983).
11. Establishment records are rejected in the following cases:
    (a) Where initial employment is over 200, and there is absolute decline of more than 85 per cent.
    (b) For primary and manufacturing industry, where employment expands

239

by 300 per cent and initial employment was less than 200 *or* final year employment more than 500.

(c) For services, where employment expands by 300 per cent and initial employment was less than 100 OR final year employment more than 200.

12. It is possible that the errors pointed out by Birch and McCracken occurred in the (unedited) cross-sectional files, rather than the longitudal files used by Brookings for their growth analysis.

13. There appears to be some discrepancy between the 25 per cent figure implied by Figure 3.2, and the Brookings suggestion that 75 per cent of births are recorded in Dun and Bradstreet files by the end of the second year (Armington, Odle and Harris 1983).

14. It is not clear whether these factors are designed to estimate *all* births during the period or only those which survived.

15. The MIT approach to branch births and to deaths is described below.

16. These figures are calculated by summing 'Regular births' and 'New listing births' for Head Offices in Table 3.8.

17. For full details of the MIT estimation technique, see Birch and McCracken (1983, pp. 28–9).

18. We assume the average refers to the average rate of growth of multi-plant firms.

19. A later analysis of the effect of old reports in the DMI files (Applied Systems Institute 1985) suggests that there was not an irregular purge during 1978–80. There was, however, a major purge of old records between 1982 and 1984 which seriously hinders any growth study of this period.

20. It is unclear why Birch and McCracken did not use the actual employment reported by the 'Nixies' to estimate both the 'spurious death' count and the allocation of these spurious job losses between small and large firms.

21. It could be argued that Brookings, in wrongly reporting some purged records as deaths, may simply have compensated for the actual deaths which still remained on the files.

22. This section is *NOT* intended to be an alternative to the Brookings and MIT studies. Obviously, we have only a limited knowledge of the contents of the DMI file, the weighting schemes used, and the overall context of the studies. It is rather intended as an illustrative exercise to show how a particular set of 'realistic' assumptions might affect the outcome of a components of change study, when the data base suffers from the type of problems described above.

23. We make no assumption as to whether Dun and Bradstreet reporting has improved for particular industries relative to others, as we do not know the overall distribution of the sample by industry group. We simply assume that the net effect of reporting improvements leads to 20 per cent more jobs being discovered.

4 Job Generation in other OECD Countries

1. One possible explanation of this discrepancy is that there are 116 firms with more than 1000 employees which made their first appearance in the 1984 database, but started in business before 1982. Presumably such firms

would be excluded from the 1982–84 analysis as 1982 employment is unknown. This could presumably be checked by Doyle and Gallagher, and if it was the case, then this could be a powerful justification for the scaling up of fast growing firms. In the absence of such confirmation, we remain sceptical of the claim that 70 firms increased their employment from less than 20 to more than 1000 within two years.

2. It is likely that our corrected figures slightly underestimate the small firm contribution to job generation. In particular, we have scaled up expansions into the 20–500 size categories by the scaling factor for the *end year* (see Appendix). It is probable that Dun and Bradstreet do overlook a significant proportion of such firms. Thus our figures for expansions into the 20–49, 50–99 and 100–499 categories may be an underestimate.

3. For instance, a study of dissolution rates by firm size using the Dun and Bradstreet data base (Stewart and Gallagher, 1984) found that annual death rates were lower in the 500+ size category than in the smaller size groups.

5 Small Firms and the Process of Economic Development

1. The text by Pollard (1983) covers these issues.
2. The most recent and comprehensive discussion of the decline of Birmingham is found in Spencer *et al.* (1986).
3. David Trippier, the UK Small Firms Minister, quoted in Hunt (1985), expresses satisfaction that small firms are increasing their share of the labour market, and clearly regards recent trends in firm formation and self-employment as positive signs. In the same article, Professor Paul Burns suggests that Britain should aim for a small firm share of employment similar to that which exists in Italy, France and Germany.
4. For a further discussion of factors affecting the relative attractiveness of employment and self-employment, see Johnson (1981).
5. It must be recognised, however, that the evidence on 'forced' entrepreneurship in the UK is contradictory. For example, although Storey (1982) finds that between 25 per cent and 50 per cent of entrepreneurs felt that unemployment, or the prospect of unemployment was a spur to establishing their business, careful econometric work by Binks and Jennings (1986) indicated business formation rates were highest in the upswing of a cycle. Finally, however, Storey and Jones (1987) show that using cross sectional data, formation rates were highest in those sectors shedding the most jobs.
6. One very important effect of the recession and job shedding by large firms has been to increase the different forms of business. The early 1980s have seen the growth of worker co-operatives, community businesses and other third-sector businesses – primarily established by unemployed workers. For a helpful review of these developments see Nabarro *et al.* (1986).
7. For example Storey *et al.* (1987) show that manufacturing companies with only a husband and wife team of Directors are significantly less likely to exhibit growth either in terms of profitability or employment than one

established by a team of a professional Directors or a team of technicians.

8.   Dawkins (1985) reports an increase in the number of management buy-outs from around 100 in 1980 to over 200 in 1983. The projected number of buy-outs for 1985 is less than the 1983 figure, but there is a massive increase in the average value of management buy-outs. A complete review is provided in Wright and Coyne (1985).

9.   For example the Chloride Group have their main battery-producing plant at Swinton, Lancashire. The plant had a joinery shop which made wooden battery cases but in 1980 the shop manager established an independent company, with guarantees from Chloride, to provide their products from a nearby trading estate (Shutt and Whittington, 1987). Other examples include Metal Box in Leicester offering the haulage contract to their own staff (Labour Research, 1986).

10.   Howell and Frankel (1985) report that in New England there are 250 colleges and universities, 65 of which are in Greater Boston. A total of 350 000 students are enrolled to take a first degree or higher at these institutions.

11.   The study by Stevens (1982) shows that despite its success in creating employment, growth of real manufacturing wages 1973–1980 has been lowest in New England. Setting New England = 100, then the Great Lakes = 114, the New South = 104 and West Coast = 136.

12.   It is not intended to imply that these developments are unique to Massachusetts since they reflect developments which are occurring throughout the US economy. For example the Small Business Administration (1985) reports that between 1977 and 1982 women-owned businesses in the US grew by an annual rate of 6.9 per cent compared with non-farm sole proprietorships overall which grew only by 3.79. The SBA attributes this to structural shifts in favour of services, more female workers (higher activity rates) and more women having higher levels of education.

13.   The distinction closely follows that made by Brusco and Sabel (1981) who identify three types of Italian small firms – the traditional artisan, the dependent sub-contractor and the small firm in the industrial district. It is the latter type of firm which corresponds closely to the 'Bologna' model identified here. For a more recent analysis see either Piore and Sabel (1984) or Brusco (1986).

14.   As we are trying to explain a current situation which is to some extent an 'ideal type,' our analysis underplays the importance of change and dynamism among the small firms, such as the switch from subcontracting for large firms during the 1960s to different forms of market penetration in the 1970s.

15.   This section draws heavily from the work of Bagnasco and that of Brusco.

7   Public Policy Towards Small Firms

1.   This may be reflected in data on small manufacturing businesses in Northern England, where it is noted that as the number of businesses formed rose in the mid to late 1970s the number of fast-growth businesses actually *fell*. We would not wish to place too much reliance on the result

since it may merely reflect the fact that it takes some firms several years after establishment before they appear in government employment records. Nevertheless it could equally reflect the problems that small firms starting under highly competitive conditions in the late 1970s found it difficult to obtain sufficient profits to finance expansion (Storey *et al.*, 1987).

References

ANTHONY, D. (1983) 'Japan' in D.J. Storey (ed.) *The Small Firm: An International Survey* (Croom Helm, London).

APPLIED SYSTEMS INSTITUTE (1985) 'Effects of Old Reports on DMI files', Report submitted to US Small Business Administration, 29 August 1985.

ARMINGTON, C. (1983) 'Further examination of sources of recent employment growth: analysis of USEEM data for 1976 to 1980', mimeo, Business Microdata Project, Brookings Institution, March.

ARMINGTON, C. and ODLE, M. (1981) 'Associating establishments into enterprises for a microdata file of the US Business population' *Statistics of Income and Related Record Research*, Internal Revenue Service, pp. 71–76.

ARMINGTON, C. and ODLE, M. (1982) 'Small Business – How Many Jobs?' *Brookings Review*, Winter, pp. 14–17.

ARMINGTON, C., HARRIS, C., ODLE, M. (1983) 'The Formation and Growth in High Technology Businesses: A Regional Assessment', Mimeo.

ARMINGTON, C. and ODLE, M. (1984). 'US Establishment Longitudinal Microdata (USELM). The Weighted Integrated USEEM 1976–1982 sample', Business Microdata Project, Brookings Institution, 12 June.

ARMINGTON, C., ODLE, M. and HARRIS, C. (1983) 'Weighting the 1976–80 and 1978–80 USEEM files for Dynamic Analyses of Employment Growth' Business Microdata Project, Brookings Institution, April.

ATKINSON, J. (1985) 'Flexibility: Planning for an Uncertain Future' *Manpower Policy and Practice*, Vol. 1, Summer, pp. 26–29.

BAGNASCO, A. (1985) 'La costruzione sociale del mercato: strategie di inpressa e esperimenti di scala in Italia', *Stato e Mercato*, No. 13, pp. 9–45.

BANNOCK, G. (1981) *The Economics of Small Firms*, (Oxford: Basil Blackwell).

BANNOCK, G. (1986) 'V.A.T. and Small Businesses: European Experience and Implications for North America' Canadian Federation of Independent Business and National Federation of Independent Business Research and Education Foundation, Willowdale, Ontario, Canada.

BEESLEY, M.E. and WILSON, P. (1984) 'Public Policy and Small Firms in Britain' in C. Levicki (ed) *Small Business: Theory and Policy* (Acton Society Trust, London: Croom Helm).

BINKS, M. and JENNINGS, A. (1986) 'Small Firms as a Source of Economic Rejuvenation' in J. Curran, J. Stanworth and D. Watkins (ed) *The Survival of the Small Firm*, Vol. 1 (Aldershot: Gower).

BIRCH, D. (1979) 'The Job Generation Process', MIT Program on Neighborhood and Regional Change, Cambridge, Mass.

BIRCH, D. (1979) 'The Job Generation Process (Summary)', MIT Program on Neighborhood and Regional Change, Cambridge, Mass.

BIRCH, D. and McCRACKEN, S. (1983) 'The Small Business Share of Job Creation: Lessons learned from the use of a Longitudinal File', MIT Program on Neighborhood and Regional Change, March.

BODDY, M. and LOVERING, J. (1986) 'High Technology Industry in the Bristol Sub Region: The Aerospace/Defence Nexus', *Regional Studies*, Vol. 20. No. 3, pp. 217–231.

BOLLARD, A. and HARPER, D. (1986) 'Employment Generation and Establishment Size in New Zealand Manufacturing' *International Small Business Journal*, Vol. 4, No. 4, pp. 10–28.

BOLTON, J. (Chairman) (1971) *Report of the Committee of Inquiry on Small Firms*, Cmnd 4811 (London: HMSO).

BRUSCO, S. (1986) 'Small Firms and Industrial Districts: The experience of Italy' in D. Keeble and E. Wever (ed.) *New Firms and Regional Development in Europe*, (London: Croom Helm).

BRUSCO, S. and SABEL, C. (1981) 'Artisan Production and Economic Growth' in F. Wilkinson (ed.) *The Dynamics of Labour Market Segmentation*, (London: Academic Press).

BUCHTEMANN, C.F. and SCHUPP, J. (1986) 'Sozio-okonomie der Telizeit – beschaftigung in der Bundesrepublik Deutschland' Research Unit Labour Market Policy, International Institute of Management, Berlin.

BUSINESS MICRODATA PROJECT (1984) 'Constructing a Small Business Microdata Base for the Analysis of Small Business Activity', Brookings Institution, July.

BUSINESS STATISTICS OFFICE (1980) *Statistics of Product Concentration of UK Manufacturers*, PA 1006, (London: HMSO).

CANADIAN FEDERATION OF INDEPENDENT BUSINESS (1984) 'Employment Profile of Small and Medium Enterprises Based on CFIB data' Mimeo, 24 October.

CHOEFFEL, P. *et al.* (1985) 'Logiques des marches externes et internes, aspects structaraux, aspects dynamiques', Mimeo (University of Poitiers, France).

CLEVELAND COUNTY COUNCIL (1985) 'Manufacturing Employment Change in Cleveland 1965–1981' County Planning Department, Middlesbrough.

CONFEDERATION OF BRITISH INDUSTRY (1985) *Managing Change: the organisation of work*, (London: CBI).

CONTINI, B. (1984) 'Firm size and the division of labour', *Moneta e Credito*, December.

CONTINI, B. *et al.* (1984) 'The Determinants of Productivity and Employment in Italy's SME's in Manufacturing: A Cross Sectional Analysis 1973–81' (Turin: R & P).

COWLING, K. (1982) *Monopoly Capitalism* (London: Macmillan).

CREIGH, S., ROBERTS, C., GORMAN, A. and SAWYER, P. (1986) 'Self Employment in Britain: results from the Labour Force Surveys 1981–1984' *Employemnt Gazette*, June, pp. 183–194.

CROSS, M. (1981) *New Firm Formation and Regional Development* (Farnborough: Gower).

CURRAN, J. and STANWORTH, J. (1986) 'Trends in Small Firms industrial relations and their implications for the role of the small firm in economic restructuring', in A. Amin and J.B. Goddard (eds.), *Technological Change, Industrial Restructuring and Regional Development*, (London: Allen and Unwin).

DAHREMOLLER, A. (1985) 'Der Beitrag mittelstandischer Unternehmen zur Beschaftigung und zum Wachstum unter Berucksichtigung der Unternehmensfluktuation-Zwischenbericht' (Bonn, West Germany: Institut fur Mittelstandforschung).

DANIEL, W.W. and MILLWARD, N. (1983) *Workplace Industrial Relations in Britain: the DE/PSI/SSRC Survey* (London: Heinemann).

DAWKINS, W. (1985) 'Buy-outs are the fashion, but there are still a few doubts', *Financial Times*, 11 November.

DE JONG, M. (1987) 'Small Firm Policies and Job Generation in the Netherlands' in Storey and Johnson (1987a).

DEL MONTE, A. (1984) 'The Effects of Regional Policy on the Industrial Development of the South of Italy', *Mezzorgiorno d'Europa*, No. 4, pp. 563–583.

DEL MONTE, A. and GIANNOLA, A. (1978) *Il Mezzogiorno nell'Economia Italiana*, (Bologna: Il Mulino).

DEL MONTE, A. and RAFFA, M., (eds.) (1977) *Technologia e Decentramento Produtivo*, (Torino: Rosenberg and Sellier).

DEPARTMENT OF ECONOMIC DEVELOPMENT, Northern Ireland (1982) 'The contribution of Small Firms to Economic Growth in Northern Ireland' Planning and Research Branch, DED (NI), Belfast.

DEPARTMENT OF TRADE AND INDUSTRY (1985) *Burdens on Business – Report of a Scrutiny of Administrative and Legislative Requirements* (London: HMSO).

DICKEN, P. and LLOYD, P. (1978) 'Inner Metropolitan Industrial Change, Enterprise Structures and Policy Issues: Case Studies of Manchester and Merseyside' *Regional Studies* Vol. 12, pp. 181–197.

DOMBERGER, S. (1983) *Industrial Structure, Pricing and Inflation*, (Oxford: Martin Robertson).

DOYLE, J. and GALLAGHER, C.C. (1986) 'The Size Distribution, Potential for Growth and Contribution to Job Generation of Firms in the UK, 1982–1984' Research Report No. 7, Department of Industrial Management, University of Newcastle upon Tyne.

DURHAM COUNTY COUNCIL (1986) 'Manufacturing Employment Change in County Durham' County Planning Department, Durham.

ECKHART, W., von EINEM, E. and STAHL, K. (1985) 'Dynamik der Beschafligenentwicklung: Stand der Empirischen Forschung'. Mimeo.

ECKHART, W., von EINEM, E. and STAHL, K. (1986) 'Arbeitsplatz – dynamik im Sud-Nord-Gefalle' Raumforschung und Raumordnung, pp. 74–78.

EMPIRICA (1986) 'Policy Instruments to Facilitate the Creation of Small and Medium Sized Companies', Final Report for EEC, DG III F5, October (Bonn).

FIRN, J.R. and SWALES, J.K. (1978) 'The Formation of New Manufacturing Establishments in the Central Clydeside and West Midlands Connurbations, 1963–1972: A Comparative Analysis' *Regional Studies* Vol. 12, No. 2, pp. 199–213.

FLYNN, P.M. (1984) 'Lowell: A High Technology Success Story', *New England Economic Review*, Sept/Oct pp. 39–49.

FOTHERGILL, S. and GUDGIN, G. (1979) *The Job Generation Process in Britain*, Centre for Environmental Studies, Research Series 32.

FRIEDMAN, A. (1977) *Industry and Labour: Class Struggle at work and monopoly capitalism*, (London: Macmillan).

FRITSCH, M. (1984) 'Die Arbeitsplatzentwicklung in Kleinen und mitteleren Betreiben bzw Unternehmen' *Informationen zur Raumentwicklung*, Vol. 9, pp. 921–35.

GALLAGHER, C.C. and STEWART, H. (1984) *Jobs and the Business Life Cycle in the UK*, Research Report No. 2, Department of Industrial Management, University of Newcastle upon Tyne.

GALLAGHER, C.C. and STEWART, H. (1985) 'Jobs and the Business Life Cycle in the UK', Department of Industrial Management, University of Newcastle upon Tyne.

GALLAGHER, C.C. and STEWART, H. (1986) 'Jobs and the Business Life Cycle in the UK' *Applied Economics*, Vol. 18, pp. 875–900.

GANGULY, P. (1985) *U.K. Small Business Statistics and International Comparisons*, (London: Harper and Row).

GEISER, J. (1981) 'Unternechmensgrossenbezogene Wachstumschemmnisse Mittelstandischer Industriebetribe' (Gottingen: Verlag Otto Schwartz).

GIANNOLA, A. (1985) 'Il rapporto fra imprese, analisi del dibattito teorico e risultati di una ricerca empirica: dal decentramento ad un nuovo modello di relazioni interindustriali', in *Grande Impresa E Artigianato*, (Milano: Angeli).

GOVERNMENT OF CANADA, Department of Regional Industrial Expansion (1984) *A Study of Job Creation in Canada 1974–1982*.

GREENE, R. (1982) 'Tracking Job Growth in Private Industry', *Monthly Labor Review*, September, pp. 3–9.

GREGORY, M., LOBBAN, P. and THOMSON, A. (1986) 'Bargaining Structure, Pay Settlements and Perceived Pressure in Manufacturing, 1979–84: Further Analysis from the CBI data bank', *British Journal of Industrial Relations*, July 1986 pp. 214–232.

GUESNIER, B. (1987) 'Job Creation in Small and Medium Sized Firms: France' in Storey and Johnson (1987a).

HAKIM, C. (1984) 'Homework and outwork: National estimates from two surveys' *Employment Gazette*, January, 7–12.

HAMILTON, D., MOAR, L. and ORTON, I. (1981) 'Job Generation in Scottish Manufacturing Industry' Fraser of Allander Institute, University of Strathclyde.

HARRIS, C.S. (1981) 'A Comparison of Employment Data for Several Business Data Sources: County Business Patterns, Unemployment Insurance and the Brookings US Establishment and Enterprise Microdata File' Brookings Institution, Business Microdata Project.

HARRIS, C.S. (1983) 'The Magnitude of Job Loss from Plant Closings and the Generation of Replacement Jobs: Some Recent Evidence'. Brookings Institution, December.

HARRIS, C.S. (1984) 'Small Business and Job Generation: A Changing Economy or Differing Methodologies', (Harris and Associates).

HART, M. (1985) 'The Urban Labour Market Impact of New and Small Manufacturing Firms – some evidence from the Belfast Urban Area' National Small Firms Policy and Research Conference, Belfast.

HEALEY, M. (1984a) 'Industrial Change in Warwick District 1974–1983' Industrial Location Working Paper No. 6, Department of Geography, Coventry (Lanchester) Polytechnic.

HEALEY, M. (ed.) (1984b) *Urban and Regional Research: the Changing UK Data Base* (Norwich: Geo. Books).

HEALEY, M. (1985) 'Industrial Change in Nuneaton and Bedworth District 1974–1985' Industrial Location Working Paper No. 8, Department of Geography, Coventry (Lanchester) Polytechnic.

HEALEY, M. and CLARK, D. (1985) 'Industrial Decline in a local economy: the case of Coventry' *Environment and Planning A*, pp. 1351–1367.

HERTZ, L. (1982) *In Search of a Small Business Definition: An Explanation of the Small Business Definition in the USA, UK, Israel and the Peoples Republic of China*, (Washington DC: University Press of America).

HOWELL, J.M. and FRANKEL, L.D. 'Economic Revitalisation and Job Creation in America's oldest industrialised region', Paper given at AEI/Institute La Boetie Conference, Paris, 24–25, October 1985.

HOWICK, C. and KEY, A. (1980) 'Small Firms and the Inner City: Tower Hamlets' Centre for Environmental Studies, London.

HUBBARD, R. and NUTTER, D. (1982) 'Service Sector Employment in Merseyside' *Geoforum*, Vol. 13, No. 3, pp. 209–235.

HULL, C. (1985) 'Job Generation among independent West German manufacturing firms 1974–80 – evidence from four regions' *Environment and Planning C*, volume 3, pp. 215–234.

HULL, C. (1987) 'Job Generation in the Federal Republic of Germany: a review' *in* Storey and Johnson (1987a).

HUNT, J. (1985) 'Jobs before Profits?' *Chief Executive*, September, pp. 10–13.

IMRIE, R. (1986) 'Work decentralization from large to small firms: a preliminary analysis of subcontracting', *Environment and Planning*, A, Vol. 18, pp. 949–65.

JOHNSON, P. (1981) 'Unemployment and Self Employment: a survey' *Industrial Relations Journal*, vol. 12 (5), pp. 5–15.

JOHNSON, S. and STOREY, D.J. (1987) Small Firms in A. Rajan ed. (1987).

KAPLINSKY, R. (1983) 'Firm Size and Technical Change in a Dynamic Context', *Journal of Industrial Economics*, Vol. 32, No. 1, pp. 39–60.

KUTSCHER, R.E. and PERSONICK, V.A. (1986) 'Deindustrialization and the shift to services', *Monthly Labour Review*, June pp. 3–13.

LABOUR RESEARCH (1986) Vol. 7, No. 2 pp. 13–15.

LAYNE, D. (1982) 'The performance of small manufacturing units' Paper presented to conference of the International Council for Small Business, Edmonton, Canada, April.

LLOYD, J. (1986) 'CBI to urge tax changes to boost self-employment' *Financial Times*, 2 March.

LLOYD, P. and DICKEN, P. (1980) 'Small Firms and Job Generation: the experience of Manchester and Merseyside 1966–75' *NWIRU Discussion Paper*.

LLOYD, P.E. and MASON, C.M. (1984) 'Spatial variations in new firm formation in the United Kingdom: comparative evidence from Merseyside, Greater Manchester and South Hampshire: *Regional Studies*, Vol. 18, No. 3, pp. 207–20.

MACEY, R. (1982) *Job Generation in British Manufacturing Industry: Employment Change by Size of Establishment and by Region* Department of Industry Regional Research Series No. 4, (London: HMSO).

MALECKI, E. (1984) 'Military Spending and the US Defence Industry: Regional Patterns of Military Contracts and Sub-contracts', *Environment and Planning* C Vol. 12, pp. 31–41.

MARKUSEN, A. (1986) 'Defense Spending: A successful industrial policy?' *International Journal of Urban and Regional Research*, Vol. 10, No. 1, pp. 105–22.

MASON, C. (1986) 'New Manufacturing Firm Formation since the onset of Recession: A Case Study of South Hampshire: paper presented at the Ninth National Small Firms Policy and Research Conference, Gleneagles.

MASON, C.M. and HARRISON, R.T. (1986) 'The Regional Impact of Public Policy towards Small Firms in the United Kingdom' in Keeble, D. and Wever, E. eds. (1986) *New Firms and Regional Development in Europe* (London: Croom Helm).

MATTERA, P. (1985) *Off the Books: the Rise of the Underground Economy*, (London: Pluto Press).

MEAGER, N. (1985) *Temporary Work in Britain; Its Growth and Changing Rationales* Institute of Manpower Studies, Sussex.

MONOPOLIES AND MERGERS COMMISSION (1981) *Ready Mixed Concrete*, Cmnd 3854 (London: HMSO).

MONOPOLIES AND MERGERS COMMISSION (1982) *Car Parts*, HC 318, (London: HMSO).

NABARRO, R., DAVIES, R., COBBOLD, C. and N. GALLEY (1986) *Local Enterprise and the Unemployed*, (London: Calouste Gulbenkian Foundation).

OAKEY, R.P. and ROTHWELL, R. (1986) 'High Technology small firms and regional industrial growth', in A. Amin and J.B. Goddard (eds) *Technological Change, Industrial Restructuring and Regional Development* (London: George Allen & Unwin).

OECD (1985) 'Employment in Small and Large Firms: Where Have the jobs come from?' *OECD Employment Outlook*, September, pp. 64–82.

OECD (1986) 'Self Employment in OECD Countries', *OECD Employment Outlook*, pp. 43–65.

O'FARRELL, P. (1986) *Entrepreneurs and Industrial Change* Irish Management Institute, Dublin.

ONIDA, F. (1980) 'Italian exports and industrial structure in the 1970s', *Banco di Roma Review of Economic Conditions in Italy*, February.

PICKLES, A.R. and O'FARRELL, P.N. (1987) 'An analysis of Entrepreneurial behaviour from Male work histories', *Regional Studies* (forthcoming).

PIORE, M. and SABEL, C. (1984) *The Second Industrial Divide: Possibilities for Prosperity* (New York: Basic Books).

POLLARD, S. (1982) *The Wasting of the British Economy* (London: Croom Helm).

PRAIS, S. (1976) *The Evolution of Giant Firms in Britain* (Cambridge University Press).

RAINNIE, A. (1985) 'Small Firms, Big Problems: The Political Economy of Small Business' *Capital and Class* No. 25, Spring, pp. 140–168.

RAJAN, A. and PEARSON, R. (1986) *UK Occupation and Employment Trends to 1990*, (London: Butterworths).

RAJAN, A. (ed.) (1987). *Special Studies in the UK's Employment Prospects* (London: Butterworths).

RICHARDSON, G. (1985) 'Employment in the public and private sectors 1978 to 1984' *Economic Trends*, March, No. 377.

ROBINSON, J.F.F. *et al.* (1987) *Economic Development Policies: an Evaluative study of the Newcastle Metropolitan Region* (Oxford University Press).

ROWLEY, C.K. and PEACOCK, A. (1975) *Welfare Economics: A Liberal Restatement* (London: Martin Robertson).

SAUER, W. (1984) 'Small Firms and the German Economic Miracle' in Levicki, C. ed (1984) *Small Business: Theory and Policy* Acton Society Trust (London: Croom Helm).

SCOTTISH OFFICE (1980) 'Small Units in Scottish Manufacturing' *Scottish Economic Bulletin*, No. 20, pp. 16–23.

SCHIATTARELLA, R. (1984) *Mercato del Lavoro e Struttura Produttiva* (Milano: Franco Angeli).

SCHILLER, B. (1985) 'Human Capital transfers from small to large business' (Washington, DC: SBA).

SEGAL QUINCE AND PARTNERS (1985) *The Cambridge Phenomenon: High Technology Growth in a University Town* (Cambridge: Segal Quince and Partners).

SHUTT, J. and WHITTINGTON, R. (1984) 'Large Firm Strategies and the rise of small firms: The Illusion of Small Firm Job Generation', University of Manchester School of Geography, Working Paper No. 15.

SHUTT, J. and WHITTINGTON, R. (1987) 'Fragmentation Strategies and the rise of small units: Cases from the North West', *Regional Studies*, Vol. 21, No. 1, pp. 13–24.

SIDAWAY, R. (1983) 'The Self Employed' MSC Conference on Self Employment Research and Policy, July.

SPENCER, K. *et al.* (1986) *Crisis in the Industrial Heartland: A Study of the West Midlands* (Oxford University Press).

STEVENS, B. H. (1982) 'Regional Cost Inequalities and the potential for Manufacturing Recovery in the Industrial North'. Paper given at State University of New York at Albany, April.

STEWART, H. (1986) 'No good at creating jobs' *The Guardian* 21 February 1986.

STEWART, H. and GALLAGHER, C.C. (1984) 'Business insolvency, death and dissolution in the UK' Research Report 3, Department of Industrial Management, University of Newcastle upon Tyne.

STOREY, D.J. (1980a) *Job Generation and Small Firms Policy in Britain.* Centre for Environmental Studies, Policy Series 11.

STOREY, D.J. (1980b) 'Small Firms and the Regional Problem' *The Banker* November. Reprinted in Gorb, P. Dowell, P and Wilson P. eds. (1981) *Small Business Perspectives* (London: Armstrong Press).

STOREY, D.J. (1982) *Entrepreneurship and the New Firm* (London: Croom Helm).

STOREY, D.J. (1983) 'Job Accounts and Firm Size', *Area*, Vol. 15, No. 3, pp. 231–237.

STOREY, D.J. (1985a) 'Manufacturing Employment Change in Northern England 1965–78: The Role of Small Businesses in D.J. Storey (ed) *Small Firms in Regional Economic Development: Britain, Ireland and the United States*, (Cambridge University Press).

STOREY, D.J. (1985b) 'The Problems Facing New Firms' *Journal of Management Studies*, Vol. 22, No. 3, pp. 327–345.

STOREY, D.J. and JOHNSON, S. (1985) 'Job Generation in Britain: A review of recent Studies', *International Small Business Journal* Vol. 4, No. 4, pp. 29–46.

STOREY, D.J. and JONES, A.M. (1987) 'New Firm Formation – A Labour Market Approach to Industrial Entry' *Scottish Journal of Political Economy*, Vol. 34, No. 1 pp. 37–51.

STOREY, D.J., KEASEY, K., WATSON, R. and WYNARCZYK, P. (1987) *The Performance of Small Firms* (London: Croom Helm).

STOREY, D.J., WYNARCZYK, P. and JOHNSON, S. (1986) 'The High Tech Entrepreneur and his business, paper given to U.K. Science Parks Annual Conference, 10th December, London.

STOREY, D.J. and JOHNSON, S. (1987a) 'Small and Medium Sized Enterprises and Employment Creation in the EEC Countries' Report for Commission of the European Communities, DG V, Study No. 85/407.

STOREY, D.J. and JOHNSON, S. (1987b) 'Regional Variations in Entrepreneurship in the UK' *Scottish Journal of Political Economy* (forthcoming).

TEITZ, M.B. *et al.* (1981) *Small Business and Employment Growth in California.* Working Paper No. 348, Institute of Urban and Regional Development, University of California, Berkeley, March.

TOWNSEND, A. and PECK, F. (1985) 'The geography of mass redundancy', in M. Pacione (ed) *Progress in Industrial Geography*, 174–218 (London: Croom Helm).

TYNE AND WEAR COUNTY COUNCIL (1986) 'Manufacturing Employment Change in Tyne and Wear 1965–1981' County Planning Department, Newcastle upon Tyne.

US GOVERNMENT Small Business Administration (1984, 1985) *The State of Small Business: A Report of the President* (Washington DC: US Government Printing Office).

VAN GINNEKIN, C. (1985) 'Who are working in SMEs? A comparison of the characteristics of the labour force in SMEs and that in large enterprises' Zoetermeer, EIM.

WALTON, A.L. (1983) 'How Small Businesses Contribute to Job Creation – the pitfalls of a seemingly simple question' Paper presented to Conference on Industrial Science and Technological Innovation, Northwestern University, Evaston, Illinois May 1983.

WATSON, R. (1984) 'Local Government and the Business Sector: Local Authority initiatives towards Small Firms' *Local Government Policy Making.*, March, pp. 53–60.

WEINER, S. (1983) 'Arbeitsbedingungen un Klein – und Mittelbetreiben' Rationalisierungs Kuratorium der Deutschen Wirtschaft, Eschborn, West Germany.

WIETFELDT, R. (1984) 'A Study of Job Creation in Canada, 1975–1982', *Journal of Small Business in Canada*, Vol. 1. (4), Spring, pp. 8–14.

WREN, C. (1987) 'The Relative Effects of Local Authority Financial Assistance Policies', *Urban Studies* (forthcoming).

WRIGHT, M. and COYNE, J. (1985) *Management Buy-Outs* (London: Croom Helm).

Index